Study Guide

for

Essentials of Economics

Ninth Edition

Bradley R. Schiller
American University, Professor Emeritus

Cynthia Hill
Idaho State University

Prepared by
Linda Wilson

STUDY GUIDE FOR
ESSENTIALS OF ECONOMICS, NINTH EDITION

Published by McGraw-Hill Education, 2 Penn Plaza, New York, NY 10121.

Some ancillaries, including electronic and print components, may not be available to customers outside the United States.

This book is printed on acid-free paper.

1 2 3 4 5 6 7 8 9 0 QVS/QVS 1 0 9 8 7 6 5 4 3

ISBN: 978-0-07-765015-5
MHID: 0-07-765015-8

www.mhhe.com

STUDY GUIDE

Table of Contents

STUDY GUIDE

Preface

This study guide was written to accompany *Essentials of Economics*, 9th edition, by Bradley R. Schiller. The overall focus of the study guide is to reinforce the economic principles and concepts presented in the textbook. As a result, many of the problems are patterned after examples in the textbook, and the language used throughout the study guide is similar to the textbook. Each section within each chapter has a particular objective.

The *Quick Review* section provides a brief summary of the basic contents of the corresponding text chapters.

The *Learning Objectives* are restated as they appear in the text.

The section titled *Using Terms to Remember* allows students to practice using the words defined in each chapter in a crossword puzzle format.

The *True or False* and *Multiple Choice* sections help students apply economic principles in a familiar problem-solving setting. An explanation is given for each false answer. These two sections should help greatly in the preparation for exams.

The *Problems and Applications* section allows students to discover economic principles for themselves. Students not only learn the techniques that economists use, but they also discover the basis for the economic concepts they have learned.

Semester after semester, students have difficulty with the same concepts and make the same mistakes. The section called *Common Errors* addresses some of these areas and provides an explanation using appropriate economic principles.

SECTION I Basics

CHAPTER 1

The Challenge of Economics

Quick Review

- In order to produce goods and services, resources or factors of production—land, labor, capital, and entrepreneurship—are necessary. Resources are considered scarce, even though they may seem abundant, because there are *not* enough resources to satisfy all of society's wants.
- Given that resources are limited, society must make choices about what to produce. Choosing to produce one good or service means giving up the opportunity to produce something else. The best foregone alternative is referred to as the opportunity cost.
- Because of scarcity, every economy must answer three basic questions: WHAT to produce? HOW to produce? and FOR WHOM to produce?
- The WHAT question involves finding and producing the optimal (or best) mix of output.
- The production possibilities curve demonstrates the output limits for an economy given its available resources and technology. Remember that all production entails opportunity costs. Additional resources and technological advances result in an outward shift in the production possibilities curve or economic growth.
- The HOW question is focused on society's choice among techniques for producing various goods and services. Government frequently intervenes in ways that favor certain techniques.
- The FOR WHOM question involves the distribution of output. Again there is a role for markets and a role for government as it levies taxes and makes transfers.
- The responsibility for answering the WHAT, HOW, and FOR WHOM questions is jointly shared by government and the market.
- The market mechanism relies on market sales and prices to signal the goods and services society desires.
- Most economies are "mixed" because neither the market mechanism nor government alone can lead to the optimal mix of output. Market failure occurs when the market mechanism leads society to an output mix other than the optimal level; government failure occurs when intervention does not improve the outcome.
- Microeconomics is concerned with the behavior of individual households, firms, and government agencies; macroeconomics with economy-wide issues and goals.

Learning Objectives

After reading the chapter and doing the following exercises, you should be able to:

1. Explain the meaning of scarcity.
2. Define opportunity cost.
3. Recite society's three core economic questions.
4. Discuss how market and command economies differ.
5. Describe the nature of market and government failure.

Using Terms to Remember

Fill in the puzzle on the opposite page with the appropriate terms from the list of Terms to Remember in the text.

Across

1. The trade-off experienced by choosing to watch TV instead of reading your textbook.
3. The result of government intervention if it fails to improve market outcomes.
5. Represented by land, labor, capital, and entrepreneurship.
6. Economic study concerned with the behavior of individuals, firms, and government agencies.
9. Expenditure on new plant and equipment, for example.
12. Referred to as the "invisible hand" by Adam Smith.
14. Latin term meaning "other things remaining equal."
15. Economic policy supported by Adam Smith.

Down

2. The alternative combinations of goods and services that can be produced in a given time period with available resources and technology.
4. The study of the economy as a whole.
7. The use of both market signals and government directives to select the mix of output.
8. Illustrated by an outward shift of the production possibilities curve.
10. The study of how best to allocate society's scarce resources.
11. This occurs when the market produces a nonoptimal mix of output.
13. The central economic problem in which the desire for goods and services exceeds the capacity to produce them.

Puzzle 1.1

True or False: *Circle your choice and explain why any false statements are incorrect.*

T F 1. The United States is a prosperous nation because its resources are sufficient to meet the desires of its citizens.

T F 2. Resources are scarce because our desire for goods and services exceeds the ability of our resources to produce goods and services.

T F 3. The production possibilities curve demonstrates how society responds to the FOR WHOM question.

T F 4. Even if a country had unlimited resources, opportunity costs would still exist.

T F 5. An economy will be able to produce a combination of goods and services beyond its current production-possibilities curve if technology improves.

T F 6. Additional factors of production can result in economic growth.

T F 7. The best answer to the HOW to produce question for an economy is the method of production that uses the most labor.

T F 8. Adam Smith encouraged a policy of laissez faire because he believed that the market mechanism provided society with the best answers to the WHAT, HOW, and FOR WHOM questions.

T F 9. When unregulated producers damage the environment by polluting a lake, this is an example of market failure.

T F 10. Government intervention is designed to improve market outcomes so government failure is not possible.

Multiple Choice: *Select the correct answer.*

_____ 1. The United States is capable of producing more goods and services now than in 1980 because of an:
(a) Increase in the quantity of labor and capital.
(b) Increase in the quantity of labor, but *not* an improvement in technology.
(c) Improvement in technology, but *not* an increase in the quantity of capital.
(d) Increase in entrepreneurship and capital, but *not* an increase in labor.

_____ 2. Which of the following is *not* a factor of production?
(a) A computer used by an economics professor to create exams.
(b) The $10 million donated to a college by wealthy alumni.
(c) A college professor.
(d) The land on which a college is located.

_______ 3. The economic problem of scarcity exists because:
(a) We are capable of producing more than people actually want.
(b) Of opportunity costs.
(c) Society's desires exceed the capability of available resources to satisfy those desires.
(d) The world is running out of resources such as available drinking water.

_______ 4. Which of the following are considered to be scarce in the U.S. economy?
(a) Farmland and oil, but *not* workers.
(b) Machinery and workers, but *not* land.
(c) Workers, but *not* equipment and machinery.
(d) Farmland, workers and equipment.

_______ 5. You plan on staying home this weekend and studying for an economics exam. The opportunity cost of studying:
(a) Is the next-best forgone alternative use of your time.
(b) Is minimal since you like economics.
(c) Depends on how well you do on the exam.
(d) Is zero since you have a scholarship and need to make good grades to keep it.

_______ 6. The opportunity cost of building a new highway is:
(a) Negative, since people who use the new highway will reduce their travel time.
(b) Society's next best alternative use of the resources that are used to build the highway.
(c) The time lost by drivers who must take a detour during the highway construction.
(d) Minimal since the highway construction will bring new jobs to the area.

_______ 7. The market mechanism:
(a) Relies on prices and sales to send a message to producers.
(b) Eliminates market failures created by government intervention.
(c) Works through central planning by the government.
(d) Is very inefficient because consumers don't interact directly with producers.

_______ 8. A society must address the question of WHAT to produce because:
(a) The government cannot make the decision.
(b) Taxes are so high.
(c) Resources are unlimited.
(d) It cannot produce all the goods and services that the citizens desire.

_______ 9. Which of the following is definitely true about two different points on the same production-possibilities curve?
(a) There are not enough resources available to reach either point.
(b) All available resources are being utilized at either point.
(c) More output could be produced with existing resources.
(d) Society is equally well satisfied with the quantity of goods and services at either point.

_______ 10. The best answer to the HOW to produce question is the production method that:
(a) Uses the most labor.
(b) Maximizes the quantity of all resources used.
(c) Results in a combination of goods and services on the production possibilities curve.
(d) Results in a combination of goods and services outside the production possibilities curve.

_______ 11. For the United States, welfare programs are an example of:
(a) How the country has answered the FOR WHOM to produce question.
(b) How the country has answered the HOW to produce question.
(c) A laissez-faire economic approach.
(d) The "invisible hand" at work.

_______ 12. Which of the following would allow an economy to produce a combination of goods and services beyond the current production-possibilities curve?
(a) Using the best existing technology.
(b) Finding additional resources.
(c) Using government intervention to command producers to produce more.
(d) It is not possible to produce a combination of goods and services outside the current production-possibilities curve.

_______ 13. Which of the following will cause the production possibilities curve to shift outward?
(a) An increase in the amount of money in the economy.
(b) A decrease in the number of workers employed.
(c) An improvement in technology.
(d) A decrease in immigration into the United States.

_______ 14. Government intervention in the economy as a result of market failure will:
(a) Improve the mix of output produced.
(b) Worsen the mix of output produced.
(c) Decrease total output.
(d) Any of the above could occur.

_______ 15. Which of the following can be used to correct market failure?
(a) The market mechanism.
(b) Laissez-faire price and output policies.
(c) Government intervention in the form of laws and regulations.
(d) Reliance on the invisible hand.

_______ 16. The trend toward greater reliance on the market mechanism by former communist societies is evidence of:
(a) Government failure.
(b) Market failure.
(c) Scarcity.
(d) *Ceteris paribus.*

_______ 17. Based on Figure 1.6 in the text, an increase in:
(a) Other goods from O_2 to O_1 requires a decrease in health-care services from H_2 to H_1.
(b) Other goods from O_2 to O_1 requires an increase in health-care services from H_1 to H_2.
(c) Health-care services from H_1 to H_2 requires an increase in other goods from O_2 to O_1.
(d) Health-care services from H_1 to H_2 requires no change in other goods.

_______ 18. When it comes to determining the combination of goods and services to produce, most countries are considered to be a:
(a) Centrally planned economy.
(b) Market mechanism economy.
(c) Command economy.
(d) Mixed economy.

_______ 19. Which of the following is *not* an example of one of the three basic economic questions?
(a) Should we produce more military goods or more consumer goods?
(b) Which level of output should we produce so the company can earn the highest profit?
(c) Should everyone get the same amount of goods and services?
(d) Is it wrong for farmers to contaminate waterways with fertilizer?

_______ 20. Microeconomics focuses on the performance of:
(a) Individual consumers, but not government agencies.
(b) Government agencies, but not individual firms.
(c) Individual firms only.
(d) Individual consumers, firms and government agencies.

Appendix

_______ 21. If an increase in one variable results in a decrease in the other variable, a graph of the relationship between these two variables would be:
(a) A straight line.
(b) A downward sloping line.
(c) An upward sloping line.
(d) A line with a slope equal to zero.

_______ 22. When the relationship between two variables changes:
(a) There is movement from one point on the curve to another point on the curve.
(b) The curve is not affected.
(c) The entire curve shifts.
(d) The curve becomes linear.

_______ 23. A linear curve is distinguished by:
(a) Continuous changes in its slope.
(b) The same slope throughout the curve.
(c) The changing relationship between the two variables.
(d) A shift in the curve.

_______ 24. The slope of a production possibilities curve provides information about:
(a) The growth of the economy.
(b) Technological change.
(c) Opportunity costs.
(d) Income distribution.

Problems and Applications

Exercise 1

This exercise focuses on the concept of opportunity cost.

Suppose you have only 20 hours per week to allocate to study or leisure. Table 1.1 indicates the trade-off between leisure time (not studying) and the grade point average (GPA) achieved as a result of studying.

Table 1.1

	(a)	(b)	(c)	(d)	(e)
Leisure time (hours/week)	20	18	14.5	10	0
Grade point average	0	1.0	2.0	3.0	4.0

1. In Figure 1.1, draw the production possibilities curve that represents the possible combinations from Table 1.1.

Figure 1.1

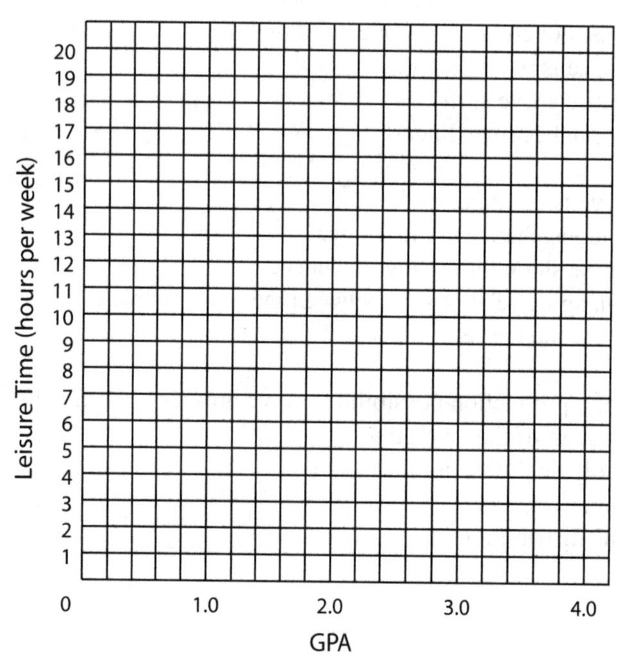

2. Using the information above, what is the opportunity cost of raising your GPA from 2.0 to 3.0?

____

3. What is the opportunity cost of raising your GPA from 3.0 to 4.0?

____

4. Why does the opportunity cost of improving your GPA increase as it moves closer to 4.0?

____

Exercise 2

This exercise provides practice in drawing and interpreting a production possibilities curve and demonstrating shifts of such a curve.

1. A production possibilities schedule showing the production alternatives between corn and lumber is presented in Table 1.2. Plot combination *A* in Figure 1.2 and label it. Do the same for combination *B*. In going from combination *A* to combination *B*, the economy has sacrificed _____ billion board feet of lumber production per year and has transferred the land to production of _____ billion bushels of corn per year. The opportunity cost of corn in terms of lumber is _____ board feet per bushel.

Table 1.2

Combination	*Quantity of corn (billions of bushels per year)*	*Quantity of lumber (billions of board feet per year)*
A	0	50
B	1	48
C	2	44
D	3	38
E	4	30
F	5	20
G	6	0

2. In answering Question 1 you determined the opportunity cost of corn when the economy is initially producing only lumber (combination *A*). Using the information in Table 1.2, plot the rest of the production possibilities combinations in Figure 1.2 and label each of the points with the appropriate letter. Connect the points to form the production possibilities curve.

Figure 1.2

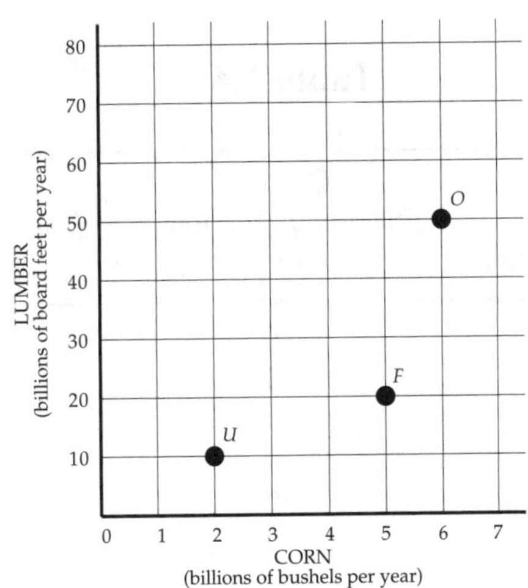

3. When Table 1.3 is completed, it should show the opportunity cost of corn at each possible combination of lumber and corn production in the economy. Opposite "1st billion bushels" insert the number of board feet per year of lumber sacrificed when the economy shifts from combination *A* to combination *B*. Complete the table for each of the remaining combinations.

Table 1.3

Corn production (billions of bushels per year)	*Opportunity cost of corn in terms of lumber (billions of board feet per year)*
1st billion bushels	______________
2nd billion bushels	______________
3rd billion bushels	______________
4th billion bushels	______________
5th billion bushels	______________
6th billion bushels	______________

4. In Table 1.3, as more corn is produced, the economy moves from combination *A* toward combination *G* and the opportunity cost of corn (falls, rises, remains the same), which illustrates the law of ______________________________.

5. Suppose that lumber companies begin to clear-cut forest areas instead of cutting them selectively. Clear-cutting improves the economy's ability to produce lumber but not corn. Table 1.4 describes such a situation. Using the information in Table 1.4, draw the new production possibilities curve in Figure 1.2 as you did the initial production possibilities curve based on Table 1.3. For which combination does clear-cutting fail to change the amount of corn and lumber produced? ______________

Table 1.4

Combination	*Corn (billions of bushels per year)*	*Lumber (billions of board feet per year)*
A'	0	75
B'	1	72
C'	2	66
D'	3	57
E'	4	45
F'	5	30
G'	6	0

6. After the introduction of clear-cutting, most of the new production possibilities curve is (outside, inside, the same as) the earlier curve. The opportunity cost of corn has (increased, decreased, not changed) as a result of clear-cutting.

7. Study your original production possibilities curve in Figure 1.2 and decide which of the combinations shown (*U, F, O*) demonstrates each of the following. (*Hint:* Check the answers at the end of the chapter to make sure you have diagrammed the production possibilities curve in Figure 1.2 correctly.)

   (a) Society is producing at its maximum potential. Combination ______.
   (b) Society has some unemployed or underemployed resources. Combination ______.
   (c) Society cannot produce this combination. Combination ______.
   (d) Society might be able to produce this combination if technology improved but cannot produce it with current technology. Combination ______.
   (e) If society produces this combination, some of society's wants will go unsatisfied unnecessarily. Combination ______.

Exercise 3

This exercise uses graphs in conjunction with opportunity cost and production possibilities.

Answer the following questions based on the information in the section of the text titled "WHAT to Produce."

______ 1. The term *peace dividend* refers to the:
   (a) Increase in consumer goods because of a decrease in military goods.
   (b) Availability of resources for the production of military goods.
   (c) Tradeoff between food and consumer goods.
   (d) Difference between a market economy and a mixed economy.

______ 2. For the United States, the share of total output devoted to military goods:
   (a) Has remained fairly constant since 1940.
   (b) Is currently about 15 percent.
   (c) Has decreased since the end of the Cold War.
   (d) Is fairly low and results in no opportunity cost.

______ 3. According to Figure 1.3 in the text, as the mix of output moves from point *S* to point *R*:
   (a) There is a decrease in the production of consumer goods.
   (b) There is an increase in the production of military goods.
   (c) The opportunity cost of more military goods is equal to the distance C_2 plus C_1.
   (d) The opportunity cost of more consumer goods is equal to the distance M_2 minus M_1.

______ 4. According to Figure 1.4 in the text, North Korea:
   (a) Has the largest army in the world in terms of number of personnel.
   (b) Has the highest opportunity cost of maintaining an army.
   (c) Spends more absolute dollars on its army than does any other country.
   (d) Has the lowest opportunity cost of maintaining an army.

_______ 5. Which of the following is the opportunity cost of maintaining an army in North Korea?
   (a) There is no opportunity cost because North Korea needs a large army to protect its citizens.
   (b) There is no opportunity cost because North Korea is producing the optimal mix of output.
   (c) Only the money spent on military equipment and salaries.
   (d) The food and other consumer goods that must be given up.

Appendix

Exercise 4

This exercise provides practice in the use of graphs.

Use Figure 1.3 below to answer the following questions.

Figure 1.3

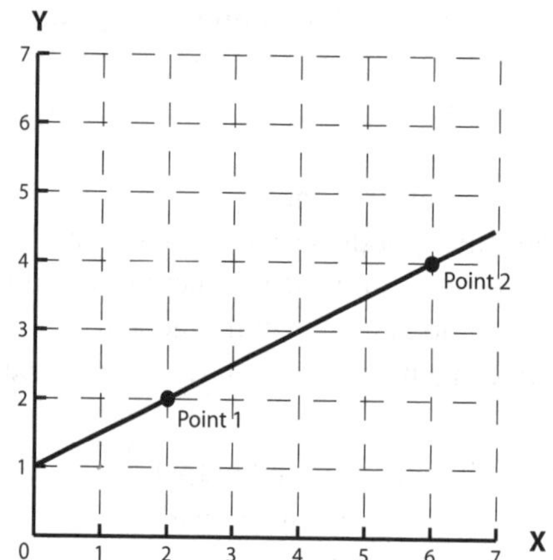

The slope of a line is the rate of change between two points or the vertical change divided by the horizontal change.

1. The vertical distance between the two points equals ________.

2. The horizontal distance between the two points equals ________.

3. The slope of the line equals ________.

4. The slope of the line is (positive, negative) because as one variable increases the other variable (increases, decreases).

5. The line has the same slope at every point implying a (constant, changing) relationship between the two variables.

6. When the slope of a line is the same at every point, the curve is (linear, nonlinear).

Common Errors

The first statement in each "common error" below is incorrect. Each incorrect statement is followed by a corrected version and an explanation.

1. Words used in economics have the same meaning as they do in our everyday conversation. *Incorrect!*
   Words that are used technically and precisely in economics *often* have different meanings when they are used more casually in everyday conversation. *Correct!*
   You must be very careful here. Words are used with precision in economics. You'll have difficulty if you confuse their everyday meanings with their economic meanings. For example, the term *capital* in economics refers to goods used in the production of other goods. In everyday usage it may mean money, machines, a loan, or even the British response to the question, "How are you feeling?"

2. Economic models are abstractions from the real world and are therefore useless in predicting and explaining economic behavior. *Incorrect!*
   Economic models are abstractions from the real world and *as a result* are useful in predicting and explaining economic behavior. *Correct!*
   You must be willing to deal with abstractions if you want to get anything accomplished in economics. By using economic models based on specific assumptions, we can make reasonable judgments about what's going on around us. We try not to disregard any useful information. However, to try to include everything (such as what cereal we like for breakfast) would be fruitless. For example, the production-possibilities curve is an abstraction. No economist would argue that it is an economy! But it certainly is useful in focusing on public-policy choices, such as the choice between guns and butter.

3. Because economics is a "science," all economists will arrive at the same answer to any given question. *Incorrect!*
   Economics is a science, but there is often room for disagreement in trying to answer a given question. *Correct!*
   Economics is a social science, and the entire society and economy represent the economist's laboratory. Economists cannot run the kind of experiments on the economy that are done by physical scientists. As a result, two economists may attack a given problem or question in different ways using different models. They may come up with different answers, but since there is no answer book, you cannot say which is right. The solution is to do more testing, refine our models, compare results, and so on. By the way, recent space exploration has given physicists cause to reevaluate some of their theories concerning our solar system, and there is much controversy concerning what the new evidence means. But physics is still a science, as is economics!

~ ANSWERS ~

Using Terms to Remember

Across

1. opportunity cost
3. government failure
5. factors of production
6. microeconomics
9. investment
12. market mechanism
14. *ceteris paribus*
15. laissez faire

Down

2. production possibilities
4. macroeconomics
7. mixed economy
8. economic growth
10. economics
11. market failure
13. scarcity

True or False

1. F Like all societies, the United States has to deal with the problem of scarcity. The United States is a prosperous nation because it uses its scarce resources efficiently.
2. T
3. F The production possibilities curve demonstrates the combinations of goods and services that society chooses to produce. It answers the WHAT question, not the FOR WHOM question.
4. F If a country had unlimited resources, then opportunity costs would *not* exist.
5. T
6. T
7. F The best answer to the HOW to produce question for an economy is the method of production with the lowest opportunity cost.
8. T
9. T
10. F Even though the goal of government intervention is to correct market failure, it may fail to improve economic outcomes or may even make the situation worse.

Multiple Choice

1. a	5. a	9. b	13. c	17. a	21. b
2. b	6. b	10. c	14. d	18. d	22. c
3. c	7. a	11. a	15. c	19. b	23. b
4. d	8. d	12. b	16. a	20. d	24. c

Problems and Applications

Exercise 1

1. **Figure 1.1 Answer**

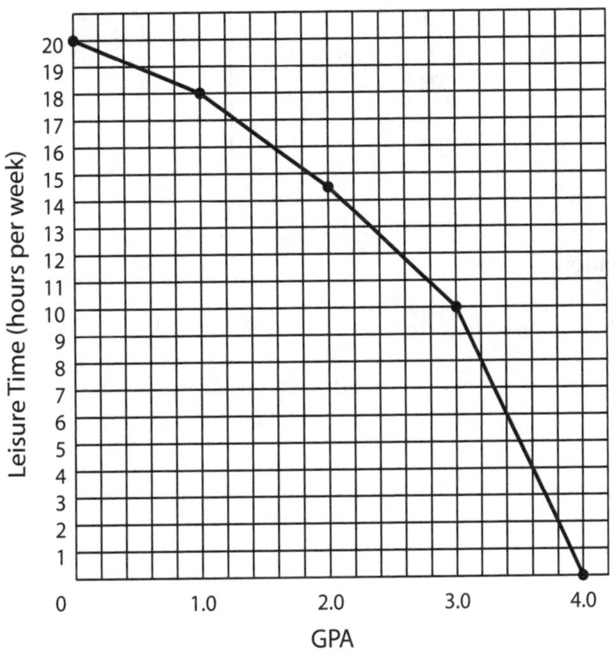

2. 4.5 hours of leisure time

3. 10 hours of leisure time

4. Higher grades are harder to get, particularly if the class is graded on a curve, with higher grades being received by a decreasing number of students.

Exercise 2

1. 2, 1, 2

2. **Figure 1.2 Answer**

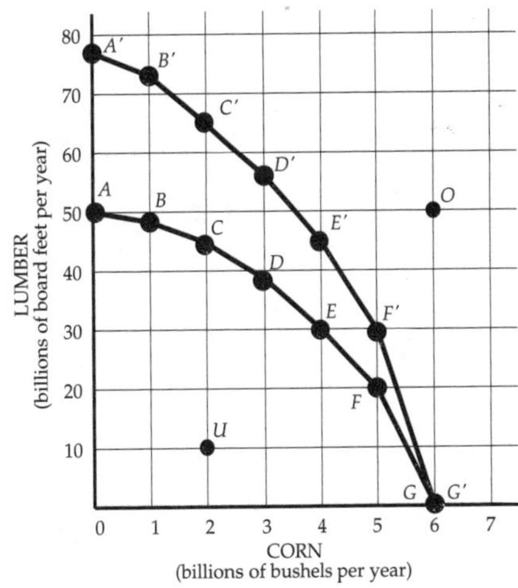

3. **Table 1.3 Answer**

Corn production (billions of bushels per year)	*Opportunity cost of corn in terms of lumber (billions of board feet per year)*
1st billion bushels	2
2nd billion bushels	4
3rd billion bushels	6
4th billion bushels	8
5th billion bushels	10
6th billion bushels	20

4. Rises, increasing opportunity costs
5. See Figure 1.2 answer, combination *G*
6. Outside, increased
7. a. *F* b. *U* c. *O* d. *O* e. *U*

Exercise 3

1. a
2. c
3. d
4. b
5. d

Exercise 4

1. 2
2. 4
3. Slope = vertical change ÷ horizontal change = 2 ÷ 4 = 1 ÷ 2 or 0.5
4. Positive, increases
5. Constant
6. Linear

CHAPTER 2

The U.S. Economy

Quick Review

- The answers to the WHAT, HOW, and FOR WHOM questions in the U.S. economy are a product of both market activity and government intervention. Economic activity is assessed using economic statistics.

- The most frequently used measure of an economy's production is gross domestic product (GDP), which is the monetary value of a nation's output. Real GDP is the measure of output adjusted for inflation. GDP for the United States, at roughly $15 trillion, is one-fifth of the world's total output.

- GDP per capita for the United States is more than five times the world's average. Abundant resources, skilled management, an educated work force, and advanced technology have contributed to the high level of output. Factor mobility and capital-intensive production have resulted in high productivity.

- GDP can be classified as consumer goods, investment goods, goods purchased by the government (federal, state, and local levels) and net exports. Consumer goods represent the largest portion of U.S. output, accounting for over two-thirds of all goods and services produced.

- The pattern of production in the United States has changed over the last century. At the beginning of the century farming was the dominant sector, then manufacturing, and now services. Service industries, including government, currently produce over 70 percent of total output.

- Business firms can be organized as sole proprietorships, partnerships, and corporations based on ownership characteristics. Even though they are fewest in number, corporations are responsible for about 80 percent of U.S. business sales.

- The government frequently regulates HOW output will be produced. Sometimes the answers to the WHAT, HOW, and FOR WHOM questions are made worse by government intervention, which is referred to as "government failure."

- Income is *not* distributed equally in the United States. Those in the highest income quintile receive half of the total U.S. income. In an attempt to make the distribution of income more equal, the government uses a system of taxes and transfers.

Learning Objectives

After reading the chapter and doing the following exercises you should be able to:

1. Explain how an economy's size is measured.
2. Describe the absolute and relative size of the U.S. economy.
3. Explain why the U.S. economy can produce so much.
4. Recount how the mix of U.S. output has changed over time.
5. Describe how (un)equally incomes are distributed.

Using Terms to Remember

Fill in the puzzle on the opposite page with the appropriate terms from the list of Terms to Remember in the text.

Across

3. The sum of consumption, investment, government expenditure, and net exports.
4. The resources used to produce goods and services.
9. Goods and services sold to other countries.
11. The knowledge and skills possessed by the labor force.
12. The quality of capital and labor contribute to the high level of ________________ in the United States.
14. The federal income tax system is an example.
15. An expansion of production possibilities.
16. Payments to individuals for which no current goods or services are exchanged.
17. A high ratio of capital to labor in the production process.

Down

1. Used as a measure of the standard of living.
2. The way total personal income is divided up among households or income classes.
5. The value of output measured in constant prices.
6. The value of output measured in current prices.
7. A firm that produces the entire market supply of a particular good or service.
8. Goods and services bought from other countries.
10. The cost or benefit of a market activity that affects a third party.
13. Includes expenditure on plant, machinery, and equipment by the business sector.

Puzzle 2.1

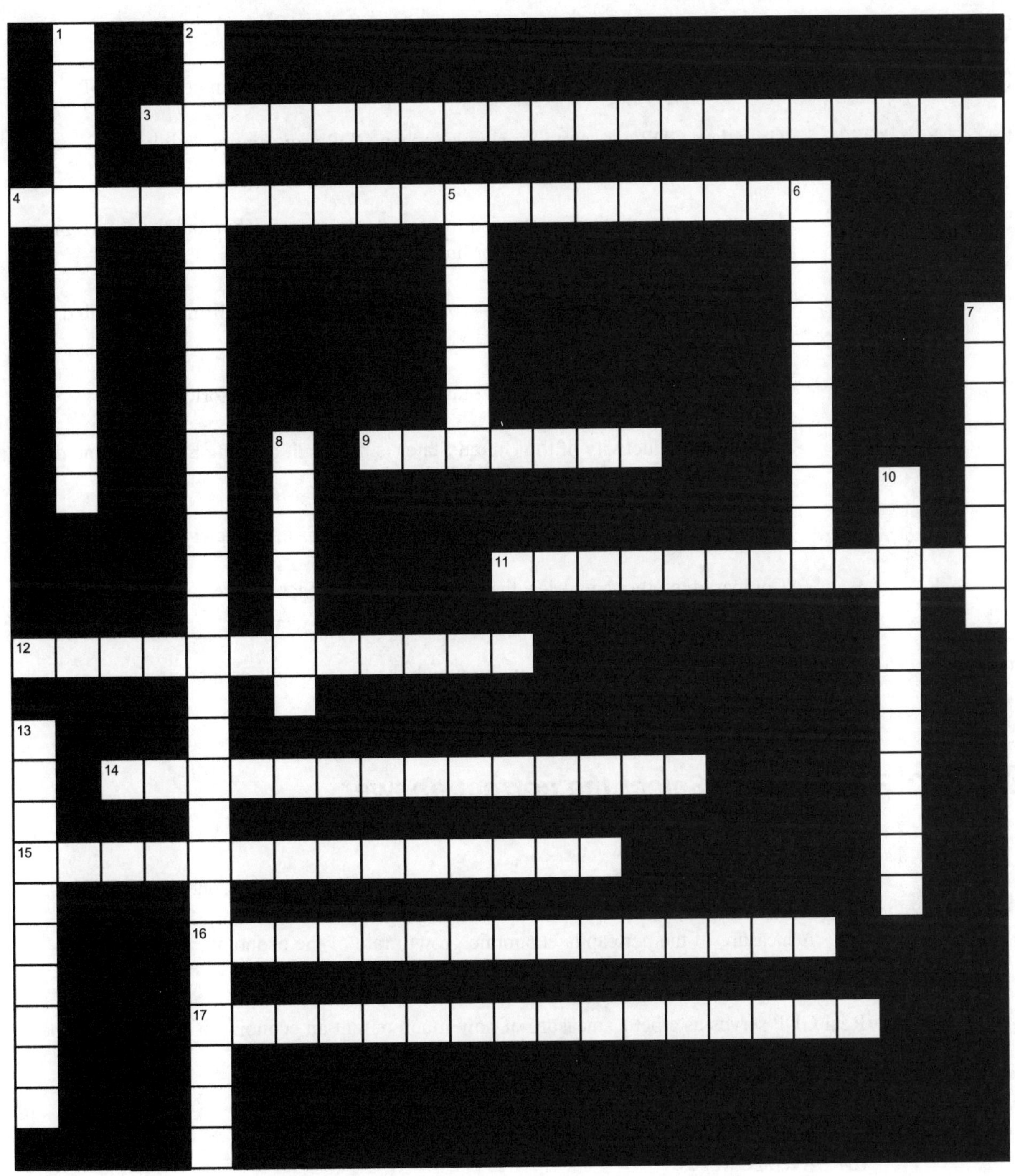

True or False: *Circle your choice and explain why any false statements are incorrect.*

T F 1. GDP measures the value of goods produced, but not services.

T F 2. In periods of rising prices, real GDP will rise more slowly than nominal GDP.

T F 3. Growth in GDP per capita is achieved when GDP grows more rapidly than population.

T F 4. Government regulation is intended to protect consumers, labor and the environment and provide a legal framework for businesses.

T F 5. Since proprietorships are the most common form of business firm in the United States, they account for the majority of business sales.

T F 6. As a percentage of GDP, service output has declined since World War II.

T F 7. The great productivity of the United States is the result of using highly educated workers in capital-intensive production processes.

T F 8. Externalities, such as pollution, result in spillover costs for society.

T F 9. Compared to other countries, the rich in the United States have a relatively high share of total income.

T F 10. A progressive tax system is one in which the tax rate falls as income rises.

Multiple Choice: *Select the correct answer.*

______ 1. GDP is:
- (a) The sum of the physical amounts of goods and services in the economy.
- (b) A dollar measure of output produced during a given time period.
- (c) A measure of the per capita economic growth rate of the economy.
- (d) A physical measure of the capital stock of the economy.

______ 2. Real GDP serves as a better measure of how much output an economy is producing than nominal GDP because real GDP measures changes in:
- (a) Prices only.
- (b) Prices and production.
- (c) Production only.
- (d) Average wages.

______ 3. On average, U.S. real GDP increases by about ____ percent per year.
- (a) One.
- (b) Three.
- (c) Five.
- (d) Seven.

_______ 4. If prices double in an economy and the quantity of output remains constant from one year to the next, then:
(a) GDP is four times larger in the second year than in the first.
(b) Real GDP is the same in the second year as in the first.
(c) On average, the population should be twice as well off in the second year as in the first.
(d) GDP per capita will definitely increase.

_______ 5. *Ceteris paribus,* which of the following is true concerning economic growth?
(a) It causes an increase in imports.
(b) It results in a decrease in government spending.
(c) It causes an increase in GDP because of inflation.
(d) It causes an increase in real GDP because of increased production possibilities.

_______ 6. Which of the following is true about U.S. GDP?
(a) Consumer goods account for approximately two-thirds of total output.
(b) Investment goods account for the second largest share of total output.
(c) Government services account for approximately one-half of total output.
(d) Net exports account for the second largest share of total output.

_______ 7. Which of the following is *not* an example of investment, as economists use the term?
(a) A new automobile manufacturing facility.
(b) New computers purchased by a private college for the President's Office.
(c) The $10,000 worth of stock that you hold as part of your retirement plan.
(d) The costumes purchased by a store to sell for Halloween.

_______ 8. Which of the following expenditures is the most important in expanding a country's production possibilities?
(a) Investment goods.
(b) Consumer goods.
(c) Government services.
(d) Net exports.

_______ 9. If the percentage of output for a given country changes from being primarily manufactured goods to primarily services, there has been a change in the:
(a) FOR WHOM question.
(b) WHAT question.
(c) WHY question.
(d) HOW question.

_______ 10. U.S. net exports are:
(a) Negative since the value of exports is less than the value of imports.
(b) Positive since the United States produces more output than any other country.
(c) Negative since foreigners purchase more U.S. output than the United States purchases from foreigners.
(d) Equal to the value of imports plus the value of exports.

_______ 11. GDP is equal to the sum of consumption, investment, net exports and:
(a) Government purchases.
(b) Income transfers.
(c) Saving.
(d) Human capital.

_______ 12. Which of the following sectors contributes the largest absolute amount to U.S. GDP?
(a) Farming.
(b) Services.
(c) Government.
(d) Manufacturing.

_______ 13. Foreign trade has become increasingly significant to the United States economy because of the:
(a) Low quality of factors of production in the United States.
(b) Reduction of educated workers in the United States.
(c) The growing share of manufacturing in the United States.
(d) Reduction of trade barriers between the United States and other countries.

_______ 14. Which of the following would *not* be included in U.S. GDP?
(a) A car made by a U.S. firm in Mexico.
(b) California wine purchased by a French businesswoman.
(c) A motorcycle made by a Japanese producer in Kansas.
(d) The meals prepared by a Mexican restaurant in Dallas.

_______ 15. Which of the following contributes to the high levels of GDP that the United States is able to produce?
(a) Equitable distribution of income.
(b) Labor intensive production.
(c) Government expenditure on welfare.
(d) Capital intensive production.

_______ 16. In terms of sales and control of assets, which of the following is the largest type of business firm in the United States?
(a) Proprietorships.
(b) Partnerships.
(c) Corporations.
(d) Nonprofit organizations.

_______ 17. The personal distribution of income tends to be more equal in:
(a) The United States but *not* other developed countries.
(b) Centrally planned economies such as North Korea.
(c) Developed countries, in general.
(d) Poor countries, in general.

_______ 18. If government intervention causes the economy to produce inside the production possibilities curve, this is known as:
(a) Market failure.
(b) Government failure.
(c) Externalities.
(d) Income inequality.

_______ 19. In the United States, the richest fifth of households receives:
(a) One-fifth of all the income.
(b) The same amount of income as the poorest fifth receives.
(c) The same amount of income as the second quintile receives.
(d) Approximately half of all the income.

_______ 20. Which of the following is true concerning income inequality in the United States?
(a) The United States is so prosperous that there is no income inequality to address.
(b) The federal income tax and transfer payments make the inequality worse.
(c) The federal income tax and transfer payments help to reduce the inequality.
(d) The federal income tax and transfer payments are so effective that the inequality is reduced almost completely.

Problems and Applications

Exercise 1

Each year an economic report on the state of the U.S. economy is prepared called *The Economic Report of the President.* It summarizes the essential features of the economy's performance and describes the policy initiatives that are likely to be undertaken. This exercise uses the kind of information that is developed in this publication.

Table 2.1 shows the real GDP and the nominal GDP for the years 2005-2012. (Your answers may differ from those in the answer section due to rounding.)

Table 2.1 Real GDP and nominal GDP, 2005-2012

Year	*Real GDP (in billions of dollars per year)*	*Nominal GDP (in billions of dollars per year)*	*Percentage growth in real GDP*	*Percentage growth in nominal GDP*	*U.S. population (in millions)*	*GDP per capita (in dollars per year)*
2005	$12,623	$12,623	--------	--------	295,517	_______
2006	12,959	13,377	_______	_______	298,380	_______
2007	13,206	14,029	_______	_______	301,231	_______
2008	13,162	14,292	_______	_______	304,094	_______
2009	12,758	13,974	_______	_______	306,772	_______
2010	13,063	14,499	_______	_______	309,350	_______
2011	13,299	15,076	_______	_______	311,592	_______
2012	13,591	15,682	_______	_______	313,914	_______

1. Using the information in Table 2.1 and the formula below, calculate the percentage growth in nominal and real GDP for each of the years 2005-2012 and insert your answers in the appropriate columns.

$$\text{Percentage growth in real GDP} = \frac{\text{real GDP}_t - \text{real GDP}_{t-1}}{\text{real GDP}_{t-1}} \times 100\%$$

where t = current year
$t - 1$ = previous year

For example, for 2006 real GDP grew by the following percentage:

$$\frac{\text{real GDP}_{2006} - \text{real GDP}_{2005}}{\text{real GDP}_{2005}} \times 100\% = \frac{\$12{,}959 - \$12{,}623}{\$12{,}623} \times 100\% = 2.66\ \% \text{ or } 2.7\ \%$$

2. T F When nominal GDP grows, real GDP must also grow.

3. By what nominal-dollar amount did nominal GDP grow from 2005 to 2012? $________

4. By what constant-dollar amount did real GDP grow from 2005 to 2012? $________

5. The U.S. population for the years 2005–2012 is presented in column 6 of Table 2.1. Using nominal GDP in column 3, calculate GDP per capita in column 7.

6. T F When GDP rises, GDP per capita must also rise.

Exercise 2

This problem is designed to help you understand the major uses of total output in the United States and their contribution to GDP.

1. First calculate the level of GDP for 2012, then calculate the percentage of total output accounted for by each of the expenditure categories in Table 2.2 below. (Your answers may differ from those in the answer section due to rounding.)

Table 2.2 U.S. national-income aggregates, 2012 (billions of dollars per year)

Expenditure categories	*(billions of dollars per year)*	*Percentage of total output*
Consumer goods and services	$11,121	________
Investment goods	2,059	________
Exports	2,183	________
Imports	2,743	________
Federal government purchases	1,214	________
State and local government purchases	1,849	________
GDP	$________	

2. Which of the GDP categories is the largest percentage of total output? ________________

3. Are net exports positive or negative in Table 2.2? ________________

4. T F When net exports are negative, an economy uses more goods and services than it produces.

Exercise 3

The following problem shows how to determine whether a tax structure is progressive or not.

Suppose Table 2.3 describes the incomes and taxes for individuals in the countries of Alpha and Omega.

1. Calculate the following:
   (a) The percentage of income paid in taxes at each income level for the citizens of Alpha (column 3 of Table 2.3).

(b) The percentage of income paid in taxes at each income level for the citizens of Omega (column 5 of Table 2.3).

Table 2.3 Taxes on income in Alpha and Omega

(1) Income	*(2) Taxes paid in Alpha*	*(3) Tax rate in Alpha*	*(4) Taxes paid in Omega*	*(5) Tax rate in Omega*
$25,000	$5,000	________%	$2,500	________%
50,000	10,000	________	7,500	________
75,000	15,000	________	15,000	________
100,000	20,000	________	22,000	________

2. In the country of Alpha, is the tax on income progressive? ________

3. In the country of Omega, is the tax on income progressive? ________

4. Which of the following is the most logical approach if an economy wants to redistribute income to the poor?
   (a) A flat or constant tax structure.
   (b) A progressive tax structure.

Common Errors

The first statement in each "common error" below is incorrect. Each incorrect statement is followed by a corrected version and an explanation.

1. Income and output are two entirely different things. *Incorrect!*
   Income and output are two sides of the same coin. *Correct!*
   This is fundamental. Every time a dollar's worth of final spending takes place, the seller must receive a dollar's worth of income. It could not be otherwise. Remember, profits are used as a balancing item. Don't confuse the term *income* with the term *profit*. Profits can be negative, whereas output for the economy cannot.

2. Comparisons of GDP per capita between countries tells you which population is better off. *Incorrect!*
   Comparisons of GDP per capita between countries are only indicators of which population is better off. *Correct!*
   Simple comparisons of GDP per capita ignore how the GDP is distributed. A country with a very high GDP per capita that is unequally distributed may provide a living standard that is below that of another country with a lower GDP per capita but which is more equally distributed. Other problems with comparisons of GDP per capita result from exchange-rate distortions, differences in mix of output in two countries, and how the economy is organized. GDP per capita is an indicator only of the amount of goods and services each person could have, not what they do have.

3. Equity and equality of income distribution mean the same thing. *Incorrect!*
   Equity and equality of income distribution mean different things. *Correct!*
   Many arguments over the division of the income pie, are laced with the terms *equity* and *equality* used interchangeably. They are not interchangeable. Equality of income distribution means that each person has an equal share. Equity of income distribution implies something about fairness. In a free society some will surely be more productive than others at doing what society wants done. The brain surgeon's services have greater value than the hairdresser's. The surgeon's income will exceed that of the hairdresser—that is, they will be unequal, but is that inequitable? This is a matter of judgment. It's safe to say, however, that if one were not allowed to keep some of the rewards for being more productive than average, our economy would suffer. An equitable distribution of income in our society will require some inequality. How much? There is no sure answer to that question.

~ ANSWERS ~

Using Terms to Remember

Across

3. gross domestic product
4. factors of production
9. exports
11. human capital
12. productivity
14. progressive tax
15. economic growth
16. income transfers
17. capital intensive

Down

1. per capita GDP
2. personal distribution of income
5. real GDP
6. nominal GDP
7. monopoly
8. imports
10. externality
13. investment

True or False

1. F GDP measures the value of both goods and services produced.
2. T
3. T
4. T
5. F Proprietorships are the most common form of business firm, but they are typically quite small and account for only about 12 percent of business sales.
6. F As a percentage of GDP, U.S. service output has increased since World War II, but manufacturing output has declined.
7. T
8. T
9. F Compared to other countries, the rich in the United States have a relatively low share of total income.
10. F A progressive tax system is one in which the tax rate *rises* as income rises.

Multiple Choice

1. b	5. d	9. b	13. d	17. c
2. c	6. a	10. a	14. a	18. b
3. b	7. c	11. a	15. d	19. d
4. b	8. a	12. b	16. c	20. c

Problems and Applications

Exercise 1

1. **Table 2.1 Answer**

Year	*Real GDP (in billions of dollars per year)*	*Nominal GDP (in billions of dollars per year)*	*Percentage growth in real GDP*	*Percentage growth in nominal GDP*	*U.S. population (in millions)*	*GDP per capita (in dollars per year)*
2005	$12,623	$12,623	------	------	295,993	42,646
2006	12,959	13,377	2.7	6.0	298,818	44,766
2007	13,206	14,029	1.9	4.9	301,696	46,500
2008	13,162	14,292	- 0.3	1.9	304,543	46,929
2009	12,758	13,974	- 3.1	- 2.2	307,240	45,482
2010	13,063	14,499	2.4	3.8	309,776	46,805
2011	13,299	15,076	1.8	4.0	312,036	48,315
2012	13,591	15,682	2.2	4.0	314,278	49,898

2. F
3. $3,059 billion
4. $968 billion
5. See Table 2.1 Answer, column 7.
6. F

Exercise 2

1. **Table 2.2 Answer**

Expenditure categories	*(billions of dollars per year)*	*Percentage of total output*
Consumer goods and services	$11,121	70.9
Investment goods	2,059	13.1
Exports	2,183	13.9
Imports	2,743	17.5
Federal government purchases	1,214	7.7
State and local government purchases	1,849	11.8
GDP	$15,683	

2. Consumer goods and services
3. Negative
4. T

Exercise 3

1. (a) See column 3 in Table 2.3.
   (b) See column 5 in Table 2.3.

Table 2.3 Answer

(1) *Income*	*(2)* *Taxes paid in Alpha*	*(3)* *Tax rate*	*(4)* *Taxes paid in Omega*	*(5)* *Tax rate*
$25,000	$5,000	20.0%	$2,500	10.0%
50,000	10,000	20.0	7,500	15.0
75,000	15,000	20.0	15,000	20.0
100,000	20,000	20.0	22,000	22.0

2. No. As income increases, the tax rate remains constant at 20%. (column 3)

3. Yes. As income increases, the tax rate increasesfrom 10% to 22%. (column 5)

4. b (A progressive tax is the most logical choice if an economy wants to redistribute income to the poor.)

CHAPTER 3

Supply and Demand

Quick Review

- Participation in the market by consumers, businesses, and government is motivated by the desire to maximize something: utility for consumers, profits for businesses, and general welfare for the government.

- Interactions in the marketplace involve either the factor market, where factors of production are bought and sold, or the product market, where goods and services are bought and sold.

- The demand curve represents buyer behavior. It slopes downward and to the right, showing that buyers are willing and able to purchase greater quantities at lower prices, *ceteris paribus*. The supply curve represents producer behavior. It slopes upward and to the right, indicating that producers are willing and able to produce greater quantities at higher prices, *ceteris paribus*.

- Movements along a demand curve result from a change in price and are referred to as a "change in quantity demanded." Shifts in a demand curve result from a change in a nonprice determinant—tastes, income, other goods, expectations, the number of buyers—and are referred to as a "change in demand."

- Movements along a supply curve result from a change in price and are referred to as a "change in quantity supplied." Shifts in a supply curve result from a change in a nonprice determinant—technology, factor costs, other goods, taxes and subsidies, expectations, the number of sellers—and are referred to as a "change in supply."

- Market demand and market supply summarize the intentions of all those participating on one side of the market or the other.

- Equilibrium price and quantity are established at the intersection of the supply and demand curves. At any price other than the equilibrium price, disequilibrium will occur.

- Price ceilings are set below the equilibrium price and result in shortages; price floors are set above the equilibrium price and result in surpluses. In either case, the market does not clear.

- The market mechanism relies on the forces of demand and supply to establish market outcomes (prices and quantities) in both product and factor markets. The market mechanism thus can be used to answer the WHAT, HOW, and FOR WHOM questions. This laissez-faire approach requires that government not intervene in the economy.

Learning Objectives

After reading the chapter and doing the following exercises you should be able to:

1. Explain why people participate in markets.
2. Describe what market demand and supply measure.
3. Depict how and why a market equilibrium is found.
4. Illustrate how and why demand and supply curves shift.
5. Explain how market shortages and surpluses occur.

Using Terms to Remember

Fill in the puzzle on the opposite page with the appropriate terms from the list of Terms to Remember in the text.

Across

3. The amount by which quantity demanded exceeds quantity supplied.
7. The price at which quantity demanded equals quantity supplied.
9. The willingness and ability to sell various quantities of a good at alternative prices.
11. The willingness and ability to buy a particular good at some price.
15. The assumption by economists that nothing else changes.
18. Where businesses purchase the factors of production.
20. The direct exchange of one good for another.
21. Economic policy advocated by Adam Smith.
22. Refers to the inverse relationship between price and quantity.

Down

1. Occurs because of a change in one of the determinants such as income or tastes.
2. The _____ _____ describes the buying intentions of consumers at alternative prices.
3. The sum of all producers' sales intentions.
4. Occurs when government intervention fails to improve economic outcomes.
5. A table showing the quantities of a good a consumer is willing and able to buy at alternative prices.
6. Where goods and services are exchanged.
8. The use of market price and sales to signal desired output.
10. The result of a price set above the equilibrium price.
12. Creates a market surplus.
13. An upper limit imposed on the price of a good.
14. Refers to the direct relationship between price and quantity.
16. The value of the most desirable forgone alternative.
17. The sum of individual demands.
19. Any place where goods and services are bought and sold.

Puzzle 3.1

True or False: *Circle your choice and explain why any false statements are incorrect.*

T F 1. We rely on others to produce most goods and services for us because we are better off when we specialize in what we produce best and trade for (i.e., purchase) other goods and services.

T F 2. A market exists only at those physical locations where exchange takes place.

T F 3. Based on the law of demand, a higher price causes an increase in quantity demanded.

T F 4. A market-demand curve can be found by adding together the separate demands of the individual consumers at each price.

T F 5. The supply curve of an individual producer is based on the expected demand in the market.

T F 6. The supply curve for gasoline will shift when the price of gasoline increases, *ceteris paribus*.

T F 7. The law of supply reflects the concept that it takes a higher price to induce greater output because costs per unit typically increase as output increases.

T F 8. If the price of a good is equal to the equilibrium price, there are no shortages or surpluses.

T F 9. At the equilibrium price for houses, everyone who desires a house is able to get one.

T F 10. If the actual price of a good is greater than the equilibrium price, a shortage results.

Multiple Choice: *Select the correct answer.*

_______ 1. People benefit by participating in the market because:
(a) Resources are no longer limited.
(b) Someone else is more proficient than you at producing a particular good.
(c) Market participation allows specialization and, ultimately, higher levels of consumption.
(d) Participants in the market do not have to make choices.

_______ 2. The goals of the principal participants in a market economy are to maximize:
(a) Income for consumers, profits for businesses, and taxes for government.
(b) Satisfaction for consumers, society's welfare for businesses, and taxes for government.
(c) Satisfaction for consumers, profits for businesses, and society's welfare for government.
(d) Society's general welfare.

_______ 3. Consumers:
(a) Provide dollars to the factor market.
(b) Receive dollars from the factor market.
(c) Receive dollars from the product market.
(d) Receive goods and services from the factor market.

_______ 4. In the U.S. economy, foreigners participate in:
(a) Both the product and factor markets.
(b) The product market only.
(c) The factor market only.
(d) Foreigners do not participate in the U.S. economy.

_______ 5. According to the law of demand, a demand curve:
(a) Exceeds the economy's ability to produce because people have unlimited wants.
(b) Slopes upward to the right.
(c) Is a horizontal, or flat, line.
(d) Slopes downward to the right.

_______ 6. Which of the following does *not* cause a shift in the demand curve?
(a) The income of consumers.
(b) Desire for the good.
(c) The price of the good itself.
(d) The number of consumers.

_______ 7. Given a downward-sloping market demand curve for computer tablets, if the price of tablets decreases from $350 to $250 then, *ceteris paribus*, the:
(a) Quantity demanded of tablets will increase.
(b) Quantity demanded of tablets will decrease.
(c) Supply of tablets will increase since sellers know that consumers will buy more.
(d) Demand for tablets will decrease.

_______ 8. *Ceteris paribus*, a rightward shift of the demand curve causes the equilibrium price to _____ and the equilibrium quantity to _____.
(a) Decrease; increase
(b) Increase; increase
(c) Decrease; decrease
(d) Increase; decrease

_______ 9. Which of the following will typically cause a decrease in the demand for automobiles?
(a) An increase in the price of automobiles.
(b) An increase in consumers' income.
(c) An increase in gasoline prices.
(d) Consumer expectations that the price of automobiles will be higher next year.

_______ 10. Which of the following provides the best example of the law of supply?
(a) Falling labor costs cause an increase in supply.
(b) Improved technology shifts the supply curve to the right.
(c) Some producers leave the industry, and the supply curve shifts to the left.
(d) Producers are willing to supply a greater quantity of a good at a higher price.

_______ 11. A movement along a supply curve is referred to as a change in the:
(a) Producer quotient.
(b) Quantity supplied.
(c) Output ratio.
(d) Law of demand.

_______ 12. Given an upward-sloping market supply curve for video game systems, if the price of video game systems falls from $290 to $250 then, *ceteris paribus*, the:
(a) Supply of video game systems will increase.
(b) Quantity supplied of video game systems will increase.
(c) Quantity supplied of video game systems will decrease.
(d) Demand for video game systems will decrease.

_______ 13. *Ceteris paribus*, a leftward shift of the supply curve causes the equilibrium price to _____ and the equilibrium quantity to _____.
(a) Increase; decrease
(b) Increase; increase
(c) Decrease; decrease
(d) Decrease; increase

_______ 14. A market is said to be in equilibrium when:
(a) Demand is fully satisfied at all alternative prices.
(b) The quantity demanded equals the quantity supplied.
(c) The buying intentions of all consumers are realized.
(d) The supply intentions of all sellers are realized.

_______ 15. In a market, the equilibrium price is determined by:
(a) The behavior of buyers but *not* the behavior of sellers.
(b) The behavior of sellers but *not* the behavior of buyers.
(c) What the government thinks is fair.
(d) The behavior of buyers and sellers.

_______ 16. When demand increases, *ceteris paribus*, the equilibrium price will also increase because:
(a) A shortage exists at the old equilibrium price.
(b) A surplus exists at the old equilibrium price.
(c) The quantity demanded has increased.
(d) The quantity supplied has decreased.

_______ 17. If the government establishes a price ceiling in the form of rent controls, this results in a:
(a) Shortage of housing.
(b) Surplus of housing.
(c) Market equilibrium for housing.
(d) Better market outcome for everyone because the price of housing is lower.

_______ 18. A market surplus is:
(a) Caused by a price ceiling.
(b) The amount by which the quantity supplied exceeds the quantity demanded at a given price.
(c) A situation that occurs when the equilibrium price is set too high by the government.
(d) The amount by which the quantity demanded exceeds the quantity supplied at a given price.

_______ 19. An effective price floor results in pressure to:
(a) Reduce prices because of surpluses.
(b) Raise prices because of surpluses.
(c) Reduce prices because of shortages.
(d) Raise prices because of shortages.

______ 20. A laissez-faire economic policy would advocate:
(a) The production of goods and services that are needed rather than demanded.
(b) Price ceilings to make goods and services more affordable for consumers.
(c) Government determination of WHAT to produce.
(d) Markets without government interference.

Problems and Applications

Exercise 1

This exercise provides practice in graphing demand and supply curves for individual buyers and sellers as well as graphing market-demand and market-supply curves.

1. Suppose you are willing and able to buy 20 gallons of gasoline per week if the price is $2.00 per gallon, but if the price is $6.00 per gallon you are willing and able to buy only the bare minimum of 10 gallons. Complete the demand schedule in Table 3.1.

Table 3.1 Your demand schedule for gasoline

Price (dollars per gallon)	*Quantity (gallons per week)*
$2.00	________
6.00	________

2. Use your demand schedule for gasoline in Table 3.1 to draw the demand curve in Figure 3.1. Assume the demand curve is a straight line.

Figure 3.1 Your demand curve for gasoline

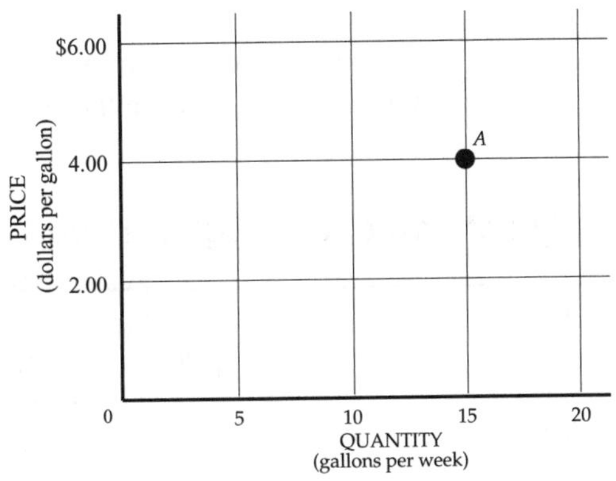

If you have drawn the demand curve correctly, it should pass through point *A*.

3. Suppose that 999 other people in your town have demand curves for gasoline that are just like yours in Figure 3.1. Fill out the town's market-demand schedule in Table 3.2 at each price. (Remember to include your own quantity demanded along with everyone else's at each price.)

Table 3.2 Market-demand schedule for gasoline in your town

Price (dollars per gallon)	*Quantity (gallons per week)*
$2.00	________
6.00	________

4. Using the market-demand schedule in Table 3.2, draw the market-demand curve for gasoline for your town in Figure 3.2. Assume the curve is a straight line and label it *D*.

Figure 3.2 Market-supply and market-demand curves for gasoline in your town

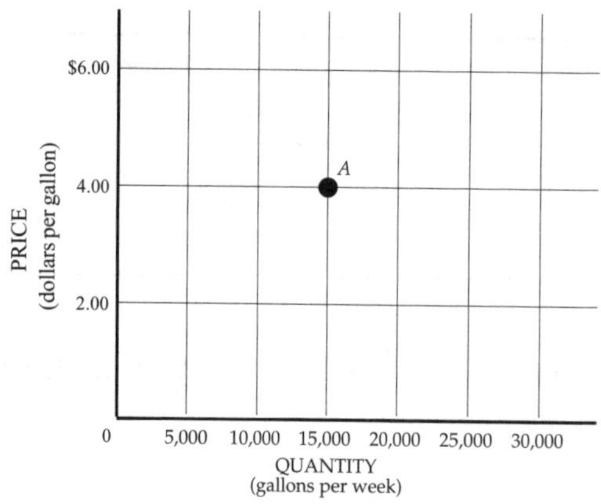

If you have drawn the demand curve correctly, it should pass through point *A*.

5. Suppose the friendly neighborhood gas station is willing to sell 250 gallons at $2.00 per gallon, and at $6.00 it is willing to sell 1,250 gallons per week. Fill in the supply schedule for this gas station in Table 3.3

Table 3.3 Supply schedule for neighborhood gas station

Price (dollars per gallon)	*Quantity (gallons per week)*
$2.00	________
6.00	________

6. Graph the supply curve in Figure 3.3 based on information in Table 3.3 and label it *S*. Assume the supply curve is a straight line.

Figure 3.3 Supply curve for neighborhood gas station

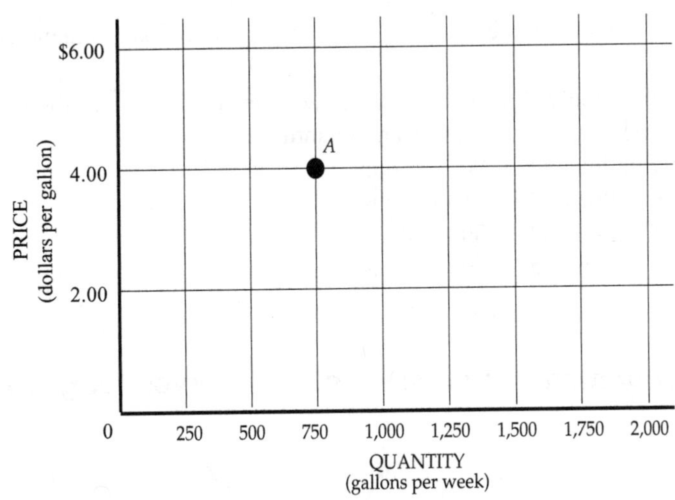

If you have drawn the supply curve correctly, it should pass through point *A*.

7. Suppose that 19 other gas stations in your town have the same supply schedule as your neighborhood gas station (Table 3.3). Fill out the market-supply schedule for gasoline of the 20 gas stations in your town in Table 3.4.

Table 3.4 Market-demand schedule for gasoline in your town

Price (dollars per gallon)	*Quantity (gallons per week)*
$2.00	______
6.00	______

8. Using the market-supply schedule in Table 3.4, draw the market-supply curve for gasoline for your town in Figure 3.2. Assume the market-supply curve is a straight line. If you have drawn the curve correctly, it should pass through point *A*. Label the supply curve *S*.

9. The equilibrium price for gasoline for your town's 20 gas stations and 1,000 buyers of gasoline (see Figure 3.2) is:
   (a) Above $4.00.
   (b) Exactly $4.00.
   (c) Below $4.00.

10. At the equilibrium price:
   (a) There is a shortage.
   (b) There is a surplus.
   (c) There is an excess of inventory.
   (d) The quantity demanded equals the quantity supplied.

Exercise 2

This exercise shows the market mechanics at work in shifting market-demand curves.

1. In Figure 3.4, the supply (S_1) and demand (D_1) curves for gasoline as they might appear in your town are presented. The equilibrium price and quantity are:
   (a) \$2.00 per gallon and 20,000 gallons.
   (b) \$4.00 per gallon and 20,000 gallons.
   (c) \$4.00 per gallon and 15,000 gallons.
   (d) \$6.00 per gallon and 15,000 gallons.

Figure 3.4 Market-demand and market-supply curves for gasoline in your town

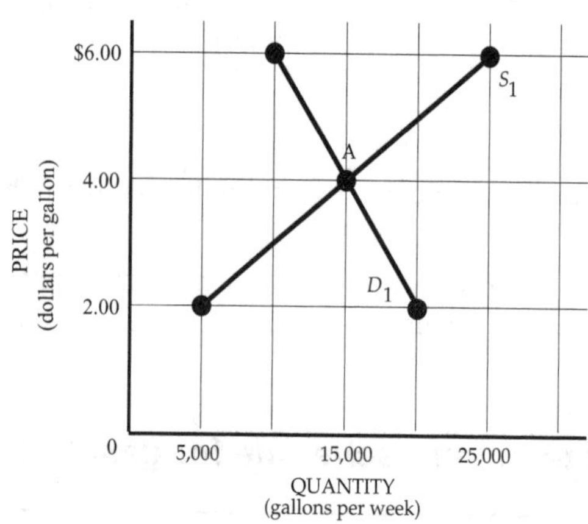

2. Assume that one-half of the people in your town move away. Because of this, suppose that the remaining buyers are willing and able to buy only half as much gasoline at each price as was bought before. Draw the new demand curve in Figure 3.4 and label it D_2.

3. When the number of buyers in a market changes, the market-demand curve for goods and services shifts and there is a change in (demand, quantity demanded).

4. When half of the buyers move from your town and the demand curve shifts, the new equilibrium price:
   (a) Is above the old equilibrium price.
   (b) Remains the same as the old equilibrium price.
   (c) Is below the old equilibrium price.
   (*Hint:* See the second demand curve, D_2, in Figure 3.4.)

5. Given the new demand curve, if the market price remains at the old equilibrium of \$3.00 then:
   (a) A surplus of gasoline will occur.
   (b) A shortage of gasoline will occur.
   (c) The quantity demanded will equal the quantity supplied.

6. When there is a surplus in a market, prices are likely to fall because:
   (a) Buyers do not wish to buy as much as sellers want to sell.
   (b) Sellers are likely to offer discounts to eliminate expensive excess inventories.
   (c) Buyers who cannot buy commodities at the current market price are likely to make offers to buy at lower prices that sellers will now accept.
   (d) All of the above.

7. When there is a leftward shift of the market-demand curve, market forces should push market prices:
   (a) Upward and market quantity downward.
   (b) Upward and market quantity upward.
   (c) Downward and market quantity upward.
   (d) Downward and market quantity downward.

8. When there is a rightward shift of the market-demand curve, market forces should push market prices:
   (a) Upward and market quantity downward.
   (b) Upward and market quantity upward.
   (c) Downward and market quantity upward.
   (d) Downward and market quantity downward.

Exercise 3

This exercise gives practice in computing market-demand and market-supply curves using the demand and supply curves of individuals in a market.

1. Table 3.5 shows the weekly demand and supply schedules for various individuals. Fill in the total market quantity that these individuals demand and supply.

Table 3.5 Individual demand and supply schedules

Price	*$1.00*	*$2.00*	*$3.00*	*$4.00*
Buyers				
Albert's quantity demanded	4	3	2.5	1.5
Becca's quantity demanded	4.5	4	3	2.5
Alan's quantity demanded	4	3	2	1
Total market quantity demanded	____	____	____	____
Sellers				
Caitlyn's quantity supplied	1	3	4.5	6
Carlie's quantity supplied	2	3	4.5	6
Tyler's quantity supplied	1	2	3	4
Emilio's quantity supplied	1	2	3	4
Total market quantity supplied	____	____	____	____

Use the data in Table 3.5 to answer Questions 2-4.

2. Construct and label market-supply and market-demand curves in Figure 3.5.

3. Identify the equilibrium point and label it *EQ* in Figure 3.5.

4. What is true about the relationship between quantity demanded versus quantity supplied at a price of $3.00 in Figure 3.5?

   ____

Figure 3.5 Market-supply and market-demand curves for buyers and sellers

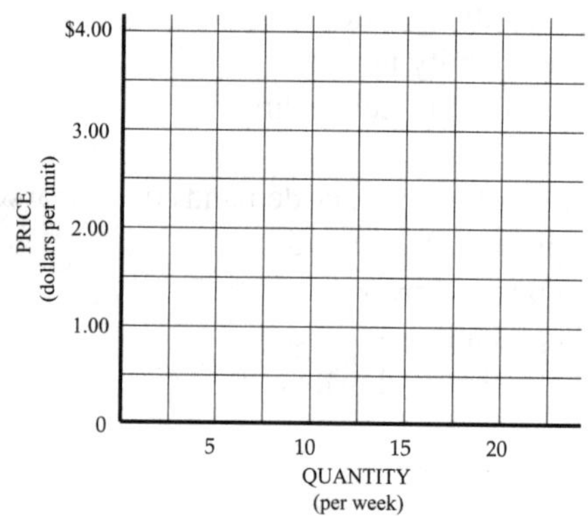

Exercise 4

This exercise provides examples of events that would shift the demand or supply curve. It is similar to a problem at the end of the chapter in the text.

Figure 3.6 Shifts of curves

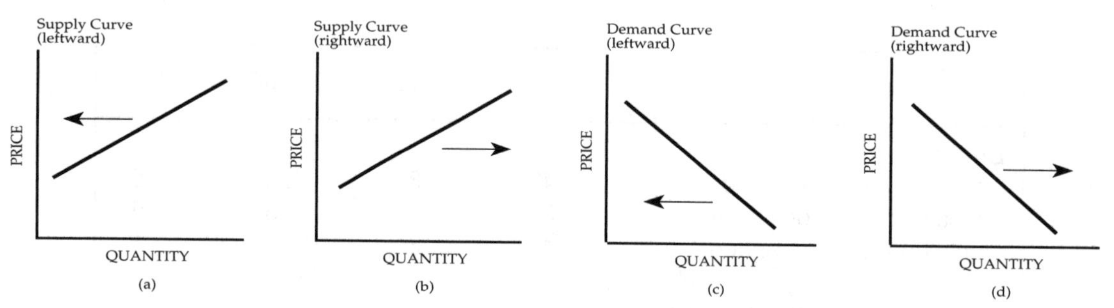

Choose the letter of the appropriate diagram in Figure 3.6 that best describes the shift that should occur in each of the following situations. The shifts are occurring in the market for U.S. defense goods. (*Hint*: Ask yourself if the change first affects buyers or sellers. Refer to the nonprice determinants for demand and supply listed in the text if necessary.)

_____ 1. Because of increased protectionism for steel, domestic steel producers are able to raise the price of specialty steel, which is a key resource in the production of defense goods.

_____ 2. A new process for creating microchips is developed that reduces the cost of materials needed to produce nuclear submarines.

_____ 3. As a result of worldwide terrorist threats, new buyers enter the market to purchase defense goods.

_____ 4. A country that previously bought U.S. defense goods enters into a peace agreement.

_____ 5. Because of heightened concerns about national security, additional U.S. firms begin producing defense weapons.

Common Errors

The first statement in each "common error" below is incorrect. Each incorrect statement is followed by a corrected version and an explanation.

1. Market price is the same thing as equilibrium price. *Incorrect!*
   The market price moves by trial and error (via the market mechanism) toward the equilibrium price. *Correct!*
   When demand and supply curves shift, the market is temporarily out of equilibrium. The price may move along a demand or supply curve toward the new equilibrium.

2. Since the quantity bought must equal the quantity sold, every market is always in equilibrium by definition. *Incorrect!*
   Although quantity bought equals quantity sold, there may be shortages or surpluses. *Correct!*
   Although the quantity *actually* bought does equal the quantity *actually* sold, there may still be buyers who *are willing and able* to buy more of the good at the market price (shortages exist) or sellers who are willing and able to sell more of the good at the market price (surpluses exist). If the market price is above the equilibrium price, there will be a surplus of goods (inventories). Prices will be lowered by sellers toward the equilibrium price. If the market price is below the equilibrium price, there will be a shortage of goods. Prices will be bid up by buyers toward the equilibrium price.

3. A change in price changes the demand for goods by consumers. *Incorrect!*
   A change in price changes the quantity demanded by consumers in a given time period. *Correct!*
   Economists differentiate between the terms *quantity demanded* and *demand.* A change in the quantity demanded refers to a movement along the demand curve due to a change in the price of the good itself. A change in demand refers to a shift of the demand curve due to a change in tastes, income, price and availability of other goods, or expectations.

4. A change in price changes the supply of goods produced by a firm. *Incorrect!*
   A change in price changes the quantity of a good supplied by a firm in a given time period. *Correct!*
   Economists differentiate between the terms *quantity supplied* and *supply.* A change in the quantity supplied refers to a movement along a supply curve due to a change in price. A change in supply refers to a shift of the supply curve due to a change in technology, factor costs, other goods, taxes and subsidies, expectations, or number of sellers.

~ ANSWERS ~

Using Terms to Remember

Across

3. market shortage
7. equilibrium price
9. supply
11. demand
15. *ceteris paribus*
18. factor market
20. barter
21. laissez faire
22. law of demand

Down

1. shift in demand
2. demand curve
3. market supply
4. government failure
5. demand schedule
6. product market
8. market mechanism
10. market surplus
12. price floor
13. price ceiling
14. law of supply
16. opportunity cost
17. market demand
19. market

True or False

1. T
2. F A market exists anywhere goods and services are bought and sold.
3. F Based on the law of demand, a higher price causes a *decrease* in quantity demanded.
4. T
5. F Supply represents the intentions of the sellers only (i.e., the quantities of goods they are willing and able to offer for sale at various prices).
6. F When the price of gasoline increases, the quantity supplied increases. This results in a movement along the supply curve.
7. T
8. T
9. F Only those buyers who are willing and able to purchase a house at the equilibrium price will be able to get a house.
10. F If the actual price of a good is greater than the equilibrium price, a *surplus* results. If the actual price of a good is *less* than the equilibrium price, a *shortage* results.

Multiple Choice

1. c
2. c
3. b
4. a
5. d
6. c
7. a
8. b
9. c
10. d
11. b
12. c
13. a
14. b
15. d
16. a
17. a
18. b
19. a
20. d

Problems and Applications

Exercise 1

1. **Table 3.1 Answer**

p	*q*
$2.00	20
6.00	10

2. **Figure 3.1 Answer**

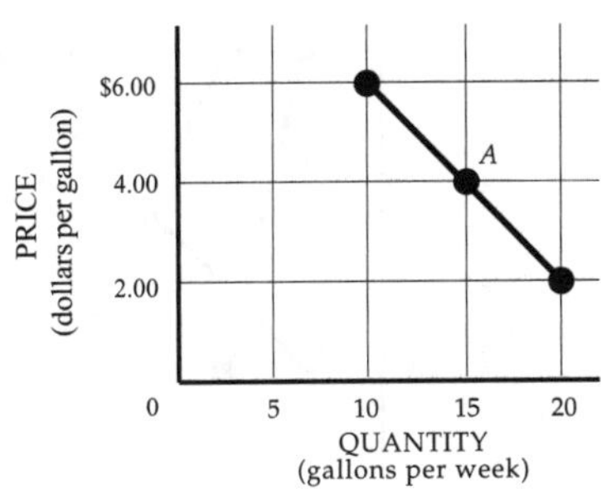

3. **Table 3.2 Answer**

p	*q*
$2.00	20,000
6.00	10,000

4. **Figure 3.2 Answer**

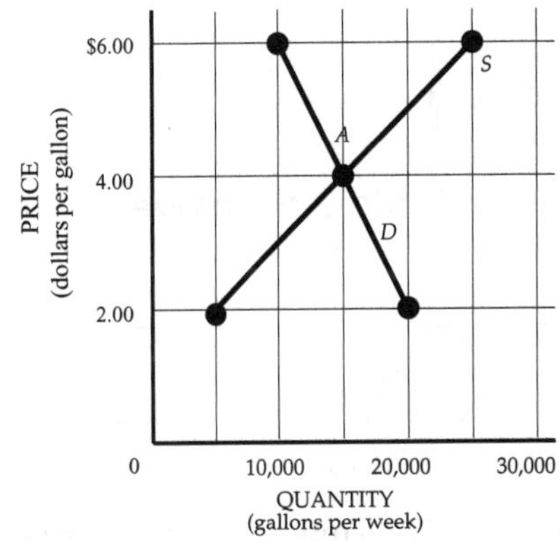

5. **Table 3.3 Answer**

p	*q*
$2.00	250
6.00	250

6. **Figure 3.3 Answer**

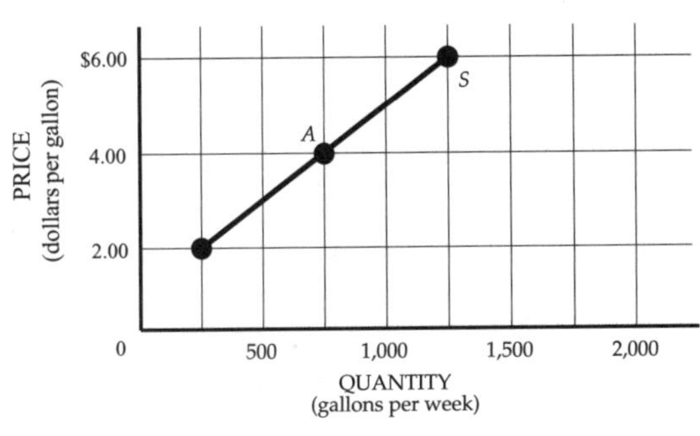

7. **Table 3.4 Answer**

p	*q*
$2.00	5,000
6.00	25,000

8. See Figure 3.2 Answer.
9. b
10. d

Exercise 2

1. c
2. **Figure 3.4 Answer**

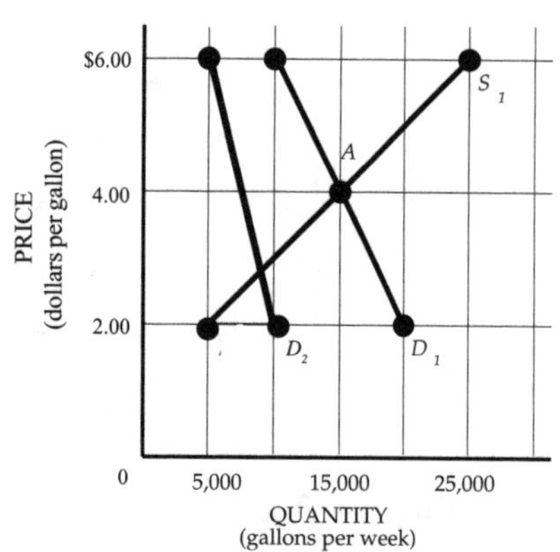

3. Demand
4. c
5. a
6. d
7. d
8. b

Exercise 3

1. **Table 3.5 Answer**

Price	*$1.00*	*$2.00*	*$3.00*	*$4.00*
Buyers				
Total market quantity demanded	12.5	10	7.5	5
Sellers				
Total market quantity supplied	5	10	15	20

2. **Figure 3.5 Answer**

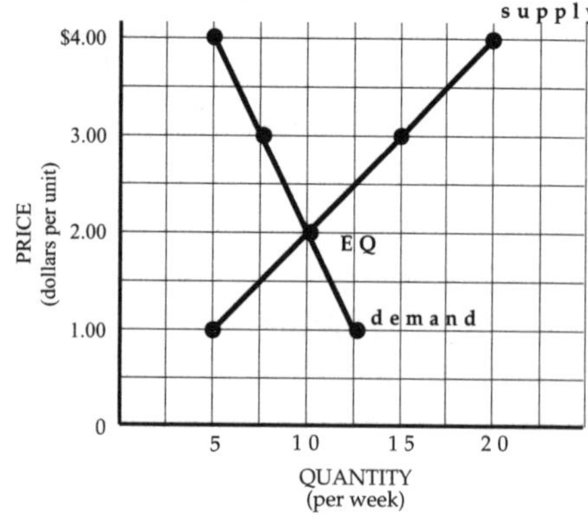

3. See point *EQ* in Figure 3.5.
4. At $3.00, the quantity supplied is greater than the quantity demanded or there is a surplus of 7.5 units (15 units minus 7.5 units equals 7.5 units).

Exercise 4

1. a
2. b
3. d
4. c
5. b

SECTION II Microeconomics

CHAPTER 4

Consumer Demand

Quick Review

- Economic theory about consumer behavior focuses on demand—the willingness and ability to buy specific quantities of a good or service at various prices—and does not try to explain why people want the things they do.

- Utility is the satisfaction obtained from a particular good or service. Total utility is the total amount of satisfaction from consuming a particular quantity of a good or service; marginal utility is the satisfaction from consuming an *additional* unit of a good or service.

- The law of diminishing marginal utility says that the satisfaction from consuming additional units of a good or service decreases as more of the good or service is consumed. This provides the basis for the law of demand, which states that the quantity demanded will increase only if price falls, in a given time period, *ceteris paribus.*

- The law of demand says that consumers will buy more of a good at a lower price than at a higher price, *ceteris paribus.* The nonprice determinants of demand—tastes, income, expectations, and the price and availability of other goods—are held constant when the demand curve is drawn. If any of these determinants change, the demand curve will shift.

- Price elasticity of demand is a measure of the responsiveness of quantity demanded to a given change in price. It is calculated between two points on a given demand curve by dividing the percentage change in quantity demanded by the percentage change in price.

- The coefficient (E) that results from the elasticity calculation is always negative because of the law of demand, so its absolute value is used. If $|E| > 1$, demand is elastic; $|E| < 1$, demand is inelastic; and $|E| = 1$, demand is unitary elastic.

- Price elasticity determines the impact of a price change on total revenue ($P \times Q$). If price falls and demand is elastic, total revenue will increase; if price falls and demand is inelastic, total revenue will decrease. The opposite is true for price increases.

- The determinants of price elasticity include the price of the good relative to income, the availability of substitutes, and the designation of the good as a necessity or a luxury.

- Advertising is intended to increase the willingness of consumers to purchase a good. If advertising is successful, the demand curve will shift to the right and may also become less elastic.

Learning Objectives

After reading the chapter and doing the following exercises you should be able to:

1. Explain why demand curves slope downward.
2. Describe what the price elasticity of demand measures.
3. Depict the relationship of price elasticity, price, and total revenue.
4. Recite the factors that influence the degree of price elasticity.
5. Discuss how advertising affects consumer demand.

Using Terms to Remember

Fill in the puzzle on the opposite page with the appropriate terms from the list of Terms to Remember in the text.

Across

3. In the cartoon in the text, the fifth slice of pizza does not provide as much satisfaction as the first slice because of the law of _______________.
5. Says that the quantity demanded of a good increases as its price falls, *ceteris paribus*.
9. This value must always be increasing as long as marginal utility is positive.
10. Influenced by tastes, income, expectations, and other goods.
11. The quantity of a product sold times the price at which it is sold.

Down

1. Measures the response of consumers to a change in price.
2. The satisfaction obtained by consuming one additional unit of a good or service.
4. The assumption that everything else is constant.
6. The sum of individual demands.
7. The satisfaction obtained from goods and services.
8. A successful advertising campaign is one that shifts the _______________ to the right.

Puzzle 4.1

True or False: *Circle your choice and explain why any false statements are incorrect.*

T F 1. One goal of economic theory is to explain and predict how consumers will spend their incomes.

T F 2. The expectation that price will change in the future has the same effect on demand as a change in the current price of the good.

T F 3. Market demand is the sum of individual demands.

T F 4. The law of demand differs from the law of diminishing marginal utility in that it takes into account what a consumer is able to pay for a good, not just the consumer's desire for the good.

T F 5. According to the law of diminishing marginal utility, the *total utility* you get from a product declines as more of the product is consumed.

T F 6. The price elasticity of demand is said to be inelastic when the percentage change in the quantity demanded of a good is greater than the percentage change in the good's price.

T F 7. If the price elasticity of demand is equal to 0.85, then a 1 percent decrease in price will result in a 0.85 percent increase in quantity demanded.

T F 8. If the price elasticity of demand is elastic, an increase in the price increases total revenue.

T F 9. The price elasticity of demand for Pop's Pizza is more elastic than the price elasticity of demand for pizza in general.

T F 10. A successful advertising campaign causes the demand curve to shift to the right and may even cause it to become less elastic.

Multiple Choice: *Select the correct answer.*

_______ 1. Which of the following is true about the difference between demanding a good and desiring a good?
(a) Goods that are demanded are goods that are needed to survive while goods that are desired are typically luxuries.
(b) Consumers not only desire but are also able to pay for demanded goods.
(c) Desired goods typically sell at a higher price than demanded goods.
(d) Goods that are demanded have a more price inelastic demand than goods that are desired.

_______ 2. Which of the following does *not* influence consumer demand?
(a) The consumer's tastes or preferences.
(b) The consumer's income.
(c) The price and availability of other goods.
(d) The producer's behavior.

_______ 3. According to the text, the typical U.S. consumer spends the largest portion of their income on:
(a) Housing.
(b) Medical care.
(c) Gasoline.
(d) Electricity.

_______ 4. *Ceteris paribus* means (in demand theory):
(a) Nothing is allowed to change.
(b) The determinants of demand may change, but all else must be held constant.
(c) Only one determinant is being changed while all other determinants remain unchanged.
(d) Consumers try to keep all things constant so that prices will be lower.

_______ 5. Suppose a student loses her job and is unable to find another. Which of the following is most likely to occur?
(a) Her demand curve for goods and services will remain unchanged.
(b) She will move up along her demand curve as she purchases fewer goods.
(c) She will move down along her demand curve as she purchases fewer goods.
(d) Her demand curve for goods and services will shift to the left.

_______ 6. Demand for a luxury good is usually considered to be:
(a) Relatively elastic.
(b) Relatively inelastic.
(c) Unitary elastic.
(d) Perfectly elastic.

_______ 7. Which of the following is an example of the law of diminishing marginal utility?
(a) Root beer gives me zero satisfaction, so I never buy it.
(b) The more I study for an economics test, the more I want to do something else.
(c) The longer I go to school, the more I appreciate the value of an education.
(d) Since water is more of a necessity than diamonds, water is more valuable.

_______ 8. *Ceteris paribus*, the shape of the demand curve indicates that:
(a) As price increases the demand curve shifts to the right.
(b) The quantity demanded of a good decreases as its price falls in a given time period.
(c) As marginal utility diminishes, consumers are willing to buy additional quantities of a good only at higher prices.
(d) As marginal utility declines, so does the customer's willingness to pay.

_______ 9. With greater consumption, total utility:
(a) Falls continually.
(b) Increases continually.
(c) Increases as long as marginal utility is positive.
(d) Increases only if marginal utility increases.

_______ 10. If you consume one more plate of food at an all-you-can-eat buffet and your total satisfaction decreases, the marginal utility from the additional plate must be:
(a) Positive.
(b) Negative.
(c) Increasing.
(d) Zero.

_______ 11. A change in a determinant of demand for a good causes a:

(a) Shift in the demand curve.
(b) Change in marginal utility.
(c) Change in a consumer's willingness or ability to buy the good.
(d) All of the above.

_______ 12. Which of the following is the best explanation of why we typically pay a relatively low price for water?

(a) Additional units of water are normally not worth much to us.
(b) Because water is normally abundant, the total utility we receive from water is relatively low.
(c) Because water is normally abundant, the marginal utility we receive from water is relatively high.
(d) Although additional units of water are normally worth a lot to us, the supply of water is so great we refuse to pay a high price for these additional units.

_______ 13. If a good has a zero price, or is free, a consumer should consume:

(a) An infinite amount of the good.
(b) The good until total utility is zero.
(c) The good until the marginal utility of the last unit is zero.
(d) The good until marginal utility of the last unit is maximized.

_______ 14. The concept of elasticity:

(a) Compares the absolute change in quantity demanded with the percentage change in price.
(b) Provides evidence of the way total revenue changes when price changes.
(c) Shows what the slope of the demand curve is.
(d) Shows what the slope of the supply curve is.

_______ 15. Suppose a local government wants to reduce traffic congestion on a bridge by imposing a toll. The toll will be most effective if the price elasticity of demand for the bridge is:

(a) Inelastic.
(b) Elastic.
(c) Unitary.
(d) Impossible to tell without more information on, for example, substitute routes available.

_______ 16. *Ceteris paribus*, if tennis balls and tennis rackets are complementary goods, an increase in the price of tennis balls will cause:

(a) A decrease in the quantity demanded of tennis balls and a decrease in demand for tennis rackets.
(b) An increase in the quantity demanded of tennis balls and a decrease in demand for tennis rackets.
(c) A decrease in the quantity demanded of tennis balls and an increase in demand for tennis rackets.
(d) An increase in the quantity demanded of tennis balls and an increase in demand for tennis rackets.

_______ 17. A new alternative band typically draws larger crowds than its venues can seat. By which of the following means can the band reduce the size of the crowd and simultaneously earn more revenue?
(a) By raising tickets prices when demand for tickets is elastic.
(b) By raising tickets prices when demand for tickets is inelastic.
(c) By reducing tickets prices when demand for tickets is elastic.
(d) By reducing tickets prices when demand for tickets is inelastic.

_______ 18. According to a News Wire article in the text, in addition to the increase in the federal tobacco tax, a number of states are considering raising their tobacco tax in hopes of generating additional revenue. In order for a tax hike to raise revenue, the price elasticity of demand for cigarettes must be:
(a) Less than 1.
(b) Greater than 1.
(c) Equal to 0.
(d) Equal to 1.

_______ 19. If the price elasticity of demand is 1.2, and a firm increases its price by 10 percent, the quantity sold by the firm will, *ceteris paribus*:
(a) Rise by 12 percent.
(b) Rise by 8.33 percent.
(c) Fall by 12 percent.
(d) Fall by 8.33 percent.

_______ 20. When a firm advertises, it is attempting to:
(a) Increase the elasticity of demand for the product.
(b) Shift the supply curve to the right.
(c) Decrease the demand for the product.
(d) Increase the product's perceived marginal utility.

Problems and Applications

Exercise 1

This exercise will help you to draw demand curves using demand schedules. It should also give you practice in constructing market-demand curves.

1. Market demand is:
(a) The total quantity of a good or service that people are willing and able to buy at alternative prices in a given period of time, *ceteris paribus*.
(b) The sum of individual demands.
(c) Represented as the horizontal sum of individual demand curves.
(d) All of the above.

2. Table 4.1 presents a hypothetical demand schedule for cars manufactured in the United States.

Table 4.1 Demand for U.S. cars

Price	*Number of U.S. cars (millions per year)*
$20,000	9.0
18,000	10.0

Graph this demand curve in Figure 4.1.

Figure 4.1

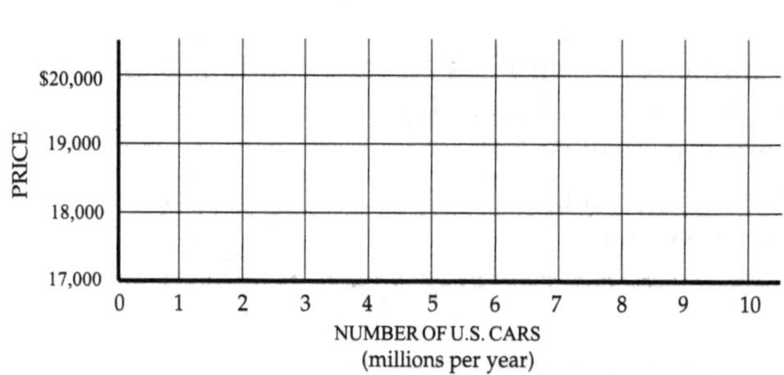

3. Table 4.2 presents a hypothetical demand schedule for cars manufactured abroad and imported into the United States.

Table 4.2 Demand for imported cars

Price	*Number of imported cars (millions per year)*
$20,000	1.0
18,000	2.0

Graph this demand curve in Figure 4.2.

Figure 4.2

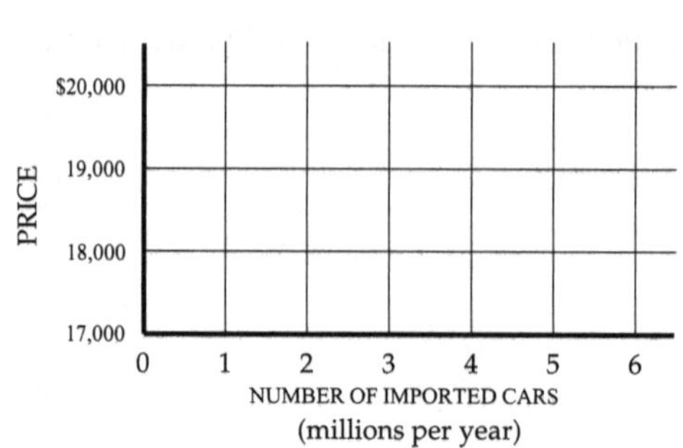

4. Suppose that the price for imported cars is the same as the price for cars manufactured in the U.S. In Table 4.3 calculate the demand schedule for cars (both imported and U.S. produced) at the two prices shown.

Table 4.3 Market demand for new cars

Price	*Total number of new cars (millions per year)*
$20,000	______
18,000	______

5. In Figure 4.3 draw the total market-demand curve for both imported and U.S. produced cars.

Figure 4.3

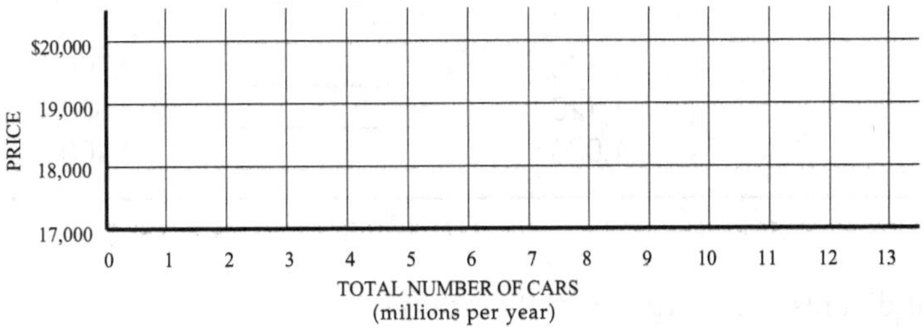

Exercise 2

This exercise shows the relationship between total and marginal utility. It also gives practice in identifying the law of diminishing marginal utility.

Suppose there are two types of entertainment you enjoy—an evening at home with friends and an "event" entertainment, such as a sports event or a rock concert. The number of times that you experience each type of entertainment during a month determines the total utility of each type of entertainment for that month. Suppose Table 4.4 represents the total utility you achieve from consuming various quantities of the two types of entertainment.

1. Compute the marginal utility of each type of entertainment by completing Table 4.4.

Table 4.4 Total and marginal utility of two types of entertainment per month

Days of entertainment per month	Evening at home		Event	
	Total utility	Marginal utility	Total utility	Marginal utility
0	0	________	0	________
1	170	________	600	________
2	360	________	1,250	________
3	540	________	1,680	________
4	690	________	2,040	________
5	820	________	2,350	________
6	930	________	2,550	________
7	1,030	________	2,720	________
8	1,110	________	2,820	________
9	1,170	________	2,820	________
10	1,170	________	2,760	________
11	1,120	________	2,660	________
12	1,020	________	2,460	________

2. The law of diminishing marginal utility means:
   (a) The total utility of a good declines as more of it is consumed in a given time period.
   (b) The marginal utility of a good declines as more of it is consumed in a given time period.
   (c) The price of a good declines as more of it is consumed in a given period of time.
   (d) All of the above.

3. The law of diminishing marginal utility is in evidence in Table 4.4 for:
   (a) Both types of entertainment.
   (b) Home entertainment only.
   (c) Event entertainment only.
   (d) Neither type of entertainment.
   (*Hint*: You should be able to tell by looking at the marginal utility columns in Table 4.4. Does the marginal utility become smaller as you go down the column?)

4. In Figure 4.4 graph the total utility curve for evenings at home.

Figure 4.4

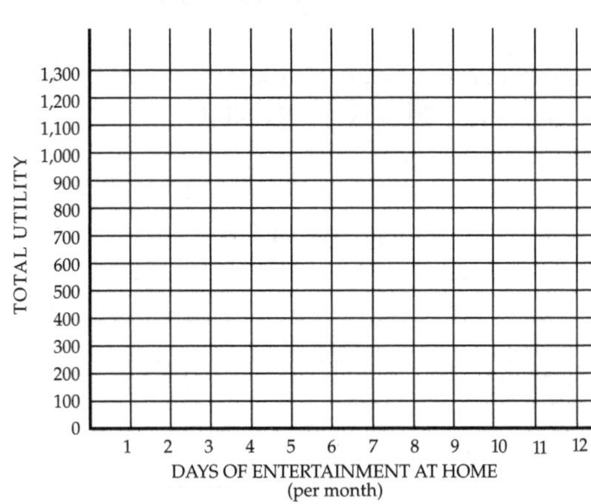

5. In Figure 4.5 graph the marginal utility curve for evenings at home.

Figure 4.5

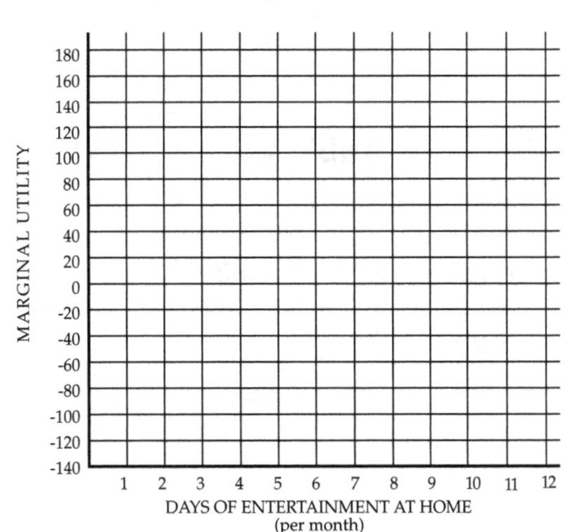

6. On the basis of the two graphs above, marginal utility is zero only at the point where total utility:
   (a) Is zero.
   (b) Reaches a maximum.
   (c) Is rising.
   (d) Reaches a minimum.

7. When total utility is rising, then it is certain that marginal utility is:
   (a) Rising.
   (b) Negative.
   (c) Positive.
   (d) Zero.

Exercise 3

This exercise examines the relationship between the price elasticity of demand and total revenue.

1. Figure 4.6 shows the demand curve for a good. Find the quantity demanded of the good for each price given in Table 4.5. Calculate the total revenue generated at each price. Then use Table 4.5 to answer Questions 2-4.

Figure 4.6

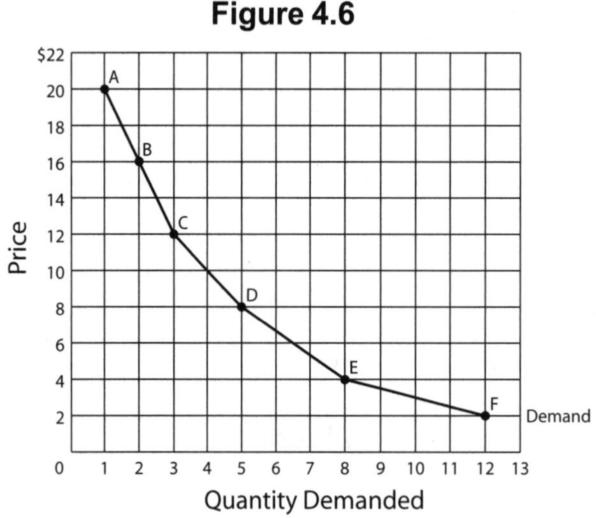

Table 4.5

	Price	X	*Quantity demanded*	=	*Total revenue*
A	$ 20		_____		_____
B	16		_____		_____
C	12		_____		_____
D	8		_____		_____
E	4		_____		_____
F	2		_____		_____

2. Based on Table 4.5, total revenue is maximized at a price of _____ and a quantity of _____ units.

3. As price decreases from $4 per unit to $2 per unit total revenue (increases, decreases, stays the same). In this case the price elasticity of demand is (elastic, inelastic, unitary elastic).

4. As price decreases from $16 per unit to $12 per unit total revenue (increases, decreases, stays the same). In this case the price elasticity of demand is (elastic, inelastic, unitary elastic).

5. Calculate the price elasticity of demand if:
   (a) The price of a good increases by 10% and the quantity demanded decreases by 5%. ______
   (b) The price of a good increases by 10% and the quantity demanded decreases by 15%. ______
   (c) In which case (a or b) will an increase in price result in an increase in total revenue? ______

6. The price elasticity of demand is influenced by:
   (a) The price of the good relative to income.
   (b) The availability of substitutes.
   (c) Whether the good is a luxury or a necessity.
   (d) All of the above.

Common Errors

The first statement in each "common error" below is incorrect. Each incorrect statement is followed by a corrected version and an explanation.

1. Figures 4.7a and 4.7b represent simple graphs drawn from a demand schedule.

Figure 4.7a

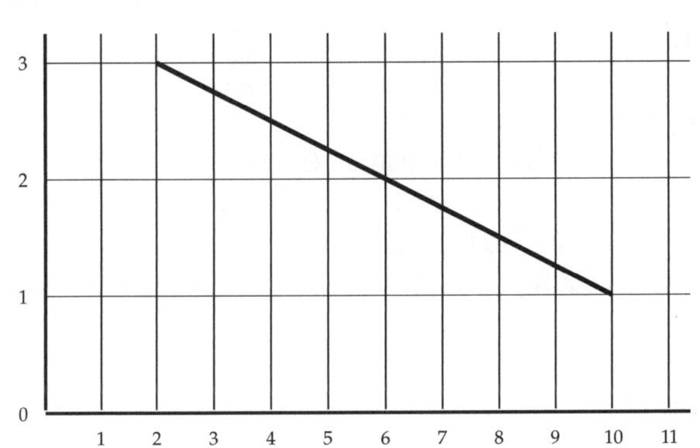

Price (dollars per unit)	*Output quantity per unit of time*
10	1
2	3

Incorrect!

Figure 4.7b

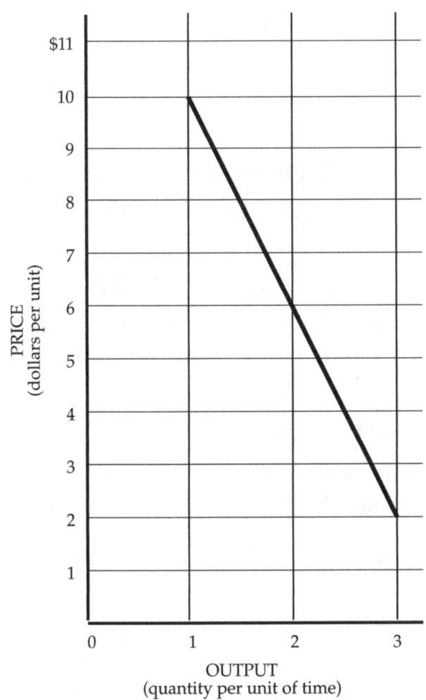

Price (dollars per unit)	*Output quantity per unit of time*
10	1
2	3

Correct!

The first graph has been drawn without any units indicated and the axes are reversed. It is something of an accidental tradition in economics to show price on the y-axis and quantity on the x-axis. This convention is sometimes confusing to mathematicians, who want to treat quantity as a function of price, according to the definition in the text. In Figure 4.7a the axes have been reversed and incorrect points have been chosen.

Be careful! When you are drawing a new graph, pay special attention to the label for each axis and the units of measure used on each axis. If you are drawing a graph from a table (or schedule), you can usually determine what should be on the axes by looking at the heading above the column from which you are reading the numbers.

Make sure price is shown on the y-axis (vertical) and quantity on the x-axis (horizontal). If you mix up the two, you may confuse a graph showing elastic demand with one showing inelastic demand.

2. The law of demand and the law of diminishing marginal utility are the same. *Incorrect!*
   The law of demand and the law of diminishing marginal utility are not the same. *Correct!*

   Do not confuse utility and demand. Utility refers only to expected satisfaction. Demand refers to both preferences and ability to pay. This distinction should help you to keep the law of diminishing marginal utility separate from the law of demand.

3. If marginal utility is diminishing, total utility is falling. *Incorrect!*
   If marginal utility is diminishing, total utility could still be increasing. *Correct!*

   Marginal utility is the change in total utility when one more unit of a good or service is consumed. When marginal utility is declining, the consumer is said to have diminishing marginal utility. However, even if marginal utility is declining, but still positive, the consumer's total utility is still increasing.

4. The formula for the price elasticity of demand is:

$$\frac{\text{Change in price}}{\text{Change in quantity}}$$

Incorrect!

The formula for the price elasticity of demand is:

$$\frac{\text{Percentage change in quantity demanded}}{\text{Percentage change in price}}$$

Correct!

Do not confuse slope and elasticity. The wrong formula above shows the formula for calculating the slope of the demand curve. The correct formula above is used to calculate the price elasticity of demand.

The concept of elasticity allows us to compare relative changes in quantity and price without having to worry about the units in which they are measured. In order to do this, we compute *percentage* changes of both price and quantity. There is a causal relationship between price and quantity. A change in price *causes* people to change the quantity they demand in a given time period. By putting the quantity changes in the numerator, we can determine if the quantity response is very large relative to a price change. If the quantity change is large, relative to the price change, then the demand is said to be elastic and $|E|$ is relatively large. If the quantity response is small relative to a price change, then demand is said to be inelastic and $|E|$ is relatively small.

5. A flat demand curve has an elasticity of zero. *Incorrect!*
   A flat demand curve has an infinite elasticity. *Correct!*

   When price remains constant, even when quantity changes, the elasticity formula requires us to divide by a zero price change. In fact, as demand curves approach flatness, the elasticity becomes larger and larger. By agreement we say it is infinite.

6. The expectation that price will change in the future has the same effect as a change in the current price. *Incorrect!*
   The expectation that price will change in the future shifts the demand curve, whereas a current price change is a movement along the demand curve. *Correct!*
   If prices are expected to rise in the near future, people will demand more of the commodity today in order to beat the rise in price. Demand increases and the quantity demanded will rise. However, if the price rises today, according to the law of demand, people will reduce their quantity demanded! Furthermore, demand itself does not change. A current price change and an expected price change have very different effects.

~ ANSWERS ~

Using Terms to Remember

Across

3. diminishing marginal utility
5. law of demand
9. total utility
10. demand
11. total revenue

Down

1. price elasticity of demand
2. marginal utility
4. *ceteris paribus*
6. market demand
7. utility
8. demand curve

True or False

1. T
2. F An expected price change will shift the demand curve while a change in the current price will result in a movement along the demand curve.
3. T
4. T
5. F According to the law of diminishing marginal utility, *marginal* utility decreases as more of a product is consumed. *Total* utility increases until marginal utility becomes negative, then it declines.
6. F The price elasticity of demand is elastic when the percentage change in the quantity demanded of a good is greater than the percentage change in the good's price.
7. T
8. F If the price elasticity of demand is elastic, an increase in price will cause total revenue to decrease.
9. T
10. T

Multiple Choice

1. b	5. d	9. c	13. c	17. b
2. d	6. a	10. b	14. b	18. a
3. a	7. b	11. d	15. b	19. c
4. c	8. d	12. a	16. a	20. d

Problems and Applications

Exercise 1

1. d

2. **Figure 4.1 Answer**

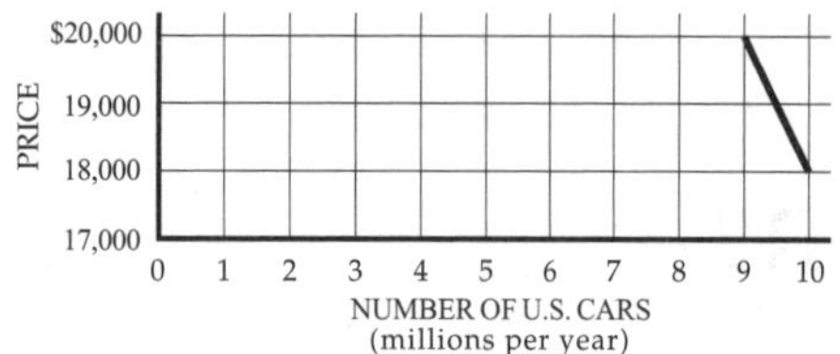

3. **Figure 4.2 Answer**

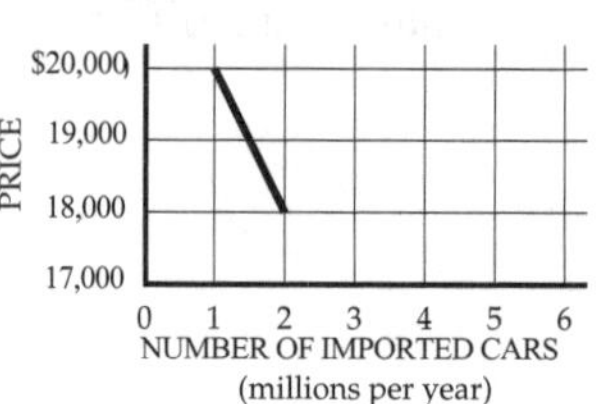

4. **Table 4.3 Answer**

Price	*Total number of cars (millions per year)*
20,000	10.00
18,000	12.00

5. **Figure 4.3 Answer**

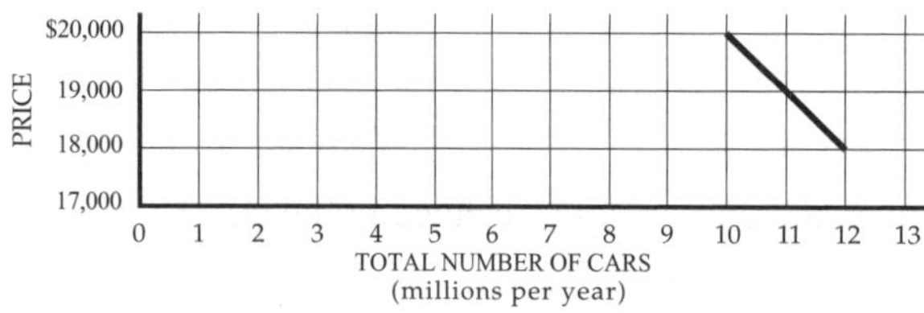

Exercise 2

1. **Table 4.4 Answer**

Days of entertainment per month	*Evening at home* Marginal utility	*Event* Marginal utility
0	—	—
1	170	600
2	190	650
3	180	430
4	150	360
5	130	310
6	110	200
7	100	170
8	80	100
9	60	0
10	0	–60
11	–50	–100
12	–100	–200

2. b
3. a

4. **Figure 4.4 Answer**

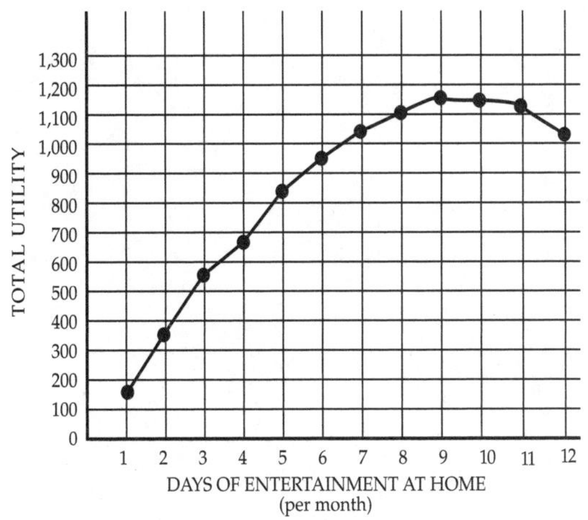

5. **Figure 4.5 Answer**

6. b
7. c

Exercise 3

1. **Table 4.5 Answer**

	Quantity demanded	*Total revenue*
A	1	$20
B	2	32
C	3	36
D	5	40
E	8	32
F	12	24

2. $8; 5
3. Decreases; inelastic
4. Increases; elastic
5. a. 0.5
   b. 1.5
   c. a
6. d

CHAPTER 5

Supply Decisions

Quick Review

- The production function determines how much output can be obtained from varying amounts of factor inputs. Every point on the production function is efficient, meaning that, given current technology, the maximum output is being produced.

- The output of any factor depends on the amount of other resources available to it. Fixed factors constrain the firm's ability to produce output. As more of a variable input is applied to a fixed input, at some point, the marginal physical product of the variable input begins to get smaller in size. This short-run situation is referred to as the *law of diminishing returns*. In the long run, all factor inputs are variable.

- The dollar costs incurred because of fixed inputs are called fixed costs; those for variable factors are called variable costs. In the short-run, even if output is zero, there are fixed costs. The total cost of producing any level of output is the sum of fixed and variable costs. Because fixed costs do not change as output changes, the rate of increase in total cost is determined by variable costs only.

- Marginal cost (MC) is the increase in total cost associated with a one-unit increase in production. Average total cost (ATC) is the total cost of production divided by the rate of output. The ATC curve starts at a high level and declines as production increases because of fixed costs. At a point the ATC curve begins to rise because of rising marginal costs that result from the law of diminishing returns. This results in a U-shaped ATC curve.

- The production decision is the short-run choice of how much output to produce with existing facilities. A producer will be willing to supply output only if price at least covers marginal costs.

- In the long run there are no fixed costs. The producer must decide whether to build, buy, or lease plant and equipment. This is the investment decision.

- Economic costs include both explicit and implicit costs associated with the use of *all* resources in the production process, whether they receive a monetary payment or not. Accounting costs include only those costs for which an explicit payment is made.

- Advances in technology shift the production function upward and the cost curves downward. Along with improved quality of inputs, technology improvements have historically been the major source of productivity growth in the U.S. economy.

Learning Objectives

After reading the chapter and doing the following exercises you should be able to:

1. Explain what the production function reveals.
2. Explain the law of diminishing returns.
3. Describe the nature of fixed, variable, and marginal costs.
4. Illustrate the difference between production and investment decisions.
5. Discuss how accounting costs and economic costs differ.

Using Terms to Remember

Fill in the puzzle on the opposite page with the appropriate terms from the list of Terms to Remember in the text.

Across

2. Explains why the marginal physical product of a variable input declines as more of it is employed with a given quantity of other inputs.
3. A technological relationship expressing the maximum quantity of a good attainable from different combinations of factor inputs.
4. The resources used to produce a good or service.
8. Costs of production that do not change when the rate of output changes.
11. The difference between total revenue and total costs.
13. Includes both explicit and implicit costs.
14. The ability and willingness to produce a good at various prices.
15. Total cost divided by the quantity produced in a given time period.

Down

1. The change in total output that occurs when an additional worker is hired.
3. The selection of the short-run rate of output.
5. The long-run supply decision.
6. A period in which some inputs are fixed.
7. This curve is typically rising because of the law of diminishing returns.
9. The market value of all resources used to produce a good or service.
10. These costs have a direct impact on how fast total costs rise.
12. A period in which all inputs are variable.

Puzzle 5.1

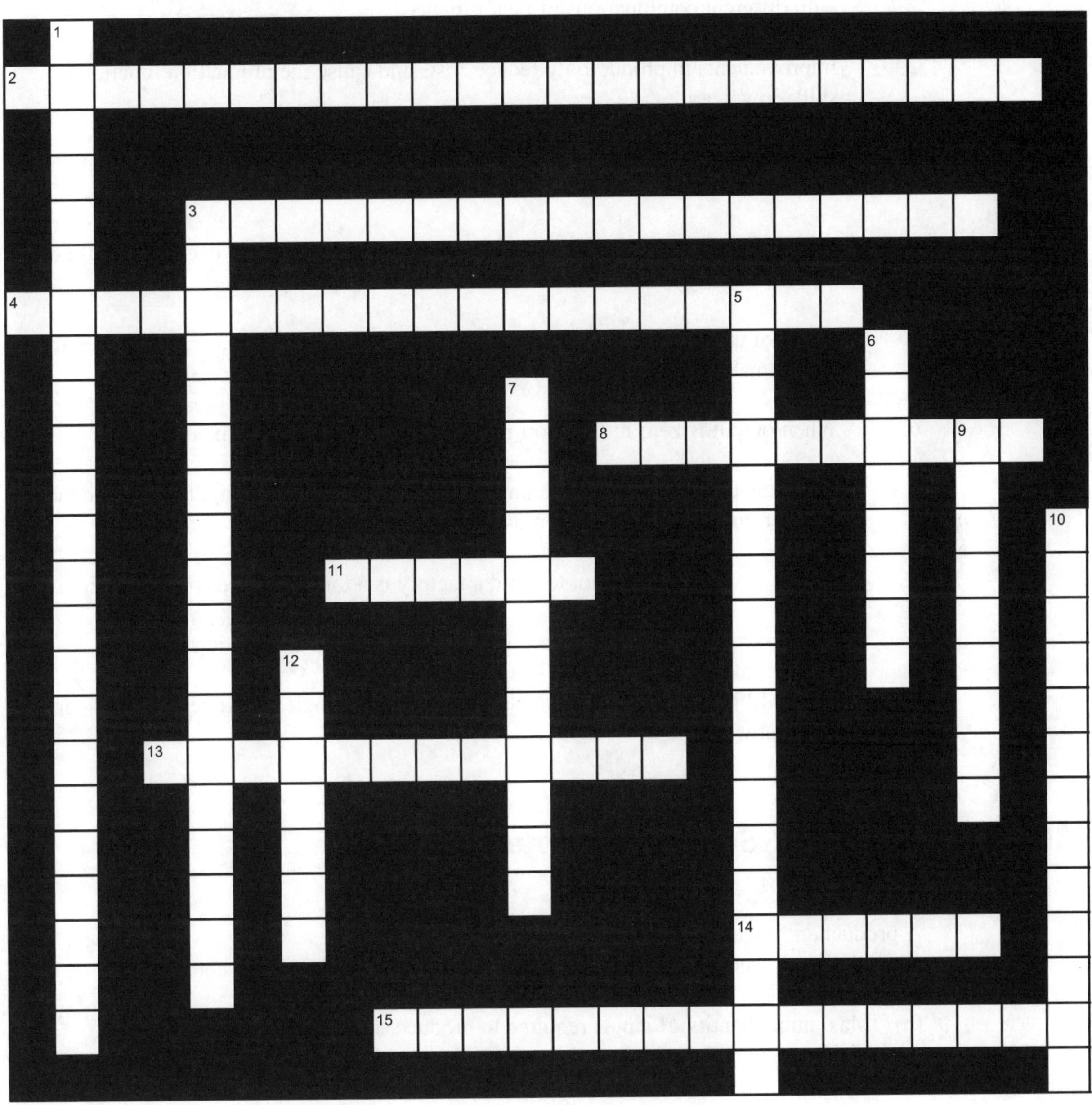

True or False: *Circle your choice and explain why any false statements are incorrect.*

T F 1. A production function tells us the maximum amount of output that can be produced with different combinations of factor inputs.

T F 2. Improvements in productivity reduce costs and cause the production function to shift downward.

T F 3. If the marginal physical product (MPP) of an input is decreasing, total output must be decreasing.

T F 4. The marginal physical product (MPP) will eventually begin to decline because of the relative scarcity of some factor inputs in the production process.

T F 5. If any of the factor inputs are fixed in a firm's decision-making process, then the firm is making a long-run decision.

T F 6. When output is zero in the short run, total costs are equal to fixed costs.

T F 7. When the cost of an additional unit of output (MC) is increasing, the average total cost per unit of output (ATC) must also be increasing.

T F 8. The issue of whether or not to build a factory is a long-run investment decision.

T F 9. Economic costs are less than accounting costs if there are implicit costs.

T F 10. If the MPP curve shifts upward because of a technological advance, the MC curve shifts upward.

Multiple Choice: *Select the correct answer.*

_____ 1. A production function shows the:
(a) Minimum amount of output that can be obtained from alternative combinations of inputs.
(b) Maximum quantity of inputs required to produce a given quantity of output.
(c) Maximum quantity of output that can be obtained from alternative combinations of inputs.
(d) Maximum profit that a firm can earn.

_____ 2. Which of the following would cause a firm's production function to shift upward?
(a) Increased investment in capital.
(b) Hiring more workers.
(c) Increased production by the firm.
(d) An increase in factor costs.

_______ 3. Assuming labor is a variable input, an increase in labor productivity will result in:
   (a) A downward shift in the MPP curve.
   (b) An upward shift in the MC curve.
   (c) A downward shift in the ATC curve.
   (d) A downward shift in the MRP curve.

_______ 4. Diminishing returns begin to occur when:
   (a) Total output begins to decline.
   (b) Marginal physical product becomes negative.
   (c) Total output begins to rise.
   (d) Marginal physical product begins to decline.

_______ 5. Declining MPP is the result of:
   (a) Inefficiency in the production process.
   (b) Adding more variable factors of production to a fixed quantity of other factors of production.
   (c) Laziness on the part of the workers.
   (d) The use of less qualified workers.

_______ 6. Refer to the table in Figure 5.1 in the text and fill in the blank in the following sentence. The law of diminishing returns begins to occur when the ________ worker is added to the production process.
   (a) First
   (b) Third
   (c) Seventh
   (d) Eighth

_______ 7. Which of the following is the best explanation of why the law of diminishing returns does *not* apply in the long run?
   (a) In the long run, firms can increase the availability of space and equipment to keep up with the increase in labor.
   (b) The MPP does not change in the long run.
   (c) In the long run, firms have more time to find better-qualified workers.
   (d) All factors of production are fixed in the long run.

_______ 8. The most desirable rate of output for a firm is the output that:
   (a) Minimizes total costs.
   (b) Minimizes marginal costs.
   (c) Maximizes total profit.
   (d) Maximizes total revenue.

_______ 9. Which of the following costs will always increase as output increases?
   (a) Total costs.
   (b) Average total costs.
   (c) Marginal costs.
   (d) Fixed costs.

_______ 10. Which of the following is equivalent to total cost?
(a) The change in marginal cost divided by the change in output.
(b) 1 divided by the MPP.
(c) Fixed costs plus variable costs.
(d) Marginal costs plus variable costs.

_______ 11. Changes in short-run total costs result from changes in:
(a) Variable costs.
(b) Fixed costs.
(c) Profit.
(d) The price elasticity of demand.

_______ 12. Marginal cost is the:
(a) Total cost divided by the quantity produced.
(b) Change in fixed cost from producing one additional unit of output.
(c) Market value of all resources used to produce a good.
(d) Change in total cost from producing one additional unit of output.

_______ 13. Which of the following is most likely a fixed cost?
(a) The cost of leasing a building to use in the production process.
(b) The cost of water used in the production process.
(c) The cost of labor used in the production process.
(d) The cost of natural gas used in the production process.

_______ 14. Marginal costs will increase as output increases if:
(a) Productivity is rising.
(b) Total variable costs are decreasing.
(c) Marginal revenue product is rising.
(d) Marginal physical product is decreasing.

_______ 15. Refer to the table in Figure 5.3 in the text. The marginal cost of the 40th unit of output is:
(a) $110.00.
(b) $11.75.
(c) $11.00.
(d) $0, because fixed costs do not change.

_______ 16. Which of the following costs must remain constant at all levels of output?
(a) Total costs.
(b) Variable costs.
(c) Fixed costs.
(d) Marginal costs.

_______ 17. When producing T-shirts, all of the following are variable costs *except* for:
(a) Cloth.
(b) Wages.
(c) Electricity.
(d) Property insurance.

_______ 18. Which of the following will always increase as output increases?
 (a) Fixed cost.
 (b) Total cost.
 (c) The production function.
 (d) Marginal physical product.

_______ 19. Economic and accounting costs will differ whenever:
 (a) There are some implicit costs incurred by the firm.
 (b) There is more than one factor of production.
 (c) There are no implicit costs incurred by the firm.
 (d) All costs incurred by the firm are explicit.

_______ 20. The planning period over which all costs are variable is the:
 (a) Production run.
 (b) Short run.
 (c) Long run.
 (d) Investment decision.

Problems and Applications

Exercise 1

This exercise shows how to compute and graph the marginal physical product from a production function.

Table 5.1 The production of jeans (pairs per day)

Capital input (sewing machines per day)	*Labor input (workers per day)*							
	0	*1*	*2*	*3*	*4*	*5*	*6*	*7*
0	0	0	0	0	0	0	0	0
1	0	15	34	44	48	50	51	46
2	0	20	46	64	72	78	81	80

1. Suppose a firm has two sewing machines and only the amount of labor input can vary. On the basis of Table 5.1, fill in column 2 of Table 5.2 to show how much can be produced at different levels of labor input when there are two sewing machines.

Table 5.2 The production of jeans with two sewing machines

(1) Labor input (workers per day)	*(2) Production of jeans (pairs per day)*	*(3) Marginal physical product (pairs per worker)*
0	_______	_______
1	_______	_______
2	_______	_______
3	_______	_______
4	_______	_______
5	_______	_______
6	_______	_______
7	_______	_______

2. Graph the total output curve in Figure 5.1.

Figure 5.1

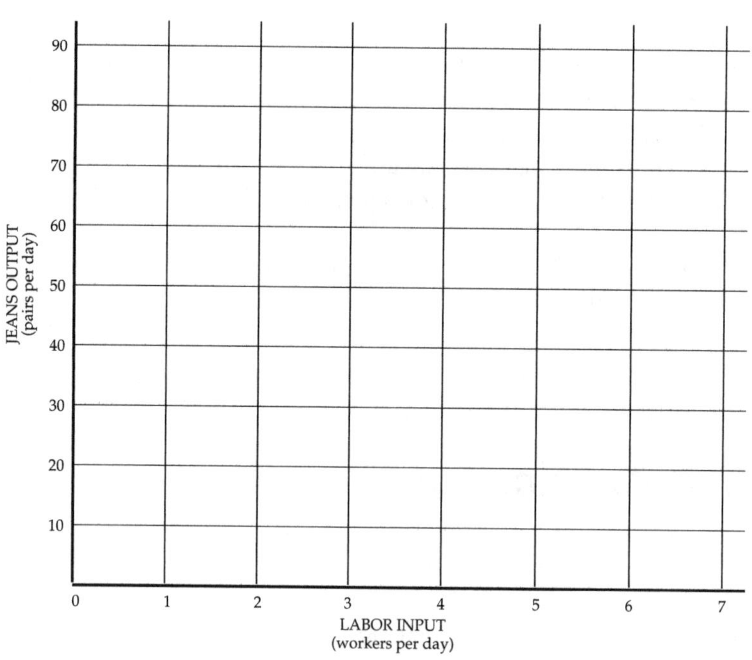

3. Compute the marginal physical product of each extra worker per day. Place the answers in column 3 of Table 5.2.

4. The law of diminishing returns states that the marginal physical product of a factor will:
   (a) Become negative as output increases.
   (b) Always decline as output increases.
   (c) Increase and then decline as output increases.
   (d) Begin to decline as more of the factor is used.

5. In Figure 5.1 above, at 5 units of labor, total output:
   (a) Is falling with increased labor usage.
   (b) Is rising with increased labor usage.
   (c) Remains constant with increased labor.

6. According to Table 5.2, marginal physical product begins to decline with the addition of the (first, second, third, fourth, fifth, sixth, seventh) worker.

7. T F When marginal physical product declines, total output declines.

Exercise 2

This exercise shows the relationship between the various costs of production.

1. Complete Table 5.3 using the information given about output and the costs of production. (*Hint*: refer to Figure 5.3 and Figure 5.4 in the text if you need help getting started.)

Table 5.3 Costs of production

Rate of Output	*Fixed Costs*	*Variable Costs*	*Total Cost*	*Average Total Cost*	*Marginal Cost*
0	$______	$______	$10	--------	-------
1	______	6	______	$______	$______
2	______	10	______	______	______
3	______	16	______	______	______
4	______	______	36	______	______
5	______	40	______	______	______
6	______	______	68	______	______

2. Graph marginal cost in Figure 5.2 and label it MC.

Figure 5.2

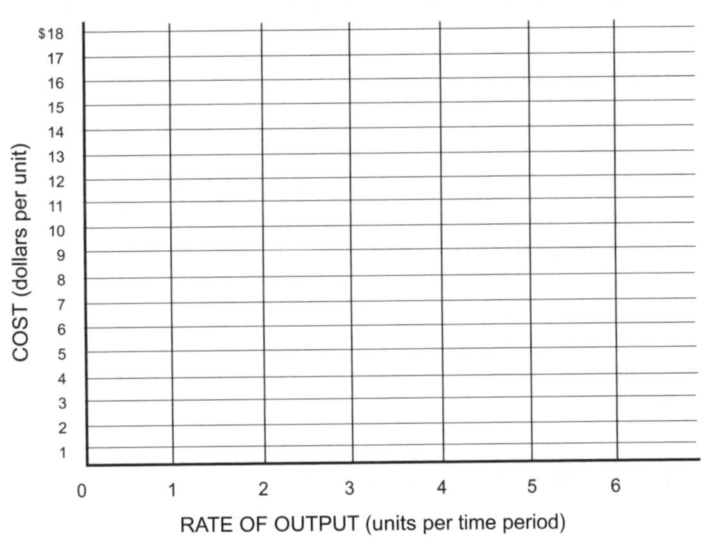

3. Graph the average total cost curve in Figure 5.2 and label it ATC. (Assume the ATC curve is equal to $8 at 3.5 units.)

4. When the average total cost curve is rising, the marginal cost curve is (above, below, equal to) the average total cost curve.

5. When the average total cost curve is falling, the marginal cost curve is (above, below, equal to) the average total cost curve.

6. The reason the average total cost curve decreases initially is because __________ costs are being spread over an increasing amount of output.

7. The reason the average total cost curve begins to rise at a point is because of rising _____________ costs.

Exercise 3

This exercise shows the relationship between fixed costs, variable costs, accounting cost, and economic cost.

1. Fixed costs are defined as:
   (a) Costs that do not change with inflation.
   (b) Costs that are set firmly (without escalator clauses) in a contract.
   (c) Costs of production that do not change when the rate of production is altered.
   (d) Average costs that do not change when the rate of production is altered.

2. Variable costs include:
   (a) Costs of production that change when the rate of production is altered.
   (b) All costs in the long run.
   (c) The difference between total and fixed costs.
   (d) All of the above.

Table 5.4 Expense statement for cupcake business (dollars per week)

Weekly expense	*Cupcakes dozen produced per week*		
	0	*100*	*200*
Lease on bakery building	$2,000	$2,000	$2,000
Mixing machines and ovens	1,200	1,200	1,200
Flour and sugar	0	500	800
Utilities (electricity, etc.)	0	250	300
Labor	0	1,250	1,500
License and inspection	500	500	500

Use the information in Table 5.4 to answer the following questions.

3. Which items are considered to be fixed costs? ______________________________

4. Calculate variable costs at an output level of 100 dozen cupcakes per week. __________

5. Calculate total costs at an output level of 100 dozen cupcakes per week. __________

6. Now assume the owner of the cupcake business buys the building she is currently leasing so she no longer has a lease expenditure. Calculate the accounting cost at an output level of 200 dozen cupcakes per week. __________

7. Assuming the owner still owns the building, calculate the economic cost at an output level of 200 cupcakes per week. Explain why there is a difference in the accounting cost and the economic cost at an output level of 200 cupcakes per week. ______________________________

   ____

Exercise 4

This exercise addresses the short-run and long-run decisions that businesses make.

1. In the short run, a firm makes the ________________ decision because some ________ are fixed.

2. In the long run, a firm can make the __________________ decision because there are no __________ costs.

3. If an oil company decides to build a new refinery, this is (an investment; a production) decision.

4. If a car maker decides to produce more SUVs in the short run by increasing the number of workers, the most important aspect of this decision is (total revenue; marginal costs).

Common Errors

The first statement in each "common error" below is incorrect. Each incorrect statement is followed by a corrected version and an explanation.

1. If marginal cost is rising, then average cost is also rising. *Incorrect!*
   If marginal cost is greater than average cost, then average cost is also rising. *Correct!*
   Marginal cost can be rising and still be less than average cost. In such a case, average cost will still decrease. Only when marginal cost is greater than average cost will average cost rise.

2. Total output starts falling when diminishing returns occur. *Incorrect!*
   Marginal output starts falling when diminishing returns occur. *Correct!*
   The law of diminishing returns describes what happens to *marginal physical product*, not total output. When diminishing returns begin to occur, MPP is still positive. Total output is increasing, but at a decreasing rate. For total output to decline, marginal physical product must be negative.

3. A firm's productivity increases when labor is willing to accept lower wages. *Incorrect!*
   A firm's productivity is not related to the wages paid to labor. *Correct!*
   Productivity is not determined by the costs of the factors of production. Productivity is determined by the amount of output that is produced by the factors of production.

4. The marginal cost curve rises because factor prices rise when more of a good is produced. *Incorrect!*
   The marginal cost curve rises because the marginal productivity of the variable factor declines. *Correct!*
   The marginal cost curve rises because marginal physical product is falling, not because of changes in resource prices. Changes in factor prices shift the whole marginal cost curve but do not explain its shape and do not affect the marginal physical product curve.

5. Marginal physical product begins to decline because inferior factors must be used to increase output. *Incorrect!*
   Declining marginal physical product occurs even if all of the factors are of equal quality. *Correct!*
   Many people incorrectly attribute diminishing returns to the use of inferior factors of production. Diminishing returns result from an increasing ratio of the variable input to the fixed input. In the case of labor, workers begin to compete for space in the work place. They start bumping into each other and marginal productivity begins to decline.

~ ANSWERS ~

Using Terms to Remember

Across

2. law of diminishing returns
3. production function
4. factors of production
8. fixed costs
11. profit
13. economic cost
14. supply
15. average total cost

Down

1. marginal physical product
3. production decision
5. investment decision
6. short run
7. marginal cost
9. total cost
10. variable costs
12. long run

True or False

1. T
2. F Improvements in productivity reduce costs and cause the production function to shift *upward.*
3. F As long as marginal product is positive, total output will be increasing.
4. T
5. F If any of the factor inputs are fixed in a firm's decision-making process, then the firm is making a *short-run* decision.
6. T
7. F The ATC will not increase until the MC is greater than the ATC.
8. T
9. F Accounting costs include only explicit costs while economic costs include both explicit and implicit costs, so economic costs are greater than accounting costs if there are implicit costs.
10. F If the MPP curve shifts upward because of a technological advance, the MC curve shifts *downward.*

Multiple Choice

1. c	5. b	9. a	13. a	17. d
2. a	6. b	10. c	14. d	18. b
3. c	7. a	11. a	15. c	19. a
4. d	8. c	12. d	16. c	20. c

Problems and Applications

Exercise 1

1. See Table 5.2 Answer, column 2.
3. See Table 5.2 Answer, column 3.

Table 5.2 Answer

(1)	*(2)*	*(3)*
0	0	—
1	20	20
2	46	26
3	64	18
4	72	8
5	78	6
6	81	3
7	80	– 1

2. **Figure 5.1 Answer**

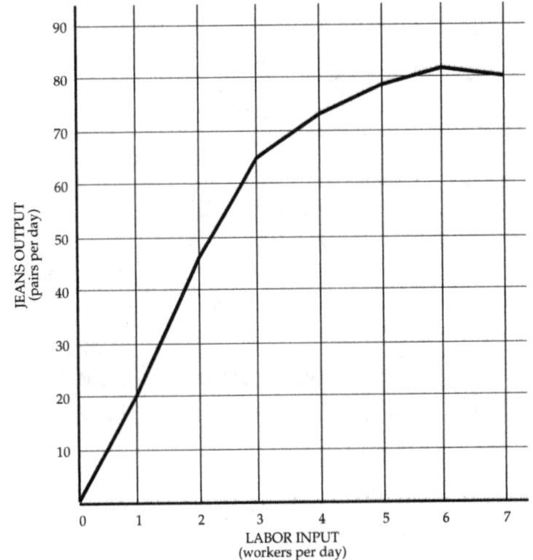

4. d
5. b
6. Third
7. F As long as marginal physical product is greater than zero, total output increases.

Exercise 2

1. **Table 5.3 Answer**

Rate of output	*Fixed costs*	*Variable costs*	*Total cost*	*Average total cost*	*Marginal cost*
0	$10	$0	$10	——	—
1	10	6	16	$16.00	$6
2	10	10	20	10.00	4
3	10	16	26	8.67	6
4	10	26	36	9.00	10
5	10	40	50	10.00	14
6	10	58	68	11.33	18

Figure 5.2 Answer

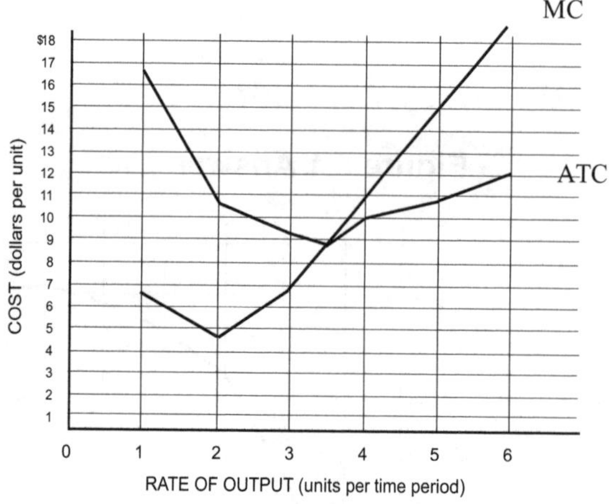

2. See the MC curve in Figure 5.2 Answer.
3. See the ATC curve in Figure 5.2 Answer.
4. Above
5. Below
6. Fixed
7. Marginal

Exercise 3

1. c
2. d
3. Lease on bakery building, mixing machines and ovens, license and inspection
4. $2,000
5. $5,700
6. $4,300
7. $6,300; The economic cost is greater than the accounting cost because the economic cost includes the implicit cost of the building; the accounting cost does not.

Exercise 4

1. Production; costs
2. Investment; fixed
3. An investment
4. Marginal costs

CHAPTER 6

Competition

Quick Review

- Market structure is determined by the number and relative size of firms in an industry. It affects the behavior of producers and influences market outcomes. Market structure ranges from monopoly to perfect competition. Monopolies have the greatest degree of market power.

- A perfectly competitive firm cannot influence the price of its output and is referred to as a price taker. It is important to distinguish the firm's demand curve from the market-demand curve. The firm's demand curve is perfectly flat because the firm produces such a small part of total market output, while the market demand curve is downward-sloping, reflecting the law of demand.

- In an effort to maximize profits, in the short run, a competitive firm will choose the rate of output where price equals marginal cost.

- A competitive firm's marginal cost curve above the average total cost curve is its short-run supply curve. The competitive market supply curve is the sum of the individual marginal cost curves.

- The determinants of supply include the price of inputs, technology, and expectations. If any of these determinants change, the firm's supply curve will shift. Market supply will shift in response to a change in the supply curve of the individual firms or if the number of firms changes.

- The existence of short-term profits will encourage new firms to enter a competitive market. As they enter, the market supply will increase and push price down along the demand curve. Profit for the competitive firm will decrease.

- The limit to the competitive price and profit squeeze is reached when price is driven down to the level of minimum average total cost (ATC). If the market price falls below the minimum ATC, firms will exit from the industry. Price stabilizes when entry and exit cease. This long-run equilibrium occurs when economic profits reach zero.

- In competitive markets there is a persistent pressure on prices and profits. Firms must keep costs as low as possible by adopting the most efficient technologies. Competitive firms must also respond quickly to changes in demand by producing the goods and services demanded by buyers in order to earn a profit. The penalty for not responding is losses and the potential failure of the firm.

Learning Objectives

After reading the chapter and doing the following exercises you should be able to:

1. Identify the unique characteristics of perfectly competitive firms and markets.
2. Illustrate how total profits change as output expands.
3. Describe how the profit-maximizing rate of output is found.
4. Recite the determinants of competitive market supply.
5. Explain why profits get eliminated in competitive markets.

Using Terms to Remember

Fill in the puzzle on the opposite page with the appropriate terms from the list of Terms to Remember in the text.

Across

2. The sole supplier of a good.
4. The price at which the quantity demanded of a good equals the quantity supplied.
7. Based on the competitive ______________ a firm should increase output if price is greater than MC.
8. The ability to alter the market price of a good or service.
9. Allows for indirect communication between producers and consumers by way of market sales and purchases.
12. The number and relative size of firms in an industry.
13. A firm that must take whatever price the market offers for the goods it produces.

Down

1. The ______________ curve shifts to the right as the result of market entry.
3. Equal to the price of the product times the quantity sold.
5. Eventually becomes zero in a competitive industry because of market entry.
6. Not significant enough to prevent entry if a market is competitive.
7. The choice of a particular short-run rate of output by producers.
9. The increase in total costs because of a one-unit increase in production.
10. An industry characterized by zero economic profit in the long run.
11. The ______________ curve is the sum of the marginal cost curves of all the firms in a competitive industry.

Puzzle 6.1

True or False: *Circle your choice and explain why any false statements are incorrect.*

T F 1. In a perfectly competitive market, prices are determined by the market, and individual firms have no control over this price.

T F 2. If Farmer James (a farmer in the wheat market, which is assumed to be perfectly competitive) doubles his production of wheat, the market price and quantity of wheat will be significantly affected.

T F 3. In a perfectly competitive market, the individual firm's demand curve is horizontal.

T F 4. In order to maximize profit, a firm should seek to maximize total revenue.

T F 5. If a perfectly competitive firm were to raise its price above the market price, its economic profit would increase.

T F 6. A perfectly competitive firm will maximize total revenue by producing at an output level where price equals marginal cost.

T F 7. As long as price is greater than marginal cost, an increase in the rate of output will cause an increase in profit.

T F 8. When economic profits exist in a perfectly competitive market, the number of suppliers will decrease and the market price will rise.

T F 9. When some firms are forced out of a market due to economic losses the result is a better use of our scarce resources.

T F 10. Competitive markets provide society with the best answer to the WHAT to produce question because competitive firms produce where price equals marginal cost.

Multiple Choice: *Select the correct answer.*

_______ 1. In which of the following types of markets does a single firm have the most market power?
(a) Perfect competition.
(b) Monopolistic competition.
(c) Oligopoly.
(d) Monopoly.

_______ 2. Which of the following is *not* a characteristic of a perfectly competitive market structure?
(a) Identical products.
(b) Low barriers to entry.
(c) Zero economic profit in the long run.
(d) Advertising to create brand loyalty.

_______ 3. The market demand curve in a perfectly competitive market is downward sloping because:
   (a) Of the law of diminishing returns.
   (b) The firms in the market have market power.
   (c) Of the law of demand.
   (d) There are economic profits in the long run.

_______ 4. Assume a perfectly competitive firm can sell 150 cartons of blueberries at $3.25 each. Which of the following is true if the firm wants to sell one more carton of blueberries?
   (a) It can sell the next carton of blueberries for $3.25.
   (b) It should raise its price in order to sell the next carton of blueberries.
   (c) It must lower its price in order to sell the next carton of blueberries.
   (d) It cannot sell an additional carton of blueberries at any price because the market is already in equilibrium.

_______ 5. A perfectly competitive firm is a price taker because:
   (a) It has no control over the selling price of its product.
   (b) It has market power.
   (c) Market demand is downward sloping.
   (d) Its products are differentiated.

_______ 6. If a perfectly competitive firm wanted to maximize its total revenues, it would produce:
   (a) The output where MC equals price.
   (b) As much output as it is capable of producing.
   (c) The output where the ATC curve is at a minimum.
   (d) The output where the marginal cost curve is at a minimum.

_______ 7. The difference between the total cost and total revenue curves at a given output is:
   (a) Marginal cost.
   (b) Average total cost.
   (c) Total profit.
   (d) Average profit.

_______ 8. Refer to Figure 6.4 in the text. If the market price of catfish is $13 per basket, this farmer should produce:
   (a) Zero baskets per hour.
   (b) Three baskets per hour.
   (c) Four baskets per hour.
   (d) Five baskets per hour.

_______ 9. Refer to Figure 6.5 in the text to help answer this question. If marginal cost is less than price, a perfectly competitive firm can increase profits (or reduce losses) by:
   (a) Increasing output.
   (b) Raising the price.
   (c) Decreasing output.
   (d) Stopping production.

_______ 10. Refer to Figure 6.5 in the text to help answer this question. If marginal cost is greater than price, a perfectly competitive firm should decrease output because:
   (a) Marginal cost is increasing.
   (b) Producing less output will add to the firm's profits (or reduce losses).
   (c) The price of the product is increasing.
   (d) Total revenue will increase.

_______ 11. Which of the following conditions always characterizes a firm that is maximizing profits in the short run?
(a) Price equals minimum average total cost.
(b) Price equals marginal cost.
(c) Economic profit equals zero.
(d) Total revenue is maximized.

_______ 12. Suppose that the cost of insecticide increases for wheat farmers and that the market is perfectly competitive. In order to maximize profits, *ceteris paribus*, wheat farmers should:
(a) Decrease output.
(b) Keep output the same since the market price did not change.
(c) Increase output.
(d) Increase price.

_______ 13. The market supply curve is calculated by:
(a) Summing the marginal cost curves of all the firms.
(b) Averaging the individual supply curves.
(c) Summing the prices from individual supply curves.
(d) Averaging individual marginal cost curves below ATC.

_______ 14. Assume the soybean market is perfectly competitive. The marginal cost curve for an individual farmer will shift downward due to all of the following *except*:
(a) Improved technology in harvesting soybeans.
(b) Increased wages that farmers pay to workers.
(c) Decreased costs for fertilizer.
(d) The expectation by farmers that factor prices will rise.

_______ 15. In a perfectly competitive market, a catfish farmer:
(a) Is able to keep other potential catfish producers out of the market.
(b) Is powerless to alter his own rate of production.
(c) Will not care if more catfish producers enter the market.
(d) Would like to keep other potential catfish producers out of the market but cannot do so.

_______ 16. In a perfectly competitive market with positive economic profits:
(a) Firms will enter until economic profits are zero.
(b) Firms will enter until accounting profits are zero.
(c) Firms will exit until economic profits are zero.
(d) No entry or exit will occur.

_______ 17. In a competitive market where firms are incurring losses, which of the following should be expected as the market moves to long-run equilibrium, *ceteris paribus?*
(a) A higher price and more firms.
(b) A lower price and more firms.
(c) A higher price and fewer firms.
(d) A lower price and fewer firms.

_______ 18. In long-run competitive market equilibrium:
(a) Marginal cost is greater than price.
(b) Price is greater than marginal cost.
(c) Economic profit is greater than zero.
(d) Price equals the minimum of average total cost.

_______ 19. When economic losses exist in the potato market, all of the following are true *except*:
(a) The goods and services that society is giving up are more valuable than the potatoes that are being produced.
(b) Society's scarce resources are *not* being used in the best way.
(c) Too many farmers are growing potatoes (assuming that the market is perfectly competitive).
(d) There is a shortage of potatoes.

_______ 20. In making a production decision, an entrepreneur:
(a) Determines the short-run rate of output.
(b) Makes a long-run decision about production.
(c) Decides whether to enter or exit the market.
(d) Determines plant and equipment.

Problems and Applications

Exercise 1

This exercise shows how the equilibrium price is determined in a competitive market and how the profit-maximizing rate of output is determined in a perfectly competitive market.

1. Using the information in Table 6.1, draw the market demand curve for chicken eggs in Figure 6.1. Label the curve *D*. (Assume the demand curve is linear.)

Table 6.1 Market demand for eggs

Quantity (millions of eggs per day)	*Price (per dozen)*
2	$2.00
3	1.50
4	1.00
5	0.50

Figure 6.1 Market demand and market supply curves

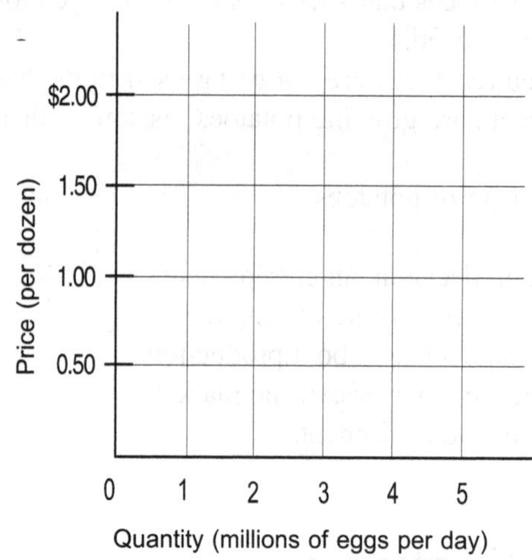

2. Using the information in Table 6.2, draw the market supply curve for chicken eggs in Figure 6.1. Label the curve *S*. (Assume the supply curve is linear.)

Table 6.2 Market supply of eggs

Quantity (millions of eggs per day)	*Price (per dozen)*
4	$2.00
3	1.50
2	1.00
1	0.50

3. Use the information in Table 6.3 to determine the marginal cost at each output level for an individual egg farmer.

Table 6.3 Production costs for an individual egg farmer

Quantity (eggs per minute)	*Total cost*	*Marginal cost*
0	$4.00	--------
1	4.40	________
2	5.30	________
3	6.80	________
4	9.00	________
5	11.80	________

4. Use the information in Table 6.3 to draw the marginal cost curve for the individual egg farmer in Figure 6.2. Label the curve *Marginal Cost.*

Figure 6.2 Costs of egg production

$3.00
2.50
2.00
1.50
1.00
0.50
Price (per dozen)
0
1
2
3
4
5
Quantity (eggs per minute)

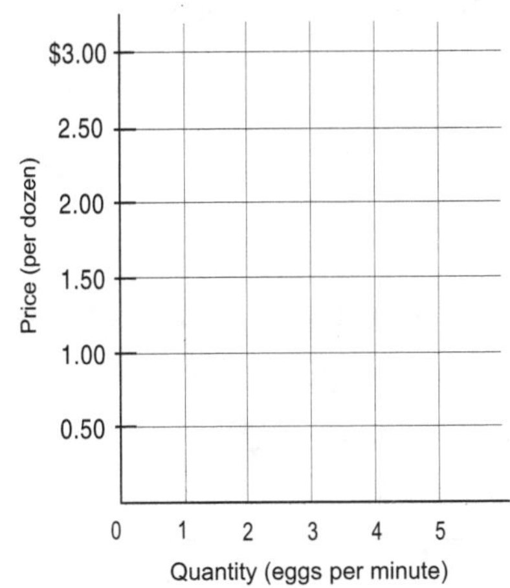

5. Use the market equilibrium price from Figure 6.1 to draw a line at the price that the individual farmer faces in Figure 6.2. Label the line *Price.*

6. According to the profit-maximization rule, this egg farmer should produce _____ eggs per minute.

7. At an output level of 2 eggs per minute, for the individual farmer, MC is (greater, less) than price and the farmer should (increase, decrease) output in order to maximize profit.

Exercise 2

This exercise provides practice in using graphs in a perfectly competitive market situation.

1. Label the three curves given in Figure 6.3 for a firm in a perfectly competitive market situation.

Figure 6.3

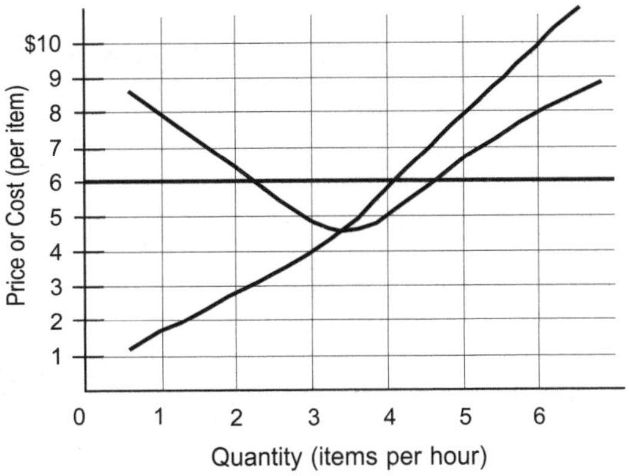

$10
9
8
7
6
5
4
3
2
1
Price or Cost (per item)
0
1
2
3
4
5
6
Quantity (items per hour)

2. What is the profit-maximizing rate of output for this firm? __________

3. Shade the area that represents total profit at the profit-maximizing rate of output.

4. Given that the firm is operating in a perfectly competitive market, does this graph indicate a short-run or a long-run situation? Explain how you know. ____

____

Exercise 3

This exercise gives you a chance to calculate total revenue, profit, and marginal cost and to find the output that will yield maximum profit.

1. Fill in the blanks for the formulas below.

   (a) Price x quantity = ______________________

   (b) (Change in total cost) ÷ (change in output) = ____________________

   (c) Total revenue – total cost = ____________________

2. After checking your answers for Question 1, complete Table 6.4.

Table 6.4 Cost and revenue data

Quantity	*Price*	*Total revenue*	*Total cost*	*Profit*	*Marginal cost*
0	$9	$_____	$5.00	$_____	———
1	9	_____	7.00	_____	_____
2	9	_____	11.00	_____	_____
3	9	_____	18.00	_____	_____
4	9	_____	27.00	_____	_____
5	9	_____	39.00	_____	_____

3. In Figure 6.4, graph price and marginal cost. Label the marginal cost curve *MC* and the price line *Price*.

Figure 6.4

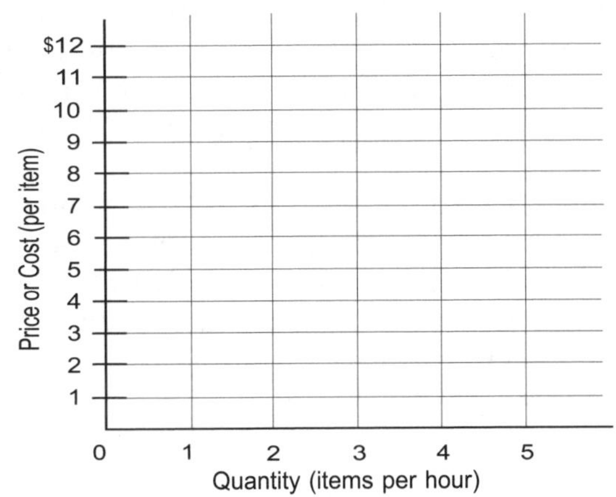

4. What is the profit maximizing level of output for this firm? __________

5. At an output level of 2 items this firm would (increase, decrease) profit by producing more.

Common Errors

The first statement in each "common error" below is incorrect. Each incorrect statement is followed by a corrected version and an explanation.

1. The demand curve for a competitive market is flat. *Incorrect!*
   The demand curve for a competitive firm is flat. *Correct!*
   Although the demand curve for an individual firm in a perfectly competitive market is flat, the demand curve for the market is still downward sloping.

2. Competitive firms do not make profits. *Incorrect!*
   Competitive firms can make economic profits in the short run. *Correct!*
   In the long run, firms enter a competitive market causing price to fall and economic profits to go to zero. In the short run, a change in demand or supply may cause price to change allowing firms to earn temporary economic profits.

3. Since competitive firms make zero profits in the long run, they cannot pay their stockholders and they should shut down. *Incorrect!*
   Since competitive firms make zero economic profits in the long run, they are able to pay all factors of production, including the skill of entrepreneurs, to keep the firms in existence. *Correct!*
   Be careful! Keep the accounting and economic definitions of such words as *profit* separate and distinct. When economists refer to profits they are referring to economic profits. If a firm is earning zero economic profits, it can still be earning a positive accounting profit. This profit is just equal to what the firm could have earned in its next best alternative.

4. A firm should always increase the rate of production as long as it is making a profit. *Incorrect!* A profitable firm should increase production rates only as long as additional revenues from the increase in production exceed the additional costs. *Correct!*

   If the increase in production generates more costs than revenue, the firm's profits will decline. In this case, continued expansion will ultimately result in zero profits. A competitive firm will maximize profits if it produces at the output level where MC = Price.

5. If a perfectly competitive firm is losing money, it can raise its price to earn a profit. *Incorrect!* Even if a perfectly competitive firm is losing money it cannot change the price it charges. *Correct!*

   Individual firms in a competitive industry have output that is so small relative to the total market output that it has no impact on the market price. If they raise their price, their customers will switch to another producer who has not raised their price. As a result, the firm's sales will decline to zero and the firm will experience an even greater loss.

~ ANSWERS ~

Using Terms to Remember

Across

2. monopoly
4. equilibrium price
7. profit maximization rule
8. market power
9. market mechanism
12. market structure
13. competitive firm

Down

1. supply
3. total revenue
5. profit
6. barriers to entry
7. production decision
9. marginal cost
10. competitive market
11. market supply

True or False

1. T
2. F In a perfectly competitive market, individual firms are so small relative to the market that a change in a firm's production will not have an impact on the market price or output.
3. T
4. F To maximize profit, a firm should produce the level of output where MC = Price.
5. F If a perfectly competitive firm were to raise its price above the market price, it would lose all of its customers.
6. F The firm will maximize total profit at this output level.
7. T
8. F When economic profits exist in a perfectly competitive market, the number of suppliers will increase, which causes the market supply curve to shift to the right, and the market price will fall.
9. T
10. T

Multiple Choice

1. d	5. a	9. a	13. a	17. c
2. d	6. b	10. b	14. b	18. d
3. c	7. c	11. b	15. d	19. d
4. a	8. c	12. a	16. a	20. a

Problems and Applications

Exercise 1

1. **Figure 6.1 Answer**

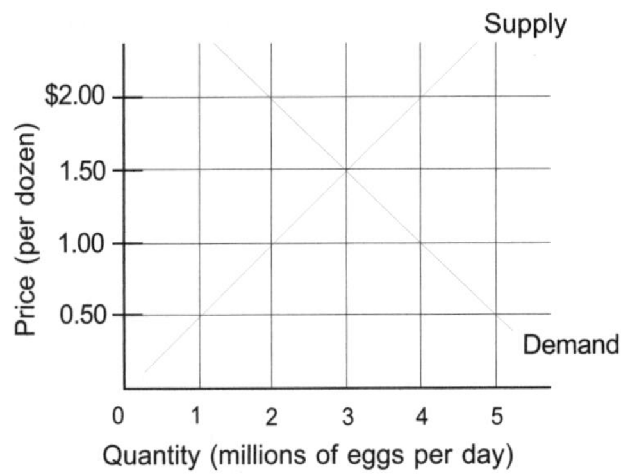

2. See Figure 6.1 Answer.

3. **Table 6.3 Answer**

Quantity	*Marginal cost*
0	------
1	$0.40
2	0.90
3	1.50
4	2.20
5	2.80

4. **Figure 6.2 Answer**

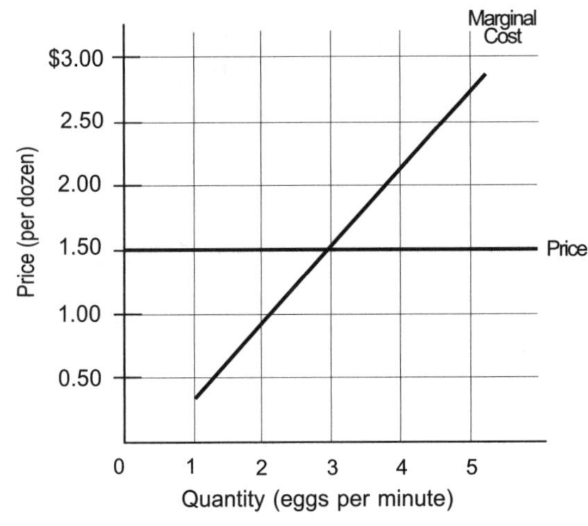

5. See Figure 6.2 Answer.
6. 3
7. Less; increase

Exercise 2

1. **Figure 6.3 Answer**

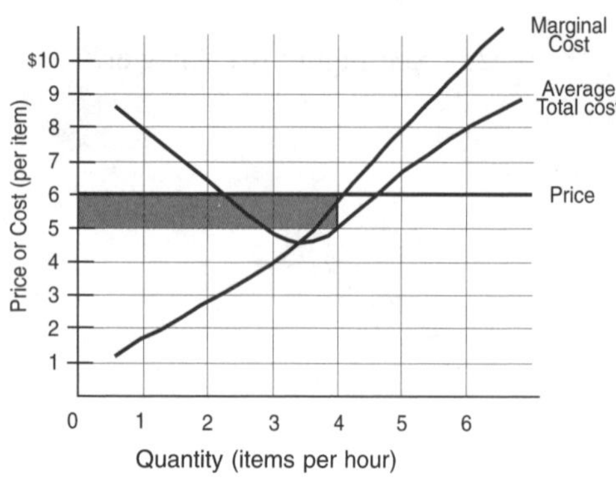

2. 4 items per hour.
3. See Figure 6.3 answer.
4. Short-run situation, because there is an economic profit and price is above the minimum of average total cost.

Exercise 3

1. a. Total revenue
   b. Marginal cost
   c. Profit

2. **Table 6.4 Answer**

Quantity	*Total revenue*	*Profit*	*Marginal cost*
0	$0.00	–$ 5.00	------
1	9.00	+ 2.00	$2.00
2	18.00	+ 7.00	4.00
3	27.00	+ 9.00	7.00
4	36.00	+ 9.00	9.00
5	45.00	+ 6.00	12.00

3. **Figure 6.4 Answer**

4. 4 items per day
5. Increase

CHAPTER 7

Monopoly

Quick Review

- Market power is the ability to alter the price of a good or service. A monopolist is the sole supplier in a given market and has market power, which it can use to influence price and output.
- The demand curve faced by a monopolist is the downward-sloping market demand curve. As a result, in order to sell more output a monopolist must lower its price for all output, so the marginal revenue curve is always less than price.
- In making the production decision, monopolists attempt to maximize profits. They produce the level of output at which marginal cost equals marginal revenue but charge a price greater than marginal revenue given by the demand curve. When compared to competitive producers with the same market demand and cost structure, monopolists charge higher prices and produce less output.
- If market demand is sufficient, monopolists will reap economic profits, which are a signal for other firms to enter the market. In order to maintain monopoly status and keep profits from being competed away, barriers to entry such as patents, legal harassment, exclusive licensing, bundled products, and government franchises are necessary.
- The existence of market power in the economy influences the answers to the WHAT, HOW, and FOR WHOM questions. By restricting output, monopolists force some resources to move to alternative production, where they earn less, and are able to keep economic profits for themselves. Monopolists tend to be less efficient than competitive firms since they are not compelled by competitive forces to adopt the newest and most efficient technologies.
- Other market structures with some monopoly characteristics include a duopoly, an oligopoly, and monopolistic competition. Each of these structures has some market power.
- Some arguments that are made in support of monopolies are: 1) economic profits give a monopoly the financial resources to pursue research and development; 2) monopoly profits may encourage entrepreneurial activity; 3) if economies of scale exist over the entire market, society will be best served by having a single firm (a natural monopoly) produce all the output; 4) potential competition, perhaps from foreign producers attracted by economic profits, is sufficient to constrain a monopoly from exploiting its market power. If a monopoly market is contestable, the threat of potential competition may cause the monopolist to behave more like a competitive market.

Learning Objectives

After reading the chapter and doing the following exercises you should be able to:

1. Define what a monopoly is.
2. Explain why price exceeds marginal revenue in monopoly.
3. Describe how a monopoly sets output and price.
4. Illustrate how monopoly and competitive outcomes differ.
5. Discuss the pros and cons of monopoly structures.

Using Terms to Remember

Fill in the puzzle on the opposite page with the appropriate terms from the list of Terms to Remember in the text.

Across

1. For a monopoly, this short-run choice is made by locating the intersection of marginal cost and marginal revenue.
3. The temporary reduction in price meant to drive competitors out of the market.
4. Used to determine the most profitable rate of production.
6. Necessary in order for a firm to retain market power.
7. The ability to set market price.
9. An imperfectly competitive industry, that is restrained by potential competition.
10. This curve lies below the demand curve at every point except the first in a non-competitive market.
12. A barrier to entry that gives one large producer an advantage over several smaller producers.

Down

1. Used to protect new inventions and acts as a barrier to entry.
2. The pricing method characteristic of competitive markets but not a monopoly.
5. Identical to the firm's demand curve in a monopoly situation.
8. Used to describe a firm that can achieve economies of scale over the entire range of market supply.
11. One producer supplies all the output for a market.

Puzzle 7.1

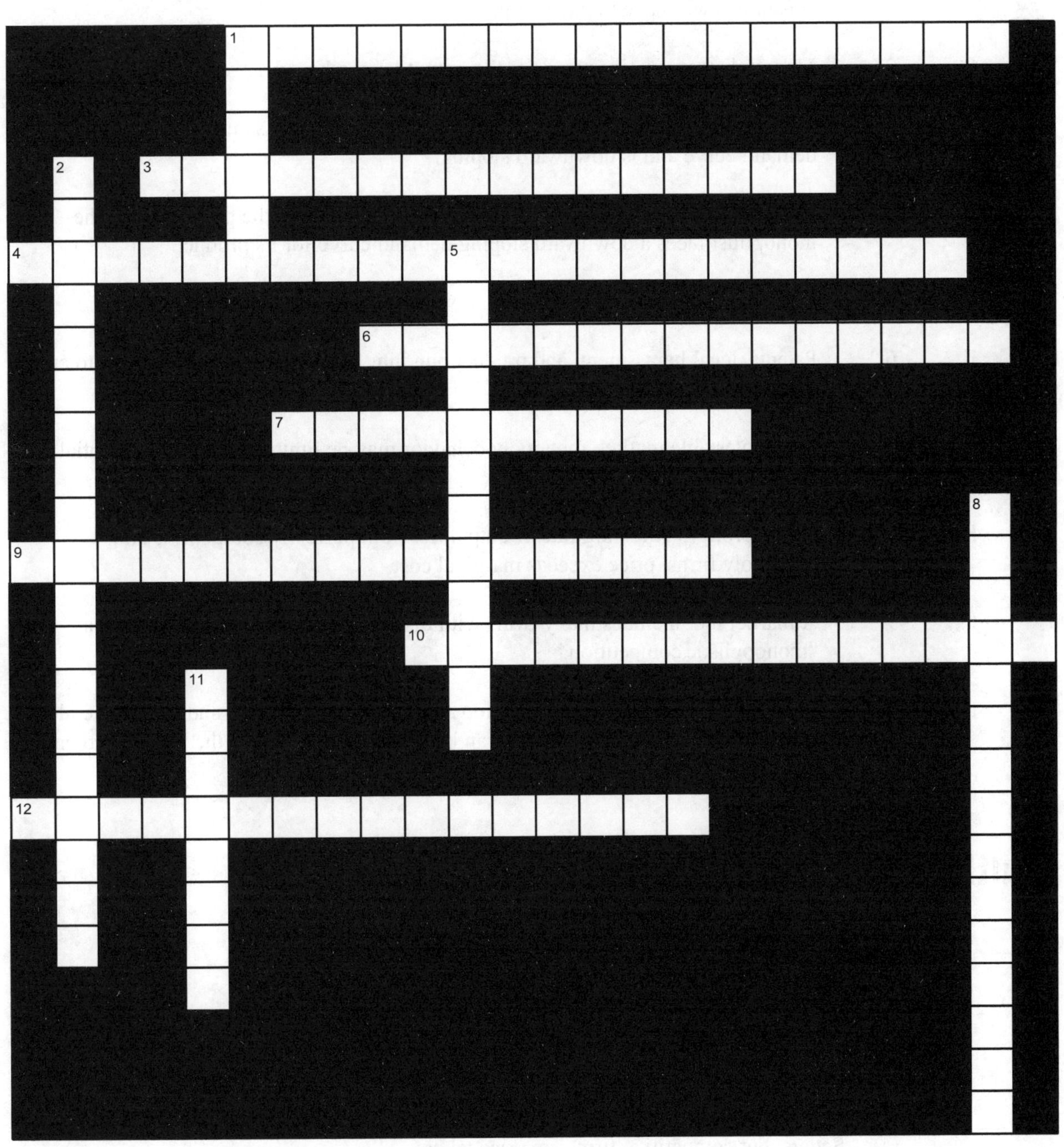

True or False: *Circle your choice and explain why any false statements are incorrect.*

T F 1. Since a monopoly firm controls the market, it can charge any price it wants and consumers will have to pay that price.

T F 2. Monopolists maximize profits at the output level where price equals marginal cost.

T F 3. For a monopolist, the demand curve facing the firm is the same as the market demand curve and is downward sloping.

T F 4. The marginal revenue curve for a monopolist is less than the price because the monopolist faces a downward sloping demand curve for its product.

T F 5. Since a monopolist is a price setter, it will earn unlimited profits.

T F 6. Patents, legal harassment, and product bundling are all examples of barriers to entry in monopoly markets.

T F 7. In a contestable market, monopoly behavior may be limited because of potential competition.

T F 8. At the profit maximizing rate of output, for both perfectly competitive and monopoly firms, price exceeds marginal cost.

T F 9. A market that includes many firms with distinct brand images is referred to as "monopolistic competition."

T F 10. Monopolists are motivated to develop and use new technology and innovative ideas because this is the only way they can keep competitors out of the market and enjoy monopoly profits.

Multiple Choice: *Select the correct answer.*

_____ 1. If a firm can change market price by altering its output, then it:
(a) Must be a monopoly.
(b) Is a price taker.
(c) Faces a vertical demand curve.
(d) Has market power.

_____ 2. Monopolists are price:
(a) Setters, but competitive firms are price takers.
(b) Takers, as are competitive firms.
(c) Takers, but competitive firms are price setters.
(d) Setters, as are competitive firms.

_______ 3. For a monopolist, the demand curve facing the firm is always:
   (a) Below the average total cost curve.
   (b) The same as the market demand curve.
   (c) Identical to the marginal revenue curve.
   (d) The same as the marginal cost curve.

_______ 4. The marginal revenue of a monopolist is:
   (a) The same as price at all output levels.
   (b) Constant up to the rate of output that maximizes total revenues.
   (c) Always less than price.
   (d) Always identical to the demand curve.

_______ 5. When a monopolist sells an additional unit of output, the marginal revenue will be lower than the price because:
   (a) The price of all the units sold will have to be lowered in order to sell the additional unit.
   (b) The monopolist faces a flat demand curve for its product.
   (c) Costs increase as more output is produced.
   (d) Economies of scale exist for monopolists.

_______ 6. Which of the following rules is always satisfied when any firm (i.e., perfectly competitive or monopoly) maximizes profit?
   (a) Price = highest level of ATC.
   (b) Price = MC.
   (c) MR = MC.
   (d) Price = MR.

_______ 7. The price charged by a profit-maximizing monopolist occurs at:
   (a) The minimum of the average total cost curve.
   (b) The price where MR = MC.
   (c) A price on the demand curve above the intersection where MR = MC.
   (d) A price on the average total cost curve below the point where MR = MC.

_______ 8. For both a monopolist and a competitive firm, production should be expanded if:
   (a) Marginal revenue is below marginal cost.
   (b) Marginal revenue is above marginal cost.
   (c) Price is below marginal cost.
   (d) Price is above marginal cost.

_______ 9. Which of the following must be true if a monopoly continues to earn an economic profit in the long run?
   (a) It produces more efficiently than a competitive market can.
   (b) Barriers to entry prevent other firms from competing away the above-normal profits.
   (c) There is a conspiracy between the government and the monopolist to maintain high prices.
   (d) It has a flat demand curve, which gives it greater revenue.

_______ 10. Which of the following is *not* a barrier to entry into a monopoly market?
   (a) Exclusive licensing.
   (b) Bundled products.
   (c) A patent.
   (d) Economic profits.

_______ 11. Compared to a competitive market with the same costs and market demand, a monopolist will produce ________ output at a ________ price.

(a) The same level of; higher.
(b) More; lower.
(c) Less; higher.
(d) The same level of; lower.

_______ 12. According to the text, which of the following barriers to entry did Polaroid use to earn and maintain monopoly profits in the instant-development camera industry?

(a) Patent protection.
(b) Exclusive licensing.
(c) Predatory pricing.
(d) Profit threats.

_______ 13. A monopoly is able to earn larger profits than a comparable competitive market by:

(a) Setting a higher price at the competitive level of output, thereby increasing total revenue.
(b) Producing a greater quantity at the competitive price, thereby increasing profits.
(c) Producing at output levels with a more favorable cost structure and charging the competitive market price, thereby increasing profits per unit.
(d) Reducing production and pushing prices up.

_______ 14. A monopolist is typically able to enjoy economic profits in the long run because of:

(a) Barriers to entry.
(b) The monopolist's ability to set prices.
(c) Economies of scale.
(d) The monopolist's ability to sell as much as it produces at the market price.

_______ 15. Suppose that a market is dominated by three firms. This type of market is known as:

(a) Perfect competition.
(b) A monopoly.
(c) Monopolistic competition.
(d) An oligopoly.

_______ 16. Monopoly might be considered to be more desirable than perfect competition because:

(a) The monopolist has more incentive to keep costs down.
(b) Economies of scale can only be fully realized by a single firm in a natural monopoly.
(c) Marginal revenue is less than price for a monopoly.
(d) It is the best way to increase output above the competitive level of production.

_______ 17. Which of the following is a redeeming quality of market power?

(a) It increases output and raises price, contributing to greater consumption of scarce resources.
(b) Monopoly profits can provide the resources with which to pursue research and development.
(c) It contributes to efficient production when there are diseconomies of scale.
(d) It provides the economic profit necessary for survival and efficient production in a market.

______ 18. Economies of scale:
(a) Allow many small firms to expand society's production possibilities.
(b) Continue no matter how large the firm becomes.
(c) Occur any time that a firm produces more output.
(d) Can be a convincing argument for allowing a monopoly to exist.

______ 19. Which of the following is the unique characteristic of natural monopolies that other monopolies do not experience?
(a) Economies of scale occur over the entire range of market output.
(b) The marginal cost curve is always above the average total cost curve.
(c) The profit-maximizing rate of output occurs where MC = Price.
(d) The characteristics are the same because all monopolies are natural monopolies.

______ 20. If a firm temporarily reduces price to drive out competition, it is engaging in:
(a) Profit sharing.
(b) Price fixing.
(c) Predatory pricing.
(d) Marginal cost fixing.

Problems and Applications

Exercise 1

This exercise provides practice in calculating total revenue and marginal revenue and shows the relationship between marginal revenue and demand.

1. Use the information given in Table 7.1 to calculate total revenue and marginal revenue.

Table 7.1 Revenue data

	Quantity	*Price*	*Total Revenue*	*Marginal Revenue*
A	0	$12.00	$______	-------
B	1	11.00	______	$______
C	2	10.00	______	______
D	3	9.00	______	______
E	4	8.00	______	______
F	5	7.00	______	______
G	6	6.00	______	______

2. For a monopoly, marginal revenue is always (greater, less) than price, after the first unit, because the firm must (raise, lower) its price to sell additional output, according to the law of demand.

3. Use the information from Table 7.1 to graph the demand curve and the marginal revenue curve in Figure 7.1. Label each curve and label the points (*B* through *G*) on the demand curve.

Figure 7.1 Demand and marginal revenue curves

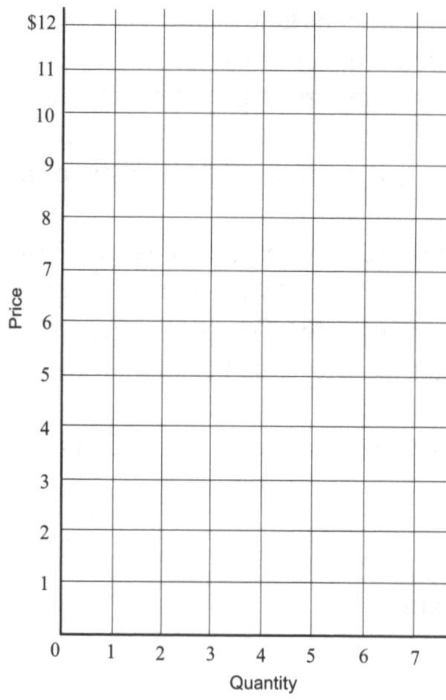

Exercise 2

This exercise reviews costs and revenues and provides further experience with profit maximization.

1. Figure 7.2 represents cost curves for a monopolist. Label the average total cost curve, the marginal cost curve, the marginal revenue curve, and the demand curve in Figure 7.2.

Figure 7.2 Cost curves and profit maximization

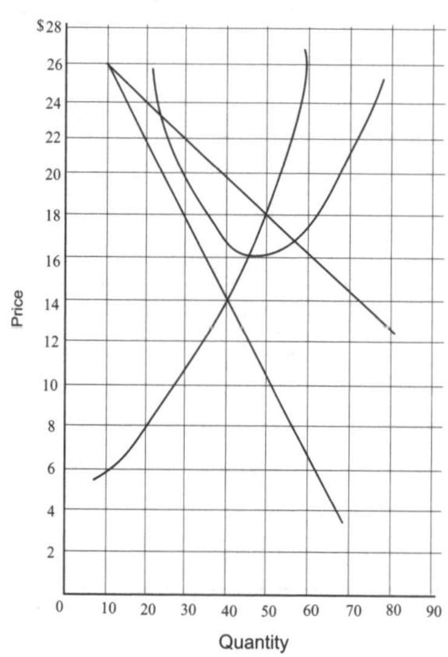

2. What is the profit-maximizing rate of output for the monopolist in Figure 7.2? _______

3. What price will the monopolist charge in Figure 7.2? _______

4. Shade the area to indicate total profit for the monopolist at the profit-maximizing rate of output in Figure 7.2.

5. Now assume the curves in Figure 7.2 represent a competitive industry. What are the profit-maximizing rate of output and price? How do they compare to the profit-maximizing rate of output and price for a monopolist? ______________________

Exercise 3

Reread the Headline article titled "Judge Says Microsoft Broke Antitrust Law" in the text.

1. What phrase indicates that Microsoft was guilty of exploiting monopoly power? __________
____

2. What barriers to entry did Microsoft use to keep other firms from competing with it?
____

3. Who were the victims of Microsoft's behavior according to the article? ______________
____

Common Errors

The first statement in each "common error" below is incorrect. Each incorrect statement is followed by a corrected version and an explanation.

1. A monopolist will maximize profit where Price = MC. *Incorrect!*
   A monopolist will maximize profit at an output level where MC = MR and use the demand curve to determine price at the same output level. *Correct!*
   The price a monopolist will charge is determined by the demand curve since it represents the maximum price that consumers are willing and able to pay. The intersection of MC and MR determines the profit-maximizing output level. The point on the demand curve directly above this intersection is used to determine the price the monopolist will charge.

2. A monopolist wants to be on the inelastic part of the demand curve. *Incorrect!*
   A monopolist wants to be on the elastic part of the demand curve. *Correct!*
   A monopolist wants to produce at the profit-maximizing rate of output or where MC = MR. If demand is inelastic, then the monopoly can usually decrease costs and increase revenues by cutting back production. This means greater profits. Remember the relationship between the elasticity of demand and total revenue from Chapter 4. If demand is inelastic, then the firm can raise price and total revenue will increase. As price rises the firm will move along the demand curve to the elastic part of the curve. So, in an effort to maximize profit, a monopolist will operate on the elastic portion of its demand curve.

3. When there are economies of scale, a firm can simply increase production rates in the short run and unit costs will decline. *Incorrect!*
   When there are economies of scale, a firm can choose a plant size designed for increased production rates at lower unit costs. *Correct!*
   Economies of scale are not realized through production decisions in the short run. They are realized through investment decisions, by the choice of an optimal-sized plant for higher production rates. Scale refers to plant size or capacity, not to production rates within a plant of a given size. Think of economies of scale in terms of investment decisions concerning choices of optimal capacity for the long run, not production decisions concerning the lowest cost production in the short run.

~ ANSWERS ~

Using Terms to Remember

Across

1. production decision
3. predatory pricing
4. profit maximization rule
6. barriers to entry
7. market power
9. contestable market
10. marginal revenue
12. economies of scale

Down

1. patent
2. marginal cost pricing
5. market demand
8. natural monopoly
11. monopoly

True or False

1. F The demand for a monopolist's product is typically not perfectly inelastic. The monopolist is constrained by the consumer's willingness and ability to purchase the product.
2. F Monopolists maximize profits at the output level where marginal cost equals marginal revenue.
3. T
4. T
5. F Even though a monopolist is a price setter, there is no guarantee that it will even earn a profit. Its profits are limited by cost and demand conditions.
6. T
7. T
8. F For perfectly competitive firms price equals marginal cost, but for a monopolist price exceeds marginal cost.
9. T
10. F Monopolists have *little motivation* to develop and use new technology and innovative ideas since they are able to keep competitors out of the market and enjoy monopoly profits without any changes.

Multiple Choice

1. d	5. a	9. b	13. d	17. b
2. a	6. c	10. d	14. a	18. d
3. b	7. c	11. c	15. d	19. a
4. c	8. b	12. a	16. b	20. c

Problems and Applications

Exercise 1

1. **Table 7.1 Answer**

Quantity	*Total revenue*	*Marginal revenue*
0	$0.00	-----
1	11.00	$11.00
2	20.00	9.00
3	27.00	7.00
4	32.00	5.00
5	35.00	3.00
6	36.00	1.00

2. Less, lower

3. **Figure 7.1 Answer**

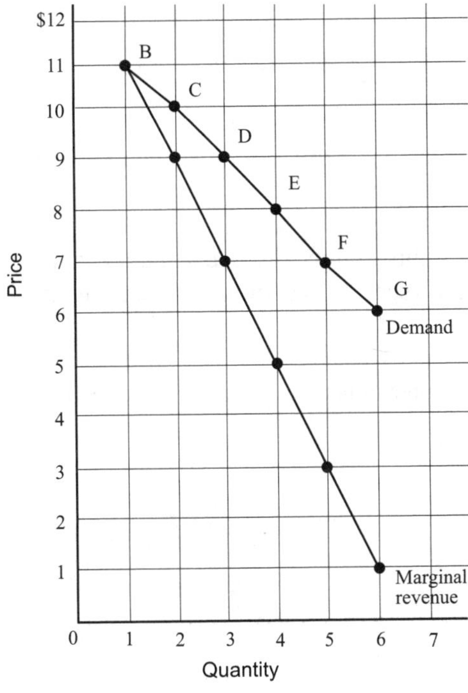

Exercise 2

1. **Figure 7.2 Answer**

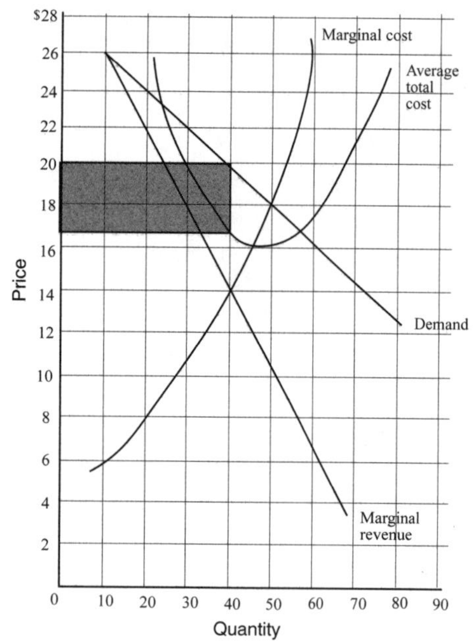

2. 40 units
3. $20 per unit
4. See Figure 7.2 Answer.
5. 50 units at $18 per unit. The price is lower and the output is greater.

Exercise 3

1. "…guilty of violating antitrust law by waging a campaign to crush threats to its Windows monopoly."

2. The barriers to entry include, "...threatening to withhold price discounts and demanding that computer makers not feature rival Netscape's browser...as a condition of licensing the Windows operating system."

3. "...corporate stars of the multibillion-dollar computer industry." The list includes Intel, Apple, IBM, and RealNetworks.

CHAPTER 8

The Labor Market

Quick Review

- The motivation to work comes from a variety of social, psychological, and economic forces. The need to have income to purchase desired goods and services is, of course, very important. Working imposes opportunity costs on the worker because leisure time must be given up when one chooses to work.

- The market supply of labor shows the total quantity of labor that workers are willing and able to supply at alternative wage rates in a given time period, *ceteris paribus*. The labor-supply curve slopes upward to the right indicating that workers will supply more labor at higher wage rates. This is true because of the increasing opportunity cost of working—the leisure time that must be given up in order to work more—and the decreasing marginal utility of income.

- The demand for labor is derived from the demand for the goods and services that the labor produces. The quantity of labor demanded will increase as the wage rate decreases so the labor-demand curve slopes downward to the right. The marginal physical product (MPP) of labor is the change in total output because of an additional worker. The demand curve for labor is the marginal revenue product (MRP) curve; it combines the productivity of labor with the price of the output. The law of diminishing returns affects both MPP and MRP.

- The hiring decision requires that managers consider the contribution of labor to the firm's revenues (called its marginal revenue product) and what it costs to hire the labor. The marginal revenue product thus sets an upper limit to the wage that will be paid to labor. Labor should be hired until the marginal revenue product declines to the level of the wage rate. Increases in the productivity of labor and increases in the market price of the output will shift the demand for labor (MRP curve) to the right.

- The market equilibrium wage is determined by the intersection of the market supply and market demand curves. A minimum wage is set above the market equilibrium wage and causes the quantity of labor supplied to exceed the quantity of labor demanded. Unemployment is the inevitable result. Labor unions must exclude some workers from the market to achieve their goals, and the displaced workers depress wages in other markets.

- It is sometimes difficult to determine the wages of certain individuals because their marginal revenue product is so difficult to calculate. In this situation opportunity wages, custom, power, and the like are used to determine the wage.

Learning Objectives

After reading the chapter and doing the following exercises you should be able to:

1. Cite the forces that influence the supply of labor.
2. Explain why the labor demand curve slopes downward.
3. Describe how the equilibrium wage and employment levels are determined.
4. Depict how a legal minimum wage alters market outcomes.
5. Explain why wages are so unequal.

Using Terms to Remember

Fill in the puzzle on the opposite page with the appropriate terms from the list of Terms to Remember in the text.

Across

2. The quantity of labor producers are willing and able to hire at alternative wages.
7. The quantity of labor people are willing and able to supply at alternative wages.
8. The wage at which the quantity demanded of labor and the quantity supplied of labor are equal.
10. The additional output because of one additional unit of input.

Down

1. Explains why the marginal physical product of labor declines as the quantity of labor increases.
3. Used by most universities to justify the compensation given to college professors according to the text.
4. Equal to marginal physical product times price.
5. The total quantity of hours people are willing and able to work at various wages.
6. The demand for labor that results from the demand for final goods and services.
9. The __________ of working is the leisure time that must be given up.

Puzzle 8.1

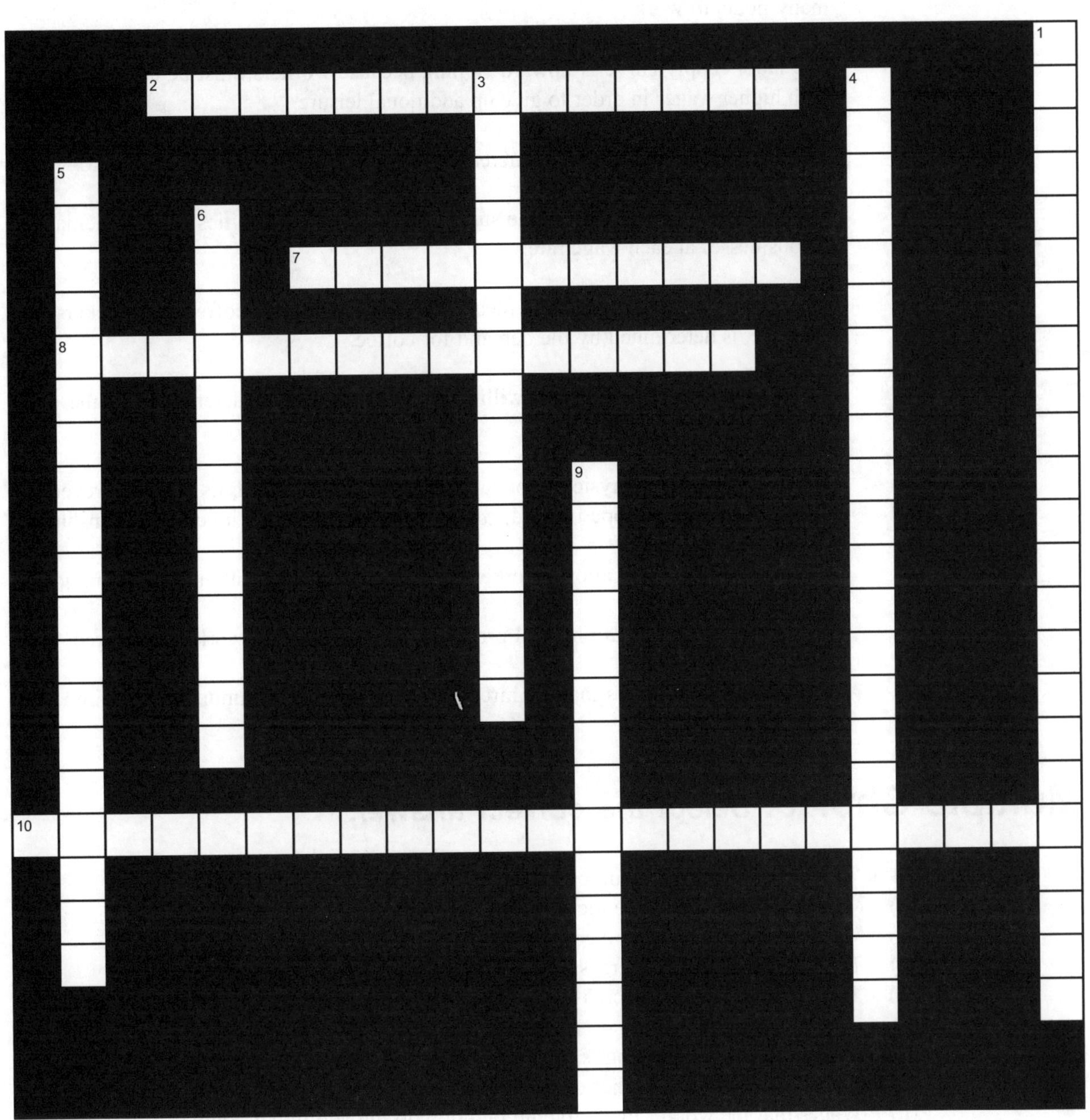

True or False: *Circle your choice and explain why any false statements are incorrect.*

T F 1. People are only concerned with maximizing their income when determining how many hours to work.

T F 2. The labor supply curve is upward sloping because workers must be compensated with higher wages in order to give up additional leisure.

T F 3. The marginal utility of income increases as total income increases.

T F 4. The market supply of labor is the summation of all the quantities of labor demanded by businesses at each wage rate.

T F 5. The concept of derived demand means that the demand for coffee bean pickers, for example, is determined by the demand for coffee.

T F 6. The highest wage that a firm is willing to pay its workers is determined by the marginal revenue product.

T F 7. If a firm's marginal physical product curve slopes downward, its marginal revenue product curve must slope upward, *ceteris paribus*, due to the inverse relationship.

T F 8. Increased productivity allows workers to get higher wages without sacrificing jobs.

T F 9. In most cases, marginal physical product increases as more workers are hired.

T F 10. The number of workers that are hired decreases when a minimum wage is imposed.

Multiple Choice: *Select the correct answer.*

_______ 1. As an individual works more and earns more income, the:
(a) Marginal utility of income increases.
(b) Marginal utility of leisure increases.
(c) Total utility of leisure increases and the total utility of income decreases.
(d) Total utility of leisure decreases and the total utility of income increases.

_______ 2. The opportunity cost of working is the:
(a) Financial cost to the worker of driving to work, parking, buying lunch, etc.
(b) Wages that the worker must give up by not working additional hours.
(c) Leisure time that must be given up.
(d) Amount of utility the worker receives when working.

______ 3. Which of the following is a reason why workers typically require higher wages in order to work additional hours?
(a) The decreasing opportunity cost of labor.
(b) The decreasing value of leisure time forgone.
(c) The inherent greed and laziness of workers.
(d) The law of diminishing marginal utility applied to additional income.

______ 4. The best way for consumers to increase the wages and number of jobs available for strawberry pickers is to:
(a) Insist that the government establish a minimum wage for strawberry pickers.
(b) Boycott strawberries until wages increase.
(c) Buy more strawberries.
(d) Insist that the sellers raise the price of strawberries.

______ 5. A firm's demand for labor is downward sloping (i.e., additional workers are worth less to employers) because:
(a) Total output decreases as more workers are hired.
(b) The marginal physical product of labor decreases as more labor is hired.
(c) The firm must raise wages to hire more workers.
(d) The price of the product declines as the firm produces and sells more.

______ 6. The marginal physical product (MPP) of labor decreases as more labor is hired because of:
(a) The law of diminishing returns.
(b) A decrease in total output.
(c) A decrease in the skills of the additional workers hired.
(d) The law of diminishing marginal utility.

______ 7. The marginal product of additional units of labor eventually diminishes because, *ceteris paribus*:
(a) Additional labor is typically less experienced.
(b) The law of increasing marginal utility is involved.
(c) The quantity of labor demanded depends on expected sales and output.
(d) Additional labor has less land and capital to work with.

______ 8. If the MPP of an additional unit of labor is 4 units per hour, product price is constant at $5.00 per unit, and the wage rate is $16.00 per hour, then:
(a) An additional unit of labor should be employed.
(b) An additional unit of labor should *not* be employed because it costs more than it is worth.
(c) The employer should reduce the level of employment.
(d) The employer should raise wages and hire more workers.

______ 9. Refer to Figure 8.3 in the text. The effect of the law of diminishing returns is not evident until the _______ worker is hired.
(a) First.
(b) Third.
(c) Fifth.
(d) Eighth.

_______ 10. A firm should continue to hire workers until the:
(a) MRP is equal to demand.
(b) MPP is equal to the market wage rate.
(c) MRP is equal to zero.
(d) MRP is equal to the market wage rate.

_______ 11. Refer to Figure 8.4 in the text. If strawberry pickers worked for zero wages (i.e., they were volunteers), how many workers should this firm hire?
(a) Zero.
(b) Two, where MRP is at a maximum.
(c) Seven, where MRP is zero.
(d) As many as possible.

_______ 12. Refer to Table 8.1 in the text. At a wage rate of $8 per hour, this firm should hire the second worker because:
(a) The value of the second worker's production is greater than $8.
(b) Total production begins to decline with the second worker.
(c) MPP begins to increase with the second worker.
(d) The price of strawberries begins to decline at a wage rate of $8.

_______ 13. If a university's football coach is paid significantly more than the university's president, the logical explanation is that the coach:
(a) Is more popular.
(b) Has a higher level of education.
(c) Has been employed at the university longer than the president.
(d) Brings more revenue to the university than does the president.

_______ 14. Which of the following is true about the equilibrium market wage?
(a) All workers are satisfied with the wage but some employers are not.
(b) All employers are satisfied with the wage but some workers are not.
(c) There is no unemployment in the market at this wage.
(d) It is always equal to the minimum wage.

_______ 15. Employment will definitely rise when productivity ________ and wages ________.
(a) Increases; rise.
(b) Increases; fall.
(c) Decreases; rise.
(d) Decreases; fall.

_______ 16. *Ceteris paribus*, if the government decides to eliminate the minimum wage, then:
(a) Wages will rise but employment will fall.
(b) Wages will fall but employment will rise.
(c) Both wages and employment will fall.
(d) Both wages and employment will rise.

_______ 17. When there is a decrease in the size of the labor force, *ceteris paribus*:
(a) Wages will rise and employment will fall.
(b) Wages will fall and employment will rise.
(c) Both wages and employment will fall.
(d) Both wages and employment will rise.

_______ 18. To maintain above-equilibrium wages, unions use which of the following forms of exclusion?
(a) Union membership.
(b) Required apprenticeship programs.
(c) Employment agreements negotiated with employers.
(d) All of the above.

_______ 19. The effect of union exclusion on nonunion workers is to:
(a) Lower the wages of nonunion workers.
(b) Cause a shortage of nonunion workers.
(c) Increase the number of jobs for nonunion workers.
(d) All of the above.

_______ 20. When the MRP of a worker is difficult to measure (e.g., a college professor or a corporate CEO) wages can be determined by:
(a) The supply of labor alone.
(b) The minimum wage.
(c) The wages the worker would receive in his or her best alternative job.
(d) The average wage of government workers.

Problems and Applications

Exercise 1

This exercise illustrates the relationship between marginal physical product and marginal revenue product for a company producing organic apple juice.

1. T F The marginal physical product (MPP) measures the change in total output that occurs when one additional worker is hired.

2. Which of the following formulas would provide a correct calculation of the marginal physical product?
(a) Quantity ÷ labor
(b) Change in quantity ÷ labor
(c) Change in quantity ÷ change in labor
(d) Change in total revenue ÷ change in labor

3. Calculate total revenue, marginal revenue product, and marginal physical product for Table 8.1.

Table 8.1 Marginal physical product and marginal revenue product

(1) Labor (workers per hour)	(2) Quantity produced (quarts per hour)	(3) Price (dollars per quart)	(4) Total revenue (dollars per hour)	(5) Marginal revenue product (dollars per worker)	(6) Marginal physical product (quarts per worker)
0	0	$3	______	—	—
1	15	3	______	______	______
2	27	3	______	______	______
3	36	3	______	______	______
4	42	3	______	______	______
5	45	3	______	______	______
6	46	3	______	______	______

4. The law of diminishing returns implies that:
   (a) Total revenue declines as additional labor is employed in a given production process.
   (b) Marginal revenue product declines as additional labor is employed in a given production process.
   (c) Marginal physical product of labor increases as additional labor is employed in a given production process.
   (d) Marginal revenue increases as additional labor is employed in a given production process.

5. T F There are diminishing returns to labor with increased production in Table 8.1.

Exercise 2

This exercise provides experience in computing and graphing derived demand as well as determining the number of workers to hire.

1. Assume you are the producer of a nutrition bar called EnerG, which sells for $2 per bar. You pay $12 an hour for labor. Complete Table 8.2.

Table 8.2 EnerG production, by labor hours

(1) Wage (dollars per hour)	(2) Labor (workers per hour)	(3) Quantity produced (bars per hour)	(4) Price of EnerG (per bar)	(5) Total revenue (per hour)	(6) Marginal revenue product (dollars per worker)
$12	0	0	$2	$______	$______
12	1	15	2	______	______
12	2	27	2	______	______
12	3	36	2	______	______
12	4	42	2	______	______
12	5	45	2	______	______
12	6	46	2	______	______

2. T F The demand curve for EnerG workers is found by plotting the marginal revenue product curve.

3. In Figure 8.1 draw the demand curve for labor using Table 8.2. Label it MRP.

Figure 8.1

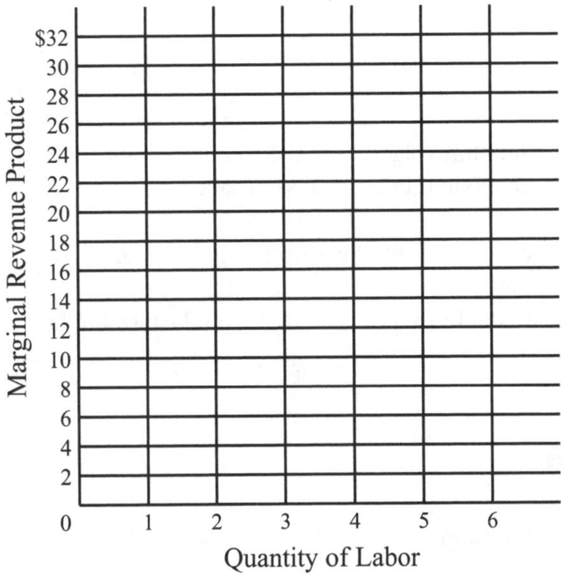

Marginal Revenue Product

$32, 30, 28, 26, 24, 22, 20, 18, 16, 14, 12, 10, 8, 6, 4, 2

0 1 2 3 4 5 6

Quantity of Labor

4. Draw a straight line at a wage of $12 in Figure 8.1 and label it *wage rate*.

5. How many workers are you willing to hire to produce EnerG bars? ________

6. How many EnerG bars will be produced per hour? ________

Exercise 3

This exercise examines the impact of a minimum wage on a labor market.

1. Figure 8.2 shows the labor market for unskilled workers. The equilibrium wage rate occurs at $ _______ per hour and at a quantity of _______ workers.

Figure 8.2

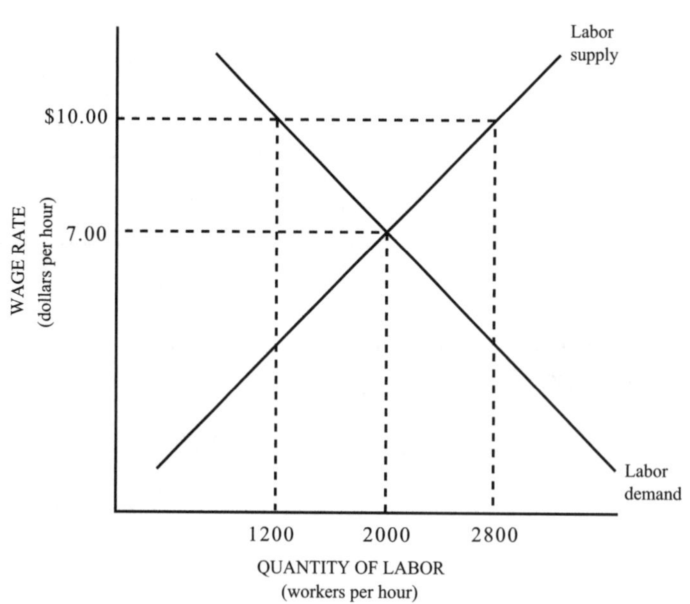

2. Now assume that a minimum wage is set at $10.00 per hour. The result of this government intervention is to create a (shortage, surplus) of labor.

3. At the minimum wage, _______ workers keep their jobs and _______ workers are unemployed.

4. An increase in labor productivity in Figure 8.2 would cause the labor (supply, demand) curve to shift to the (left, right).

Common Errors

The first statement in each "common error" below is incorrect. Each incorrect statement is followed by a corrected version and an explanation.

1. Workers demand jobs. *Incorrect!*
   Employers demand labor services and workers (employees) supply them. *Correct!*
   Demand refers to what someone is willing and able to buy. It is the employer or business who is buying the job skills of the employee. The demand curve for labor represents the behavior of the employer or business.

2. Employers employ those factors that are least expensive. *Incorrect!*
Employers want to employ those factors that are most cost-effective. *Correct!*

Companies are interested in producing a product at the lowest cost per unit. This does not necessarily mean they employ the least expensive factor. If a factor is cheap, there may be a reason. Although the labor rate per hour is less expensive in China and Mexico than in the United States, the level of productivity is also less. When productivity is factored in, it may be less expensive to produce many goods in the United States, even though the cost of labor is higher.

3. Marginal revenue product is the same as marginal revenue. *Incorrect!*
The marginal revenue product is not the same as marginal revenue. *Correct!*

The formula for marginal revenue product is:

$$\frac{\text{Change in total revenue}}{\text{Change in quantity of input}}$$

The formula for marginal revenue is:

$$\frac{\text{Change in total revenue}}{\text{Change in quantity of output}}$$

Marginal revenue shows the change in total revenue that results from one more unit of product being sold. Marginal revenue product shows the change in total revenue resulting from one more unit of an input being employed. For example, assume a competitive product market in which the product price is $5 per unit. In such a market the marginal revenue is $5. If a firm in this market hires an additional worker and the change in output is 10 units, then the marginal revenue product is $50. The additional worker added $50 to total revenue for the firm.

~ ANSWERS ~

Using Terms to Remember

Across

2. demand for labor
7. labor supply
8. equilibrium wage
10. marginal physical product

Down

1. law of diminishing returns
3. opportunity wage
4. marginal revenue product
5. market supply of labor
6. derived demand
9. opportunity cost

True or False

1. F Workers attempt to achieve a balance between more income and more leisure time.
2. T
3. F The marginal utility of income *decreases* as total income increases.
4. F The market supply of labor is the summation of all the quantities of labor supplied by workers at each wage rate.
5. T
6. T
7. F If a firm's marginal physical product curve slopes downward, its marginal revenue product curve must slope downward because MRP equals MPP times price.

8. T
9. F In most cases, marginal physical product *decreases* as more workers are hired.
10. T

Multiple Choice

1. b	5. b	9. b	13. d	17. a
2. c	6. a	10. d	14. c	18. d
3. d	7. d	11. c	15. b	19. a
4. c	8. a	12. a	16. b	20. c

Problems and Applications

Exercise 1

1. T
2. c
3. **Table 8.1 Answer**

(1) Labor	*(4) Total revenue*	*(5) Marginal revenue product*	*(6) Marginal physical product*
0	$0	—	—
1	45	$45	15
2	81	36	12
3	108	27	9
4	126	18	6
5	135	9	3
6	138	3	1

4. b
5. T

Exercise 2

1. **Table 8. 2 Answer**

(2) Labor	*(5) Total revenue product*	*(6) Marginal revenue*
0	$0	$—
1	30	30
2	54	24
3	72	18
4	84	12
5	90	6
6	92	2

2. T

3. **Figure 8.1 Answer**

4. See Figure 8.1 Answer.
5. 4 workers
6. 42 bars

Exercise 3

1. $7.00; 2000
2. Surplus
3. 1200; 1600
4. Demand, right

CHAPTER 9

Government Intervention

Quick Review

- Market failure occurs when the market mechanism causes the economy to produce a combination of goods different from the optimal mix of output, or results in an inequitable distribution of income. Market failure may prompt the government to intervene.

- There are four specific sources of market failure at the micro level: public goods, externalities, market power, and equity.

- Private goods can be consumed exclusively by those who pay, but public goods cannot. Public goods, such as national defense, are consumed jointly by all of us no matter who pays. Because the link between paying and receiving is broken, everyone seeks to be a "free rider" and benefit from purchases made by others. As a result, the market underproduces public goods, and government intervention is necessary to provide these goods.

- Externalities are costs (or benefits) of a market transaction borne by a third party. Externalities cause a divergence between social costs and private costs and lead to suboptimal market outcomes. In the case of externalities such as pollution, which impose costs on society, too much of the polluting good is produced. If the externality produces benefits, too little of the good will be produced by the market alone. Regulations and emission fees are used to reduce the external costs associated with externalities.

- Market power allows producers to ignore the signals generated in the marketplace and produce a suboptimal mix of output. Antitrust policy and laws seek to prevent or restrict concentrations of market power.

- The market mechanism tends to allocate output to those with the most income. The government responds with a system of taxes and transfer payments to ensure a more equitable distribution of income and output.

- Markets may also fail at the macro level. In this case, the problems include unacceptable levels of unemployment, inflation, and economic growth. Government intervention is intended to improve the economy and help it achieve its goals.

- Government intervention that does not improve economic outcomes is referred to as government failure.

Learning Objectives

After reading the chapter and doing the following exercises you should be able to:

1. Define what "market failure" means.
2. Explain why the market underproduces "public goods."
3. Tell how externalities distort market outcomes.
4. Describe how market power prevents optimal outcomes.
5. Define what "government failure" is.

Using Terms to Remember

Fill in the puzzle on the opposite page with the appropriate terms from the list of Terms to Remember in the text.

Across

1. The doctrine of "leave it alone."
4. Can be consumed jointly.
6. The ability to alter the market price of a good or service.
7. The costs of an economic activity incurred directly by the producer.
8. One who does not pay but still enjoys the benefits.
11. The likely outcome of government intervention according to the opinion poll in the text.
12. Exceed private costs by the amount of external costs.
13. For a ________, consumption by one person excludes consumption by others.
14. Referred to as the "invisible hand."
15. A form of government intervention to address the FOR WHOM question.

Down

2. Government intervention to alter market structure or prevent abuse of market power.
3. The most desirable combination of output attainable with existing resources, technology, and social values.
5. An imperfection in the market mechanism that prevents optimal outcomes.
9. The costs or benefits of a market activity borne by a third party.
10. A fee imposed on polluters, based on the quantity of pollution.

Puzzle 9.1

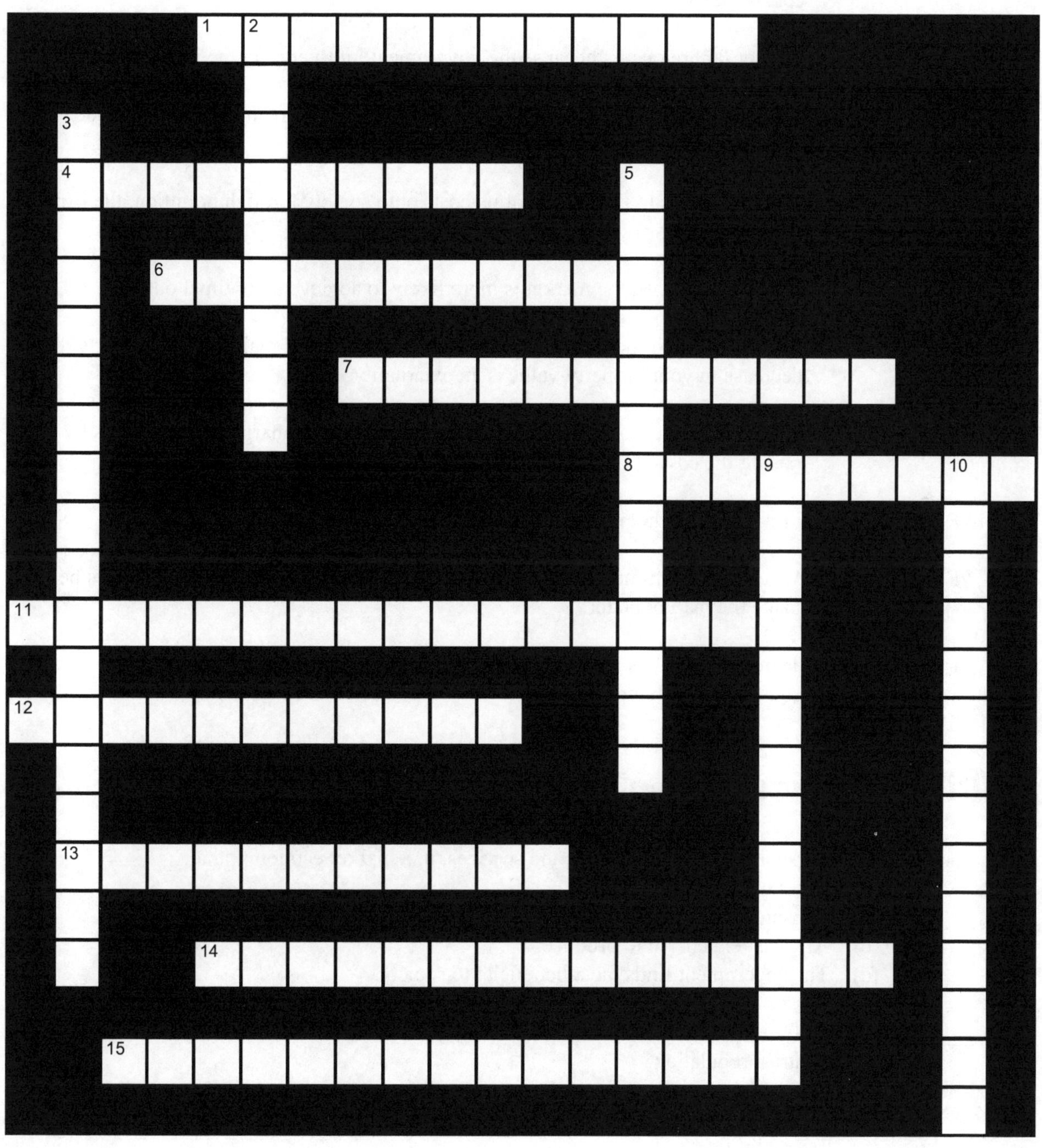

True or False: *Circle your choice and explain why any false statements are incorrect.*

T F 1. Any combination of goods and services on the production possibilities curve can be considered an optimal mix.

T F 2. Market failure occurs because the government intervenes in the marketplace.

T F 3. A public good is one for which consumption by one person does *not* preclude consumption of the same good by another person.

T F 4. If a firm is able to push some of its costs onto society through pollution, the firm will produce less output than is socially optimal.

T F 5. If free riders exist, the market is more likely to achieve an optimal outcome.

T F 6. If your next-door neighbor refuses to mow his yard and maintain his property, the decrease in your property value is an externality.

T F 7. An emission fee shifts marginal private costs closer to marginal social costs by raising the costs of production.

T F 8. Firms with market power tend to produce less output than is optimal.

T F 9. When the government responds to a market failure, the outcome will always be to make the market better.

T F 10. Transfer payments are a government response to the market's failure to provide an equitable distribution of goods.

Multiple Choice: *Select the correct answer.*

________ 1. Producers will produce the goods and services, in a market economy, that:
(a) Consumers demand.
(b) Consumers need the most.
(c) Are least expensive to produce.
(d) The government finds most beneficial to society.

________ 2. Which of the following is an example of market failure?
(a) Antitrust regulation.
(b) Marginal cost pricing.
(c) Diminishing returns.
(d) Externalities.

________ 3. Which market failure is the free-rider dilemma associated with?
(a) Externalities.
(b) Public goods.
(c) Market power.
(d) Inequity.

_______ 4. Federal, state, and local governments usually build parks because it is difficult to exclude people who don't pay for the parks from enjoying them. Which market failure is most likely involved?
(a) Inequity.
(b) Public goods.
(c) Government failure.
(d) Market power.

_______ 5. Income transfers are used to address the market failure of:
(a) Externalities.
(b) Private goods.
(c) Social costs.
(d) Inequity.

_______ 6. A private good is unique because it:
(a) Can be enjoyed exclusively by the one who purchases it.
(b) Experiences free riders.
(c) Results in market failure when provided in markets characterized by laissez-faire.
(d) Is provided most efficiently by the government.

_______ 7. When external costs result from the production of a good:
(a) Producers have an incentive to produce too little.
(b) Consumers have an incentive to consume too little.
(c) Both producers and consumers have an incentive to produce and consume too much.
(d) Producers and consumers are not affected.

_______ 8. The market will overproduce goods that have external costs because:
(a) Producers experience lower costs than society.
(b) Producers experience higher costs than society.
(c) The government is not able to produce these goods.
(d) Producers cannot keep these goods from consumers who do not pay so they have to produce greater amounts.

_______ 9. Social costs:
(a) Are less than private costs.
(b) Include private costs.
(c) Are unrelated to private costs.
(d) Do not affect society.

_______ 10. Internalizing the costs of pollution by establishing emission charges can cause:
(a) An upward shift in the polluting firm's MC curve.
(b) An upward shift in the polluting firm's ATC curve.
(c) A reduction in the polluting firm's output.
(d) All of the above.

_______ 11. Which type of market failure is addressed if a local government forbids smoking in restaurants?
(a) External costs.
(b) The failure to produce public goods.
(c) Market power by cigarette producers.
(d) Inequity in the distribution of goods.

_______ 12. The cost of environmental protection can be measured by:
(a) The difference between social benefits and social costs.
(b) The difference between marginal social benefits and marginal social costs.
(c) The opportunity cost of resources used to protect the environment.
(d) The dollar damage caused by pollution.

_______ 13. Refer to Figure 9.6 in the text. A completely successful emission fee will:
(a) Increase private marginal cost so that it intersects with price at zero output, that is, pollution is completely eliminated.
(b) Increase private marginal cost so that q_1 is produced.
(c) Increase social marginal cost so that q_0 is produced.
(d) Not impact either the private or social marginal cost.

_______ 14. Which of the following market failures provides justification for antitrust policy?
(a) Externalities.
(b) Public goods.
(c) Market power.
(d) Inequity.

_______ 15. The development of market power by a firm is considered to be a market failure because firms with market power:
(a) Produce more and charge a lower price than what is socially optimal.
(b) Tend to ignore external costs.
(c) Produce less and charge a higher price than what is socially optimal.
(d) Do not respond to consumer demand.

_______ 16. The first antitrust act to prohibit "conspiracies in restraint of trade" was:
(a) The Sherman Act.
(b) The Clayton Act.
(c) The Federal Trade Commission Act.
(d) Case decisions such as those involving AT&T and IBM.

_______ 17. The federal government's role in purchasing land for a national park is justified by considerations of:
(a) Government failure.
(b) Public goods.
(c) Market power.
(d) Macro failure.

_______ 18. If government involvement forces the economy inside the production possibilities curve, there is:
(a) Market failure.
(b) Market power.
(c) Antitrust behavior.
(d) Government failure.

_______ 19. The federal government uses a system of taxes and transfers to:
(a) Encourage the joint consumption of goods.
(b) Increase external costs and benefits.
(c) Alter the distribution of income.
(d) Reduce market power.

_______ 20. Government intervention at the macroeconomic level is intended to achieve:
(a) Market power.
(b) An increase in public goods.
(c) An equal distribution of income.
(d) Full employment and price stability.

Problems and Applications

Exercise 1

This exercise focuses on public goods versus private goods.

Assume point *A* represents the optimal mix of output in Figure 9.1. Determine which letter best represents the following situations. Then answer Questions 4-7.

Figure 9.1

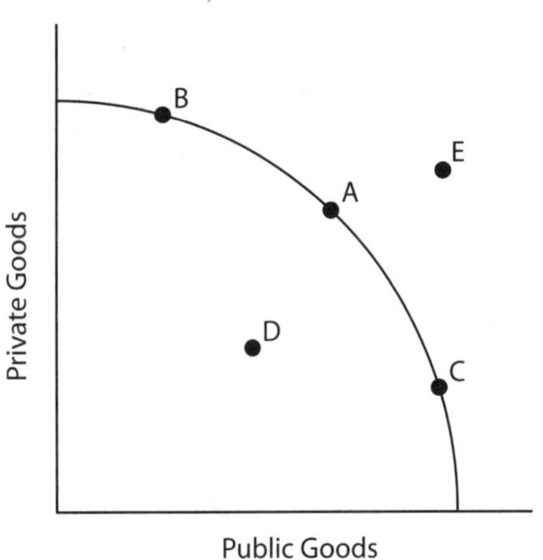

_____ 1. Government failure at the micro level that results in an overproduction of public goods.

_____ 2. The free-rider dilemma.

_____ 3. Macro failure in the market place.

4. The market mechanism tends to __________________ private goods and __________________ public goods.

5. In terms of the production possibilities curve, __________________ failures imply that society is at the wrong point on the curve and __________________ failures imply that society is inside the curve.

6. Market failures justify government __________________.

7. If government involvement fails to improve market outcomes then there is __________________ __________________.

Exercise 2

This exercise examines consumption decisions and internal versus external costs.

The market demand and market supply curves for a good are given in Figure 9.2. Assume that the consumption of the good generates external costs of $2 per unit.

1. Draw the social demand curve in Figure 9.2 and label it.

Figure 9.2

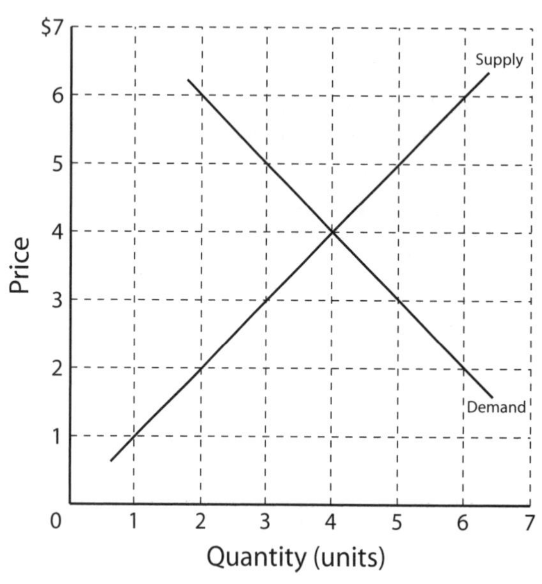

2. Market equilibrium occurs at a price of_____ and a quantity of_____ in Figure 9.2.

3. The socially optimal level of production occurs at a price of_____ and a quantity of_____.

4. External costs cause the market to produce (more, less) of the good than is optimal.

5. T F The market price of $4 does not reflect the external costs.

Exercise 3

This exercise shows how externalities affect third parties.

A chemical plant and a plastics factory are located adjacent to the same stream. The chemical plant is located upstream. The downstream plastics factory requires pure water for its production process. Its basic supply is the stream that runs past both firms.

Figure 9.3

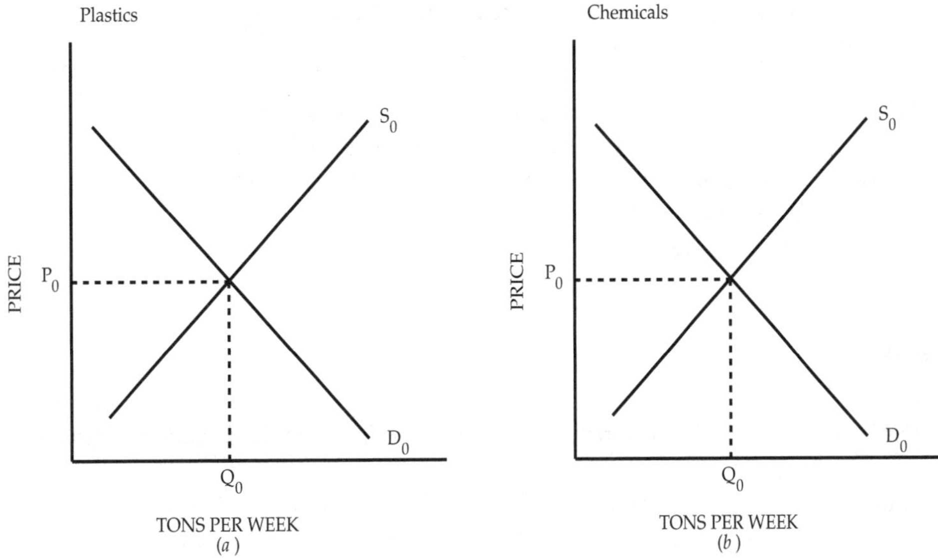

In Figure 9.3a and b, S_0 and D_0 represent the supply and demand for plastics and chemicals, respectively. Assume that the economy is initially competitive and resources are allocated efficiently. Equilibrium price and quantity are P_0 and Q_0 in each case. But then the chemical producer decides to dump waste products into the stream rather than dispose of them with the costly process that had been used.

1. In Figure 9.3b, draw a new supply curve for chemicals after the dumping in the stream begins. Label it S_1. (There are many ways to draw this curve correctly.)

2. The pollution from the chemical plant forces the plastics manufacturer to use a costly water-purifying system. Draw a new supply curve for plastics in Figure 9.3a. Label it S_1. (There are many ways to draw this curve correctly.)

3. The effect of the decision to pollute on the quantity of chemicals sold is the same as if:
   (a) A new, improved technology were discovered.
   (b) Wages to its labor force were reduced.
   (c) The Social Security tax on employers had been abolished.
   (d) All of the above were the case.

4. As a result of the chemical plant's polluting activities, the price of:
   (a) Chemicals has risen.
   (b) Chemicals has fallen.
   (c) Plastics has fallen.
   (d) Plastics has not changed.

5. As a result of the chemical plant's activities:
   (a) More chemicals are produced and sold than society desires.
   (b) More labor is used to produce chemicals than society desires.
   (c) More capital inputs are used to produce chemicals than society desires.
   (d) All of the above are the case.

6. The effect of the chemical firm's pollution is to:
   (a) Raise the price of plastics and reduce the quantity sold.
   (b) Lower the price of plastics and increase the quantity sold.
   (c) Raise the price of plastics and increase the quantity sold.
   (d) Lower the price of plastics and reduce the quantity sold.

7. The impact of the pollution on the plastics industry in this example is to:
   (a) Reduce the output of plastics below the level that society desires.
   (b) Reduce the employment possibilities in the plastics industry.
   (c) Raise the price of products made with plastics.
   (d) Do all of the above.

Exercise 4

This exercise shows the difference between private marginal costs and social marginal costs.

1. An iron-producing firm generates pollution as it mines iron ore. Assume the iron ore market is competitive. Table 9.1 depicts the private costs and social costs of the firm's iron production at each daily production rate. Complete Table 9.1.

Table 9.1 Costs of producing iron

Production rate (tons per day)	*Total private cost (dollars per day)*	*Private marginal cost (dollars per ton)*	*Total social cost (dollars per day)*	*Social marginal cost (dollars per ton)*
0	$ 0	$ ---	$ 0	$ ---
1	40	________	80	________
2	90	________	170	________
3	150	________	270	________
4	220	________	380	________
5	300	________	500	________
6	390	________	630	________
7	490	________	770	________
8	600	________	920	________
9	720	________	1,080	________
10	850	________	1,250	________
11	990	________	1,430	________
12	1,140	________	1,620	________

2. In Figure 9.4 the price of the iron in the market is $140 per ton. Draw the marginal revenue curve and label it *MR*. Draw the private marginal cost curve and label it *PMC*. Draw the social marginal cost curve and label it *SMC*.

Figure 9.4

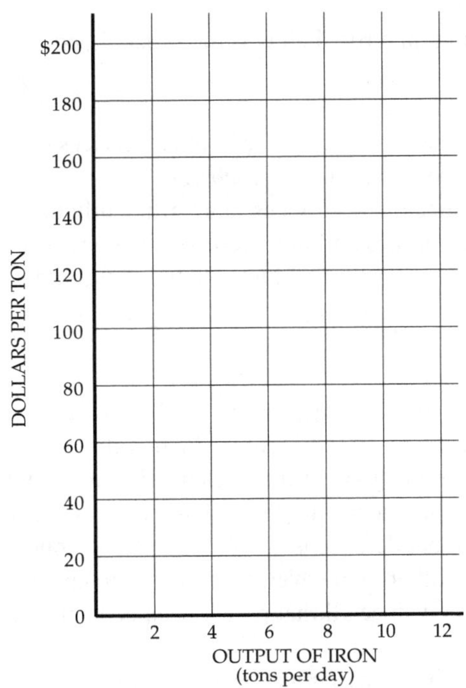

3. What is the profit-maximizing production rate for the firm if it considers only its private costs?
   (a) 5 tons per day.
   (b) 7 tons per day.
   (c) 9 tons per day.
   (d) 11 tons per day.

4. What is the profit-maximizing production rate if the firm is required to pay all social costs?
   (a) 5 tons per day.
   (b) 7 tons per day.
   (c) 9 tons per day.
   (d) 11 tons per day.

5. How much should the pollution (emission) fee be to induce the iron-producing firm to produce the socially optimal rate of output?
   (a) $2 per ton.
   (b) $20 per ton.
   (c) $40 per ton.
   (d) $100 per ton.

Common Errors

The first statement in each "common error" below is incorrect. Each incorrect statement is followed by a corrected version and an explanation.

1. Fire protection, police protection, education, and other services can be produced more efficiently by the private sector than by the public sector. *Incorrect!*
   The public sector can produce many services more efficiently than the private sector. *Correct!*
   The existence of externalities and the free-rider dilemma force society to produce some goods and services through public-sector expenditures. Many of the goods and services we take for granted (such as education and national defense) would not be produced in sufficient quantities if left to the private sector.

2. Public goods can be produced only by government. *Incorrect!*
   Public goods can be produced by government or the private sector. *Correct!*
   Whether a good is a public good or not does not depend on whether it is produced in the public or private sector. Public goods are those that are consumed jointly, by both those who pay and those who don't. National defense is a public good since one person's consumption does not prohibit consumption by another. However, landscaping to enhance the beauty of a piece of property is also a public good since all that pass by can consume or enjoy the beauty.

3. If the price of a good is too high, there must be a market failure. *Incorrect!*
   A high price does not necessarily mean there is a market failure. *Correct!*
   Sometimes markets result in outcomes that are not popular, but that does not necessarily mean that the market has failed. If the high price is merely the result of the market demand and market supply intersection and not the result of one of the sources of market failure, then there is no failure. But people still don't like the outcome.

~ ANSWERS ~

Using Terms to Remember

Across

1. laissez faire
4. public good
6. market power
7. private costs
8. free rider
11. government failure
12. social costs
13. private good
14. market mechanism
15. income transfers

Down

2. antitrust
3. optimal mix of output
5. market failure
9. externalities
10. emission charge

True or False

1. F To be considered optimal, a combination of goods and services must be the best single point on the production possibilities curve.
2. F Market failure implies that the forces of supply and demand have not led society to the optimal mix of output
3. T
4. F If a firm is able to push some of its costs onto society through pollution, the firm will produce *more* output than is socially optimal.
5. F If free riders exist, some individuals will consume the good or service without paying for it. The market is less likely to achieve an optimal outcome.
6. T
7. T
8. T
9. F When the government responds to a market failure, the outcome may be to make the market *worse*.
10. T

Multiple Choice

1. a	5. d	9. b	13. b	17. b
2. d	6. a	10. d	14. c	18. d
3. b	7. c	11. a	15. c	19. c
4. b	8. a	12. c	16. a	20. d

Problems and Applications

Exercise 1

1. c
2. b
3. d
4. Overproduce, underproduce
5. Micro, macro
6. Intervention
7. Government failure

Exercise 2

1. **Figure 9.2 Answer**

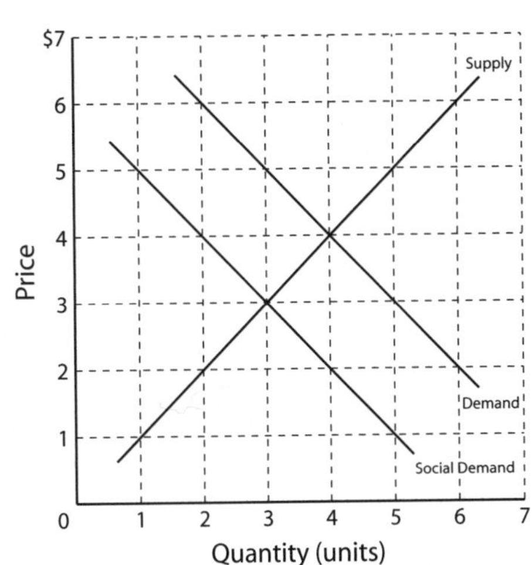

2. $4; 4 units
3. $3; 3 units
4. More
5. T

Exercise 3

1. **Figure 9.3 Answer**

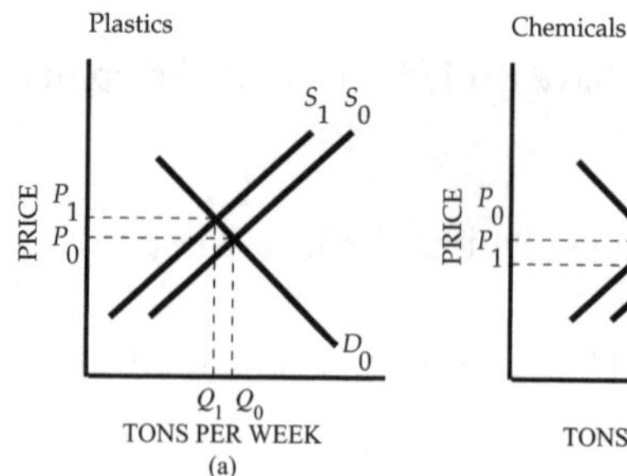

2. See Figure 9.3 Answer (*a*), line S_1.
3. d
4. b
5. d
6. a
7. d

Exercise 4

1. **Table 9.1 Answer**

Production rate	*Private marginal cost*	*Social marginal cost*
0	$ —	$ —
1	40	80
2	50	90
3	60	100
4	70	110
5	80	120
6	90	130
7	100	140
8	110	150
9	120	160
10	130	170
11	140	180
12	150	190

2. **Figure 9.4 Answer**

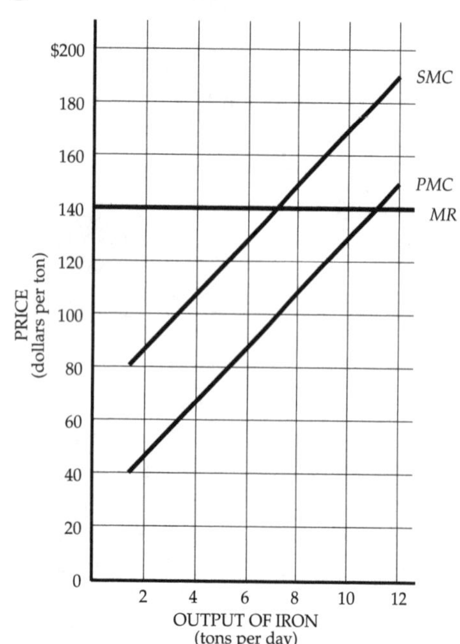

3. d
4. b
5. c

SECTION III Macroeconomics

CHAPTER 10

The Business Cycle

Quick Review

- Business cycles are alternating periods of growth and contraction in the economy. The cycle is measured by changes in the nation's real GDP. The cycles vary in length and intensity. The worst contraction experienced by the United States was the Great Depression of the 1930s. Despite the ups and downs, the U.S. economy has grown at an average of approximately 3 percent per year since 1929.

- Macroeconomic theory attempts to explain the business cycle while macroeconomic policy tries to control the cycle.

- The growth of output (GDP), the unemployment rate, and the inflation rate are used to measure the strength of the macroeconomy.

- A recession is accompanied by a higher unemployment rate for the labor force. To be counted as part of the labor force you must be over 16 years old and be employed or actively seeking employment. The unemployment rate is calculated by dividing the number of unemployed by the total labor force. The U.S. labor force is about half the size of the total U.S. population.

- Economists acknowledge four different types of unemployment. Seasonal unemployment is related to the seasons of the year. Frictional unemployment is typically short in duration and is related to the job search. Structural unemployment is caused by a mismatch between the skills of the applicants and the requirements of the available jobs. Cyclical unemployment occurs when the economy does not create enough jobs. The full employment goal is the lowest rate of unemployment that still allows for price stability.

- Inflation is an increase in the average level of prices of goods and services. Inflation acts like a tax, taking from some and giving to others, because prices do not rise at the same rate for the various combinations of goods and assets that people buy and sell.

- Inflation creates uncertainty for all of the decision-makers in the economy—households, businesses, and government.

- Inflation is typically measured using the consumer price index (CPI), a weighted average of prices paid by consumers at the retail level. The inflation rate is the percentage change in the CPI from one year to the next. The U.S. goal for price stability is an inflation rate of less than 3 percent, which reduces the conflict with full employment and allows for quality improvements.

Learning Objectives

After reading the chapter and doing the following exercises you should be able to:

1. Explain how growth of the economy is measured.
2. Tell how unemployment is measured and affects us.
3. Discuss why inflation is a problem and how it is measured.
4. Define "full employment" and "price stability."
5. Recite the U.S. track record on growth, unemployment, and inflation.

Using Terms to Remember

Fill in the puzzle on the opposite page with the appropriate terms from the list of Terms to Remember in the text.

Across

1. The number of unemployed people divided by the size of the labor force.
4. All persons over age 16 who are either working for pay or actively seeking paid employment.
10. The price of apples compared to the price of other fruit.
12. The inability of labor force participants to find jobs.
13. The lowest rate of unemployment compatible with price stability.
14. Income received in a given time period measured in current dollars.
15. Established at a rate of less than 3 percent inflation in the Full Employment and Balanced Growth Act of 1978.
16. The value of output measured in current prices is known as ____________ GDP.
17. Nominal income adjusted for inflation.
18. Alternating periods of economic growth and contraction.
19. Computed by the Bureau of Labor Statistics as the average price of consumer goods.

Down

2. The potential level of output using all resources and technology.
3. Used to measure economic growth.
5. The study of aggregate economic behavior.
6. A decrease in average prices.
7. Results in a redistribution of income and wealth.
8. The abbreviation for the total value of goods and services produced within a nation's borders.
9. Calculated as the increase in the average price level over a particular time period.
11. A decline in real GDP for two or more consecutive quarters.

Puzzle 10.1

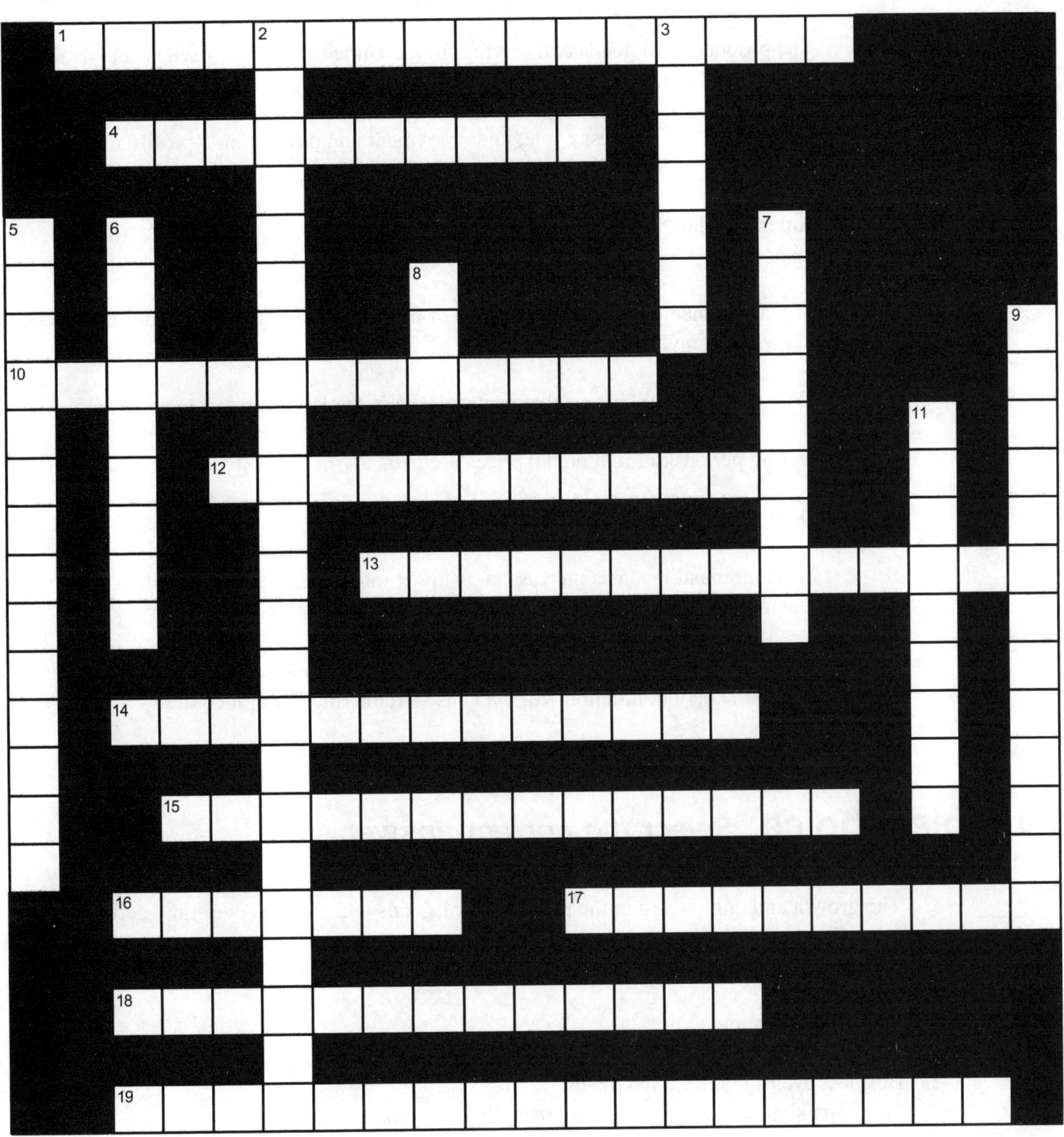

True or False: *Circle your choice and explain why any false statements are incorrect.*

T F 1. The business cycle indicates the changes in real GDP for an economy over time.

T F 2. The production of goods and services in the United States has risen steadily each year since 1929.

T F 3. Throughout the business cycle, unemployment and production typically move in the same direction.

T F 4. A person who quits one job to spend time looking for another job is part of the labor force.

T F 5. Structural unemployment is the result of insufficient demand for goods and services in the economy.

T F 6. "Full employment" means that some people in the labor force are still unemployed.

T F 7. During periods of inflation, all prices are rising.

T F 8. During periods of inflation, some people are worse off, but others are better off.

T F 9. When nominal incomes increase at a slower rate than the rate of inflation, real incomes increase.

T F 10. If all the prices and wages in the economy rise by the same percentage during the same time period, inflation will *not* cause a redistribution of income.

Multiple Choice: *Select the correct answer.*

_______ 1. The growth and contraction in the production of goods and services over time define:
(a) The business cycle.
(b) Unemployment.
(c) Inflation.
(d) Macro policy.

_______ 2. Business cycles in the United States:
(a) Are similar in length but vary greatly in magnitude.
(b) Vary greatly in length, frequency, and magnitude.
(c) Are similar in frequency and magnitude.
(d) Are similar in length, frequency, and magnitude.

_______ 3. Which of the following is *not* characteristic of a downturn in the business cycle?
(a) Higher unemployment rates.
(b) Lower prices.
(c) Lower interest rates.
(d) Higher real output.

_______ 4. Real GDP serves as a better measure of the health of the economy than nominal GDP because real GDP reflects:
(a) Changes in production only.
(b) Changes in the price level only.
(c) Changes in the price level and production.
(d) The production by factors located outside of the United States.

_______ 5. The labor force is smaller than the total population because the labor force does not include:
(a) The very young and old.
(b) People who have jobs.
(c) People looking for a job.
(d) Those who are unhappy with the job they have.

_______ 6. Which of the following would be counted as a member of the labor force?
(a) A stay-at-home mom who works 12 hours a day taking care of her children and cleaning her house.
(b) An unemployed web-page designer actively looking for employment.
(c) A student attending college.
(d) A retired member of the armed forces collecting a pension.

_______ 7. Which of the following is considered to be unemployed?
(a) Sue, who is on vacation but will soon return to the same job.
(b) Andrew, who is on welfare and not seeking employment.
(c) Anne, a college student looking for summer work.
(d) Tim, who is on strike.

_______ 8. Our full employment goal is *not* zero percent because:
(a) Frictional unemployment will always exist.
(b) Unacceptably high rates of inflation would probably result.
(c) There will always be some structural unemployment.
(d) All of the above.

_______ 9. ________ unemployment is most closely related to the growth rate of real GDP.
(a) Structural.
(b) Cyclical.
(c) Frictional.
(d) Seasonal.

_______ 10. Carlie quit her job as an economics professor at a large public university to look for a job at a small liberal arts college. While she is looking for work, Carlie is:
(a) Cyclically unemployed.
(b) Structurally unemployed.
(c) Frictionally unemployed.
(d) Seasonally unemployed.

_______ 11. Factory workers in the United States are unemployed because goods are being manufactured abroad, and at the same time there are job vacancies for high school math and science teachers. The factory workers are classified as:
(a) Structurally unemployed.
(b) Cyclically unemployed.
(c) Frictionally unemployed.
(d) Seasonally unemployed.

_______ 12. Which of the following workers qualifies as unemployed?
(a) A worker who quits his or her job and is too lazy to look for another job.
(b) A college professor during the summer months.
(c) A person who is looking for work, but cannot find a job because he has no skills.
(d) A person who is not looking for work but would take a job if offered one.

_______ 13. During periods of inflation:
(a) All prices rise.
(b) Some prices stay the same, but real income definitely falls.
(c) Real income definitely rises.
(d) On average, prices rise.

_______ 14. If the number of dollars you receive every year is the same, but prices are rising, then your nominal income ________ and your real income ________.
(a) Stays the same; rises.
(b) Stays the same; falls.
(c) Rises; falls.
(d) Falls; rises.

_______ 15. It is more useful to compare changes in relative prices than changes in average prices when trying to:
(a) Determine the redistribution of income due to inflation.
(b) Determine the inflation rate.
(c) Calculate the CPI.
(d) Calculate the unemployment rate.

_______ 16. Changes in relative prices may occur during periods of:
(a) Inflation only.
(b) Inflation and deflation, but not stable prices.
(c) Deflation only.
(d) Deflation and stable prices.

_______ 17. Inflation acts like a tax because:
(a) The government tends to benefit during periods of inflation.
(b) It takes purchasing power from some people and gives it to others.
(c) Inflation pushes everyone into higher tax brackets.
(d) Everyone loses purchasing power during periods of inflation just like everyone pays taxes.

_______ 18. Caitlyn's nominal income for 2012 was $40,000. Suppose that the inflation rate for 2012 was 5 percent. To keep her real income constant, her nominal income for 2013 must be:
(a) $2,000.
(b) $40,000.
(c) $42,000.
(d) $45,000.

_______ 19. If the CPI for 2012 was 106, then during the period between the base year and 2012:
(a) All prices increased by 6 percent.
(b) Prices of goods and services purchased by producers increased by an average of 6 percent.
(c) Prices of goods and services purchased by consumers increased by an average of 6 percent.
(d) All prices increased by an average of 106 percent.

_______ 20. The CPI tends to overestimate the rate of inflation because:
(a) Only the goods and services that consumers buy are included in the calculation.
(b) Some price increases are an indication of higher quality products.
(c) The CPI measures changes in average prices, not changes in relative prices.
(d) Some price increases are simply the result of greedy producers and sellers.

Problems and Applications

Exercise 1

This exercise focuses in calculating the unemployment rate and the relationship between the unemployment rate and the growth rate of GDP. Data from 1981-1995 is used in order to demonstrate several expansionary and contractionary economic situations.

1. Compute the unemployment rate based on the information in Table 10.1, and insert your answer in column 4.

Table 10.1 Unemployment and real GDP, 1981–95

Year	(1) Noninstitutional population	(2) Civilian labor force (thousands of persons 16 and over)	(3) Unemployment (thousands of persons 16 and over)	(4) Unemployment rate (percent)	(5) Percentage change in real GDP
1981	170,130	108,670	8,273	______	2.5
1982	172,271	110,204	10,678	______	–2.1
1983	174,215	111,550	10,717	______	4.0
1984	176,383	113,544	8,539	______	6.8
1985	178,206	115,461	8,312	______	3.7
1986	180,587	117,834	8,237	______	3.0
1987	182,753	119,865	7,425	______	2.9
1988	184,613	121,669	6,701	______	3.8
1989	186,393	123,869	6,528	______	3.4
1990	188,049	124,787	6,874	______	1.3
1991	189,765	125,303	8,426	______	–1.0
1992	191,576	126,982	9,384	______	2.7
1993	193,550	128,040	8,734	______	2.2
1994	196,814	131,056	7,996	______	3.5
1995	198,584	132,304	7,404	______	2.0

2. In Figure 10.1 graph both the unemployment rate (column 4 of Table 10.1) and the percentage change in real GDP (column 5).

Figure 10.1

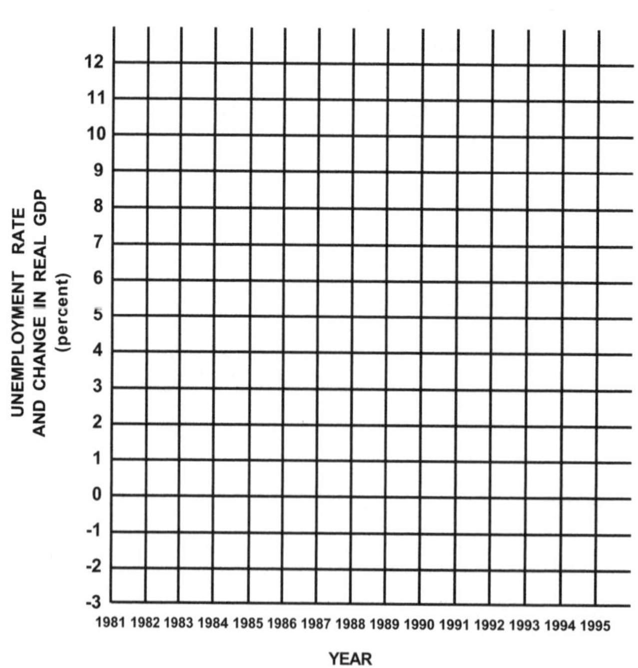

3. The relationship between the unemployment rate and the percentage change in the real GDP is best characterized as:
   (a) A direct relationship (the two indicators go up and down together).
   (b) An inverse relationship (the two indicators move in opposite directions).

4. Which indicator seems to change direction first as time passes?
   (a) Percentage change in real GDP.
   (b) The unemployment rate.

5. Which of the following kinds of unemployment is reflected in the fluctuations in Figure 10.1?
   (a) Structural unemployment.
   (b) Seasonal unemployment.
   (c) Frictional unemployment.
   (d) Cyclical unemployment.

6. During which years was the optimal unemployment rate achieved (defined by the text as somewhere between 4 and 6 percent) from 1981 through 1995? ______________________________

Exercise 2

This exercise shows the relationship between unemployment and population.

Suppose the data in Table 10.2 describes a nation's situation.

Table 10.2 Employment and unemployment

	Year 1	*Year 2*
Population	500 million	550 million
Labor force	300 million	325 million
Number of employed	276 million	276 million
Number of unemployed	________	________
Unemployment rate	___percent	___percent

1. Fill in the blanks in Table 10.2 to show the number of unemployed and the unemployment rate.

2. When the population grows and the labor force grows, but the number employed remains constant, the unemployment rate (rises, remains the same, falls).

3. If both the population and the number employed remain constant, but a larger percentage of the population enters into retirement, the unemployment rate should (rise, remain the same, fall), *ceteris paribus.*

4. The people who immigrate to the United States are generally young and of working age compared to the existing population of the United States. As greater immigration rates are permitted and if the unemployment rate stays constant, the number of people employed will (rise, remain the same, fall), *ceteris paribus.*

5. Assume each employed person contributes $35,000 worth of goods and services to GDP. If the unemployment rate falls from 8 percent to 6 percent, by how much will GDP increase? __________

Exercise 3

Identify each of the cases below as an example of seasonal, frictional, structural, or cyclical unemployment.

1. Emily, a snowboarding instructor, is unemployed during the summer months. ______________

2. Nicole, who just earned an MBA, takes several months to find her first job. ______________

3. Jake, a delivery truck driver, is laid off because of an economic downturn. ______________

4. There is a shortage of workers for jobs requiring a degree in mathematics, but Zach and his friends, who didn't complete high school, cannot find jobs. ______________

Exercise 4

This exercise explores the impact of inflation rates on the value of money held for different periods of time.

1. Use Table 10.3 in the text to find the value of $1,000 for the given inflation rate and period of time.
   a. Five years at an inflation rate of 4%. ____________
   b. Eight years at an inflation rate of 4%. ____________
   c. Ten years at an inflation rate of 2%. ____________
   d. Seven years at an inflation rate of 10%. ____________

2. In which two cases above does the $1,000 come closest to being worth the same amount? ________

3. In which case above is the $1,000 worth the least amount? ________

4. Would you lose more money if you placed $1000 under your mattress for ten years at 2% inflation or if you placed $1,000 in a cookie jar for eight years at 4% inflation? ________

Exercise 5

This exercise emphasizes the redistributions that occur because of inflation.

1. During a period of inflation, a family's income rises with inflation, but the cost of food rises more rapidly than the rate of inflation. This results in a (negative, positive) (price, wealth) effect.

2. During a period of inflation, a person owns land that increases in value at a rate greater than the rate of inflation. This person experiences a (negative, positive) (income, wealth) effect.

3. During a period of inflation, a person's nominal income remains constant. The result of this situation is a (negative, positive, zero) (price, income) effect.

Common Errors

The first statement in each "common error" below is incorrect. Each incorrect statement is followed by a corrected version and an explanation.

1. The goal for the economy is zero unemployment. *Incorrect!*
   The goal for the economy is a low level of unemployment compatible with price stability. *Correct!*

Under the Full Employment and Balanced Growth Act of 1978, the government set an unemployment goal for itself, but this goal is well short of a zero unemployment rate. As the economy approaches "full employment" there is a trade-off between employment and price stability. It would be very difficult and even undesirable to eliminate frictional or seasonal unemployment.

2. When the price of a product rises, there is inflation. *Incorrect!*
When an average of prices rises, there is inflation. *Correct!*
The price of a single product may rise while an average of prices for all products falls. Such adjustment in relative prices is essential to the most *efficient* distribution of goods and services through the market. When the average of all prices is rising, however, distribution may not be efficient and redistributions of income may occur.

3. As long as a price increase is less than the inflation rate, it does not contribute to inflation. *Incorrect!*
Every price increase contributes to a rise in the inflation rate. *Correct!*
The inflation rate is an increase in the average level of prices, and an increase in any price raises the average. Firms that buy commodities from other firms that raise prices will in turn pass the increase on to their own customers so a price increase may have an indirect effect on inflation.

4. If the economic growth rate is less than it was last quarter, this indicates a recession. *Incorrect!*
As long as the economic growth rate is positive, the economy is not in a recession. *Correct!*
The economic growth rate is measured by the percentage change in real GDP. A recession is defined as two consecutive quarters of negative growth. If the growth rate is positive, the economy cannot be in a recession.

~ ANSWERS ~

Using Terms to Remember

Across

1. unemployment rate
4. labor force
10. relative price
12. unemployment
13. full employment
14. nominal income
15. price stability
16. nominal
17. real income
18. business cycle
19. consumer price index

Down

2. production possibilities
3. real GDP
5. macroeconomics
6. deflation
7. inflation
8. GDP
9. inflation rate
11. recession

True or False

1. T
2. F The economy has been characterized by periods of economic growth and recessions.
3. F Throughout the business cycle, unemployment and production typically move in *opposite* directions.
4. T
5. F Structural unemployment occurs when workers do not have the skills that jobs require.
6. T

7. F During periods of inflation, some prices may actually fall.
8. T
9. F When nominal incomes increase at a slower rate than the rate of inflation, real incomes *decrease*.
10. T

Multiple Choice

1. a	5. a	9. b	13. d	17. b
2. b	6. b	10. c	14. b	18. c
3. d	7. c	11. a	15. a	19. c
4. a	8. d	12. c	16. d	20. b

Problems and Applications

Exercise 1

1. **Table 10.1 Answer**

Year	*(4) Unemployment rate (percent)*
1981	7.6
1982	9.7
1983	9.6
1984	7.5
1985	7.2
1986	7.0
1987	6.2
1988	5.5
1989	5.3
1990	5.5
1991	6.7
1992	7.4
1993	6.8
1994	6.1
1995	5.6

2. **Figure 10.1 Answer**

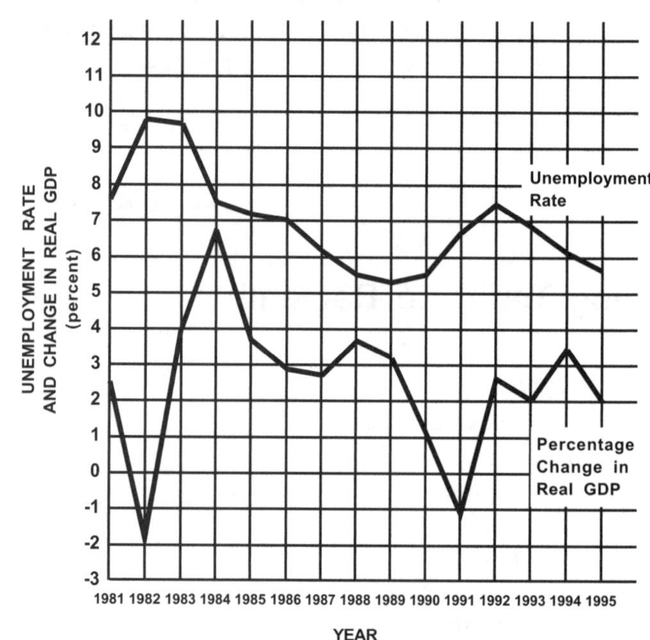

3. b
4. a, After a dramatic rise in real GDP, it takes several years for the unemployment rate to reach the lowest level.
5. d
6. 1988, 1989, 1990, 1995

Exercise 2

1. **Table 10.2 Answer**

	Year 1	*Year 2*
Population	500 million	550 million
Labor force	300 million	325 million
Number of employed	276 million	276 million
Number of unemployed	24 million (= 300 – 276)	49 million
Unemployment rate	8 percent (= 24 ÷ 300)	15 percent

2. Rises
3. Fall
4. Rise
5. $210 billion; With an additional 2 percent (8 percent – 6 percent) of the labor force now employed, there are 6 million more people employed (= 2 percent x 300 million in the labor force). Each worker can produce an average of $35,000 a year in GDP for a total of $210 billion (= 6 million x $35,000).

Exercise 3

1. Seasonal
2. Frictional
3. Cyclical
4. Structural

Exercise 4

1. a. $822
   b. $731
   c. $820
   d. $513
2. a and c
3. d
4. $1,000 in a cookie jar for eight years at 4% inflation

Exercise 5

1. Negative, price
2. Positive, wealth
3. Negative, income

CHAPTER 11

Aggregate Supply and Demand

Quick Review

- The primary outcomes of the macroeconomy include output (GDP), prices, jobs, growth, and international balances. These outcomes result from the interplay of internal market forces, external shocks, and policy levers.

- According to the classical model, the economy "self-adjusts" to deviations from the long-run growth trend and does not require intervention. The cornerstone of the classical view is flexible wages and prices, which are embedded in Say's Law, which states that "supply creates its own demand." The Great Depression weakened faith in the classical belief.

- John Maynard Keynes challenged the classical approach of laissez faire. He asserted that the economy was inherently unstable and that government intervention was necessary at times.

- Aggregate demand (AD) refers to the various quantities of output that all market participants are willing and able to buy at alternative price levels in a given period, *ceteris paribus*. It slopes downward to the right because a decrease in the price level causes an increase in real balances (real balances effect), an increase in net exports (foreign trade effect), and a decrease in the interest rate (interest rate effect).

- Aggregate supply (AS) represents the total quantity of output producers are willing and able to supply at all alternative price levels in a given time period, *ceteris paribus*. It slopes upward to the right because an increase in the price level causes profit margins to widen and factor costs to rise.

- The intersection of AS and AD determines macro equilibrium. However, macro equilibrium may occur at price and output levels that do not satisfy our macroeconomic goals concerning full employment, growth, and price stability.

- Shifts in AS and AD cause the business cycle. Macro controversies focus on the shape of AS and AD and the potential to shift the two curves. Keynesian theory focuses on the use of government spending or tax changes to shift AD. Monetary theory stresses the importance of money and credit to shift AD. Supply-side theory focuses on tax incentives and government deregulation to shift AS. Eclectic theories draw from both sides of the market.

Learning Objectives

After reading the chapter and doing the following exercises you should be able to:

1. Cite the major macro outcomes and their determinants.
2. Explain how classical and Keynesian macro views differ.
3. Explain what factors shape the aggregate demand and supply curves.
4. Tell how macro failure occurs.
5. Outline the major policy options for macro government intervention.

Using Terms to Remember

Fill in the puzzle on the opposite page with the appropriate terms from the list of Terms to Remember in the text.

Across

1. The value of output measured in constant prices.
4. The inability of labor-force participants to find jobs.
5. The use of government spending and taxes to shift the aggregate demand curve.
7. The total quantity of output demanded at alternative price levels in a given time period, *ceteris paribus.*
10. The total quantity of output producers are willing and able to supply at alternative price levels in a given time period, *ceteris paribus.*
11. An increase in the average level of prices of goods and services.
12. Occurs as a result of shifts in aggregate demand and aggregate supply.
13. The level of real output produced at full employment.

Down

2. The combination of price level and real output that is compatible with both aggregate demand and aggregate supply.
3. The use of tax cuts and government deregulation to shift the aggregate supply curve.
6. The idea that whatever is produced by suppliers will always be sold.
8. The area of study that focuses on output, jobs, prices, and growth for the entire economy.
9. The use of money and credit controls to shift the aggregate demand curve.

Puzzle 11.1

True or False: *Circle your choice and explain why any false statements are incorrect.*

T F 1. Most modern economists believe that the economy is inherently stable and government intervention will make the macro economy worse.

T F 2. According to the classical economists, government intervention in the economy was unnecessary because flexible wages and prices allowed the economy to self-adjust.

T F 3. Keynes believed that the economy was basically stable and government intervention was unnecessary.

T F 4. If, at the prevailing price level, the aggregate quantity supplied exceeds the aggregate quantity demanded, the price level will tend to fall.

T F 5. The interest-rate effect says that consumers buy fewer goods when the price level falls because the interest rate increases, which reduces borrowing.

T F 6. One reason why the quantity of real output supplied rises with the price level, *ceteris paribus*, is because profits are higher.

T F 7. Macro equilibrium never occurs at an output level that provides less than full employment, according to Keynesian economists.

T F 8. The business cycle is the result of changes in real GDP caused by shifts in aggregate demand and aggregate supply.

T F 9. Both fiscal policy and monetary policy are used to shift the aggregate supply curve.

T F 10. Supply-side policy focuses on reducing the costs of production or otherwise stimulating more output at every price level.

Multiple Choice: *Select the correct answer.*

______ 1. Possible determinants of macro outcomes include:
(a) A devastating hurricane but not population growth.
(b) Technological advances but not wars.
(c) A decrease in taxes and inflation.
(d) Population growth and spending patterns.

______ 2. Which of the following is a measure of overall economic well-being (i.e., a macro outcome) for the United States?
(a) The U.S. population growth.
(b) The U.S. price level.
(c) The level of invention and innovation.
(d) A massive flood along the Mississippi River.

_______ 3. Which of the following is consistent with the classical view of the economy?
(a) Wages are flexible but prices are not.
(b) The economy is inherently unstable.
(c) A policy of laissez faire because the economy will self-adjust to full employment.
(d) The use of government policies to stabilize the economy.

_______ 4. Say's Law implies that:
(a) Wages and prices are inflexible.
(b) Aggregate demand is greater than aggregate supply.
(c) Aggregate supply is greater than aggregate demand.
(d) The economy will always adjust to a full-employment macro equilibrium.

_______ 5. Keynes viewed the economy as inherently unstable and suggested that during an economic downturn policy makers should:
(a) Cut taxes or increase government spending.
(b) Cut taxes or reduce government spending.
(c) Raise taxes or increase government spending.
(d) Raise taxes or reduce government spending.

_______ 6. The upward slope of the aggregate supply curve can best be explained by the:
(a) Real balances effect.
(b) Interest-rate effect.
(c) Higher costs associated with higher capacity utilization rates.
(d) Concept that consumers tend to buy more goods as the price level rises.

_______ 7. *Ceteris paribus,* when the average price level in our economy rises relative to the price levels in foreign economies, U.S. consumers tend to buy ________ imported goods and ________ domestically produced goods.
(a) More; more.
(b) More; fewer.
(c) Fewer; more.
(d) Fewer; fewer.

_______ 8. The real balances effect relies on the idea that as the domestic price level falls:
(a) You will purchase less domestic output.
(b) Each bond you own will decrease in value, thus decreasing your wealth.
(c) You will begin to save more because your wealth has decreased.
(d) Each dollar you own will purchase more goods and services.

_______ 9. At the intersection of the aggregate supply and aggregate demand curves, the economy will definitely experience:
(a) Full employment.
(b) Macro equilibrium.
(c) Low levels of inflation.
(d) A GDP gap.

_______ 10. Refer to Figure 11.5 in the text. At a price of P_1 a:
(a) Surplus of output exists equal to S_1 minus D_1.
(b) Surplus of output exists equal to S_1 minus Q_E.
(c) Shortage of output exists equal to S_1 minus Q_E.
(d) Shortage of output exists equal to S_1 minus D_1.

_______ 11. Which of the following will cause the aggregate supply curve to increase, *ceteris paribus*?
(a) An increase in the cost of raw materials.
(b) An increase in the money supply.
(c) Higher business taxes.
(d) A decrease in environmental regulations.

_______ 12. Which of the following will cause the aggregate demand curve to increase, *ceteris paribus*?
(a) A natural disaster.
(b) A decrease in the money supply.
(c) A decrease in interest rates.
(d) A stock market crash.

_______ 13. If an economy is at macro equilibrium and aggregate supply increases:
(a) The unemployment rate will decrease and the price level will increase.
(b) Both the unemployment rate and price level will decrease.
(c) The unemployment rate will increase and the price level will decrease.
(d) Both the unemployment rate and price level will increase.

_______ 14. Controversies between Keynesian, monetarist, supply-side, and eclectic theories focus on:
(a) The shape and sensitivity of aggregate supply and aggregate demand curves.
(b) The existence or nonexistence of the aggregate supply curve.
(c) The importance of international balances to the economy.
(d) The usefulness of using aggregate demand and supply to analyze adjustment of the macro equilibrium.

_______ 15. According to the foreign trade effect, when the price of American-made cars rises, U.S. consumers are likely to buy:
(a) More American-made cars.
(b) Different American-made cars.
(c) More imported cars.
(d) No cars at all until they see what the market is going to do.

_______ 16. Which of the following economic perspectives focuses on aggregate demand to explain the changes in unemployment and inflation?
(a) Classical and supply-side.
(b) Keynesian and monetarist.
(c) Classical and Keynesian.
(d) New classical and Keynesian.

_______ 17. A tax cut can best be characterized as:
(a) Monetary policy only.
(b) Fiscal policy only.
(c) Both monetary and supply-side policy.
(d) Both fiscal and supply-side policy.

_______ 18. A reduction in government regulations is a policy lever most likely to be advocated by:
(a) Classical economists.
(b) Supply-side economists.
(c) Keynesians.
(d) Neoclassical economists.

_______ 19. Monetary policy involves:
(a) The use of money and credit controls to influence the macro economy.
(b) Changes in government spending.
(c) Changes in taxes.
(d) Shifting the aggregate supply curve.

_______ 20. Which of the following are policy options that the United States has used?
(a) Doing nothing but not shifting the aggregate supply curve.
(b) Shifting the aggregate demand curve but not the aggregate supply curve.
(c) Shifting the aggregate supply curve but not the aggregate demand curve.
(d) Shifting the aggregate supply and the aggregate demand curves, and doing nothing.

Problems and Applications

Exercise 1

This exercise examines the effects of fiscal policy using aggregate supply and demand curves.

Assume the aggregate demand curve (D_1) and aggregate supply curve (S_1) are those shown in Figure 11.1. Then suppose the government increases spending, which causes the quantity of output demanded in the economy to rise by $1 trillion per year at every price level. Think about whether the change causes aggregate demand or aggregate supply to shift from its initial position.

Figure 11.1

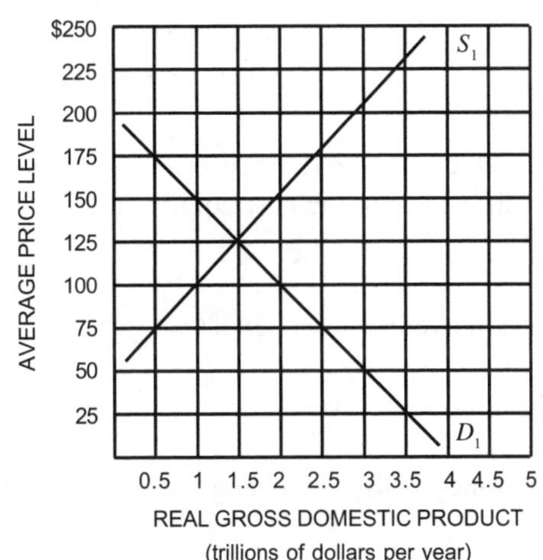

1. Draw the new aggregate demand curve (label it D_2) or aggregate supply curve (label it S_2) in Figure 11.1.

2. What is the new equilibrium average price level? ________

3. What is the new equilibrium output level? ________

4. Which school of thought would be most likely to prescribe the use of fiscal policy in this way?

____

5. The shift that occurred in Figure 11.1 is consistent with:
   (a) An increase in the price level and a lower unemployment rate.
   (b) An increase in the price level and a higher unemployment rate.
   (c) A decrease in the price level and a lower unemployment rate.
   (d) A decrease in the price level and a higher unemployment rate.

Exercise 2

Assume the aggregate demand curve (D_1) and aggregate supply curve (S_1) are those shown in Figure 11.2. Then suppose corporate taxes are reduced to encourage productivity and as a result firms supply $1 trillion more in output at every price level. Think about whether the change causes aggregate demand or aggregate supply to shift from its initial position.

Figure 11.2

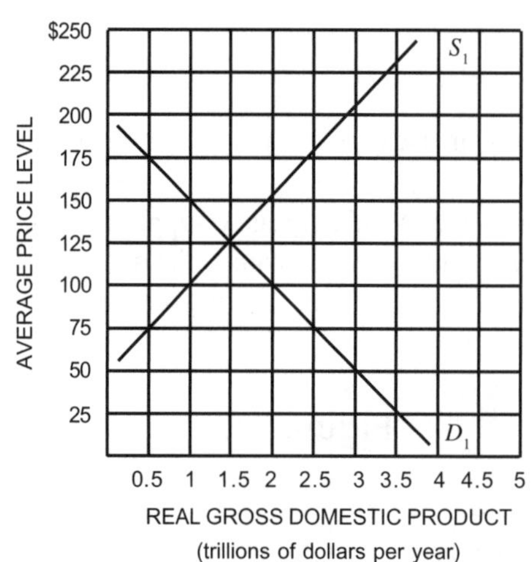

1. Draw the new aggregate demand curve (label it D_2) or aggregate supply curve (label it S_2) in Figure 11.2. Notice the difference in the new equilibrium in this exercise versus the new equilibrium in Exercise 1.

2. What is the new equilibrium average price level? ________

3. What is the new equilibrium output level? ________

4. Which type of economic policy is this tax change most consistent with? ________________

5. The shift that occurred in Figure 11.2 (above) is consistent with:
   (a) An increase in the price level and a higher unemployment rate.
   (b) An increase in the price level and a lower unemployment rate.
   (c) A decrease in the price level and a higher unemployment rate.
   (d) A decrease in the price level and a lower unemployment rate.

Exercise 3

This exercise shows how aggregate demand and supply can be used to analyze the effects of government policy. Suppose the aggregate demand curve and aggregate supply curve for all goods in an economy are presented in Figure 11.3. The economy is assumed to be on aggregate demand curve *B* in the current fiscal year.

Figure 11.3

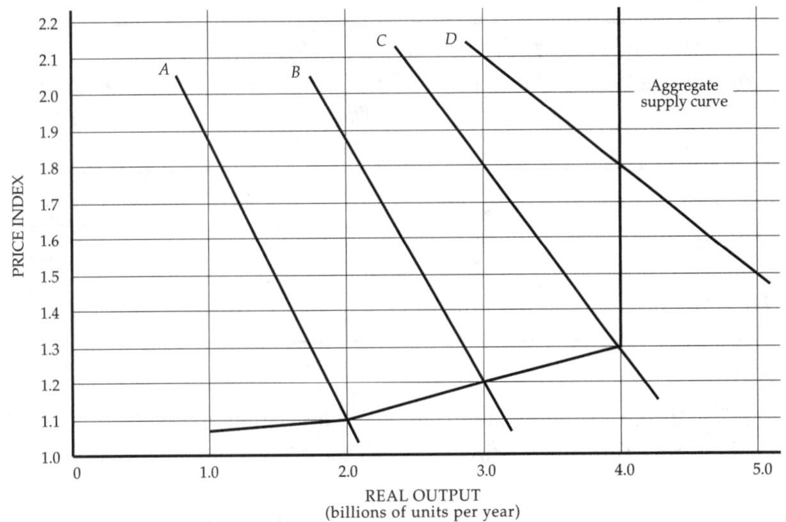

1. Four aggregate demand curves (*A*, *B*, *C*, and *D*) are shown in Figure 11.3 corresponding to four alternative government policies for the upcoming fiscal year.

   Choose the aggregate demand curve in Figure 11.3 that best portrays the expected impact of each policy. Place the letter of your choice in the blank provided. Each letter can be used more than once and some blanks will have more than one letter.

   a. ________ Money supply is expanded, taxes are cut, and government spending increases.
   b. ________ Government does nothing.
   c. ________ Government decides to balance the budget by reducing government spending and raising taxes.
   d. ________ Government increases expenditures and cuts taxes.

2. Indicate the equilibrium price index for each policy in Table 11.1.

Table 11.1 Equilibrium prices for four government policies

Aggregate demand curve	*A*	*B*	*C*	*D*
Equilibrium price index	______	______	______	______

3. Suppose the price index is currently 1.2 as shown by demand curve *B* in Figure 11.3. Compute the inflation rate under each of the four policies assuming the supply curve remains the same. The formula is:

$$\frac{\text{equilibrium price index} - 1.2}{1.2} \times 100\ \%$$

Enter your answers for each policy in the appropriate blank of column 1 in Table 11.2.

Table 11.2 Inflation rates, equilibrium output, and unemployment rates under four different government policies

Aggregate demand curve	(1) Equilibrium price change	(2) Equilibrium output (billions of units per year)	(3) Unemployment rate
A	_____%	_____	_____%
B	_____	_____	_____
C	_____	_____	_____
D	_____	_____	_____

4. In column 2 of Table 11.2 indicate the equilibrium output associated with each of the policies. Use Figure 11.3 to find this information.

5. Which of the following should be used to calculate the unemployment rate?
   (a) The population divided by the labor force times 100%.
   (b) The number of people employed divided by the population times 100%.
   (c) The number of people counted as unemployed divided by the labor force times 100%.
   (d) The number of people unemployed divided by the population times 100%.

6. Table 11.3 shows hypothetical data for the U.S. population, the labor force, the number of people who are employed, and the number of people who are unemployed at each production rate for the economy. Compute the unemployment rate at each production rate in the table.

Table 11.3 Computation of the unemployment rate

Production rate (billions of units per year)	2	3	4
Population (millions)	200	200	200
Labor force (millions)	100	100	100
Number of people unemployed (millions)	15	8	5
Number of people employed (millions)	85	92	95
Unemployment rate (percent)	_____	_____	_____

7. Using the information in Table 11.3, complete column 3 in Table 11.2, which shows the unemployment rate corresponding to each government policy.

8. In this case, the government's dilemma is that:
   (a) It cannot reach an unemployment level of 5 percent without experiencing inflation of at least 8 percent.
   (b) It cannot reach stable prices (0 percent increase) without experiencing an unemployment rate of 8 percent or more.
   (c) When it improves the economy in one sense by holding inflation below 8 percent, unemployment increases, which means the economy is worse off in another sense.
   (d) All of the above statements are true.

9. Which of the four aggregate demand curves places the economy closest to full-employment output with moderate inflation?
   (a) Aggregate demand curve *A*.
   (b) Aggregate demand curve *B*.
   (c) Aggregate demand curve *C*.
   (d) Aggregate demand curve *D*.

Exercise 4

Reread the News Wire article in the text titled "Hurricane Damage to Gulf Ports Delays Deliveries, Raises Costs." Then answer the following questions.

1. As a result of the hurricanes, the (AD, AS) curve shifted to the (left, right).

2. Based on the article, which aspects of the transportation industry were affected? ____________

   ____

3. How are the rising costs associated with the hurricanes expected to affect the U.S. economy?

   ____

Common Errors

The first statement in each "common error" below is incorrect. Each incorrect statement is followed by a corrected version and an explanation.

1. Full employment is achieved at the equilibrium GDP. *Incorrect!*
   Full employment is not necessarily achieved at the equilibrium GDP. *Correct!*
   When resources are fully employed, no additional goods and services can be produced. However, equilibrium GDP refers to the equality between the aggregate demand for goods and services and the aggregate supply of goods and services, not to any particular level of resource employment.

2. Aggregate demand (supply) and market demand (supply) are the same. *Incorrect!*
   Aggregate demand (supply) and market demand (supply) are very different quantities. *Correct!*
   Market demand (supply) represents the demand (supply) for an individual product. The aggregate demand (supply) represents the demand (supply) for all goods in the economy. The market demand and supply curves are used in microeconomic analysis to help determine equilibrium price and quantity in an individual market. The aggregate demand and supply curves are used in macroeconomic analysis to determine the equilibrium level of prices and output for the economy as a whole.

3. The AD and AS curves can be drawn anywhere on the graph. *Incorrect!*
   The AD and AS curves are drawn in specific locations on the graph to depict a given condition in the economy. *Correct!*
   The AD and AS curves must be drawn in a position to indicate the state of the economy that is being described (e.g., full employment, a recession, inflation, or stagflation).

4. The economy can spend no more than its income. *Incorrect!*
   The economy can spend more than its current income. *Correct!*

The economy can spend more than its current income by drawing down inventories of goods or by consuming capital (allowing it to depreciate) without replacing it. If the economy consumes more than its current income, it will experience negative savings and negative investment.

~ ANSWERS ~

Using Terms to Remember

Across

1. real GDP
4. unemployment
5. fiscal policy
7. aggregate demand
10. aggregate supply
11. inflation
12. business cycle
13. full-employment GDP

Down

2. equilibrium
3. supply-side policy
6. Say's Law
8. macroeconomics
9. monetary policy

True or False

1. F Most modern economists believe that some government intervention is necessary for the macro economy to perform properly.
2. T
3. F Keynes believed that the economy was inherently unstable and that fiscal policy should be used to improve it.
4. T
5. F According to the interest-rate effect, when the price level falls, the interest rate declines, which stimulates more borrowing.
6. T
7. F Macro equilibrium does not guarantee full employment; it only guarantees that aggregate demand equals aggregate supply.
8. T
9. F Fiscal policy and monetary policy both attempt to shift the aggregate demand curve, not the aggregate supply curve.
10. T

Multiple Choice

1. d	5. a	9. b	13. b	17. d
2. b	6. c	10. a	14. a	18. b
3. c	7. b	11. d	15. c	19. a
4. d	8. d	12. c	16. b	20. d

Problems and Applications

Exercise 1

1. See Figure 11.1 Answer, D_2.

Figure 11.1 Answer

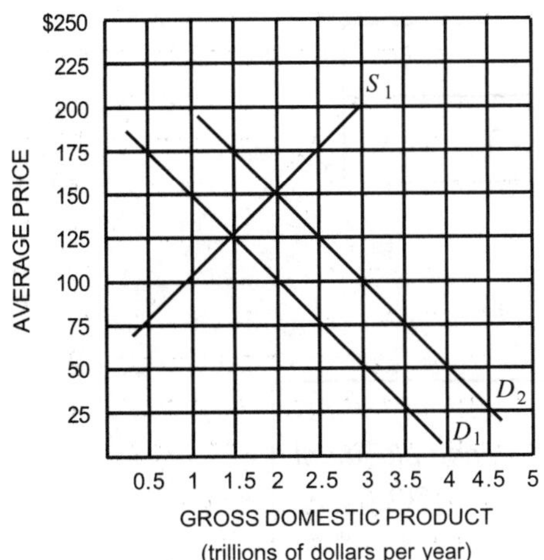

2. $150
3. $2 trillion
4. Keynesian
5. a

Exercise 2

1. See Figure 11.2 Answer, S_2.

Figure 11.2 Answer

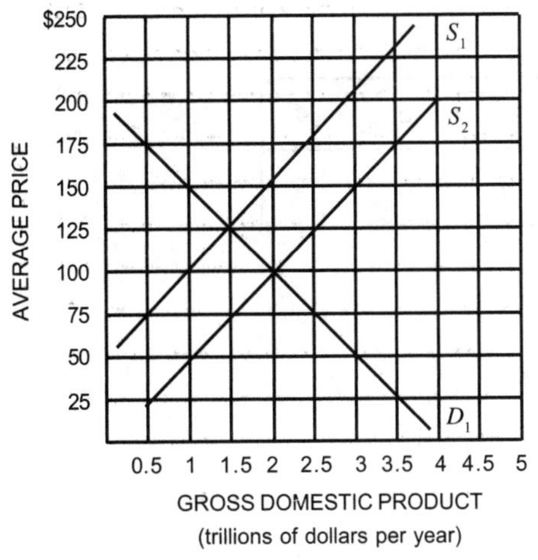

2. $100
3. $2 trillion
4. Supply-side policy
5. d

Exercise 3

1. a. *C* or *D*
   b. *B*
   c. *A*
   d. *C* or *D*

2. **Table 11.1 Answer**

Aggregate demand curve	*A*	*B*	*C*	*D*
Equilibrium price index	1.1	1.2	1.3	1.8

3. See Table 11.2 Answer, column 1.

Table 11.2 Answer

Aggregate demand curve	*(1) Equilibrium price change*	*(2) Equilibrium output (billions of units per year)*	*(3) Unemployment rate*
A	8.3%	2.0	15%
B	0.0	3.0	8
C	8.3	4.0	5
D	50.0	4.0	5

4. See Table 11.2 Answer, column 2.
5. c
6. **Table 11.3 Answer**

Production rate (billions of units per year)	*2*	*3*	*4*
Unemployment rate (percent)	15	8	5

7. See Table 11.2 Answer, column 3.
8. d
9. c

Exercise 4

1. AS; left
2. Ports, waterways, shipping terminals, warehouses, navigation channels, roads, and rail lines
3. The article states: "The rising costs could put more downward pressure on growth, particularly for industries dependent on key products that typically flow through the region. ... The rising cost of forest products like lumber could add to the price tag for rebuilding the region, while grain companies could see their exports become less competitive."

CHAPTER 12

Fiscal Policy

Quick Review

- The government can use fiscal policy to change the level of aggregate demand. Aggregate demand is composed of consumption, investment, government spending, and net exports.

- Consumption refers to all household spending on goods and services. Investment refers to spending by business on new plant and equipment and net changes in inventory. Government spending includes expenditures on goods and services at the state, federal, and local level. It does not include spending in the form of income transfers (payments for which no goods or services are exchanged) such as social security payments. Net exports is the difference between spending on exports and spending on imports.

- Aggregate demand represents a schedule of planned purchases that will change as the price level changes, as illustrated by the aggregate demand curve. Equilibrium (macro) will occur where aggregate demand and aggregate supply intersect, but this may not be at the level that achieves our price level, income, and employment goals.

- If the economy is in equilibrium at an output level other than the full-employment output level, there is a GDP gap. Fiscal policy can be used to move the economy to full employment.

- If equilibrium is less than full employment, the government can provide fiscal stimulus by increasing spending or cutting taxes. As a result of increased spending, additional consumption is generated, which impacts aggregate demand. This is known as the multiplier process. The multiplier is equal to $1 \div (1 - \text{MPC})$ and is used to determine the cumulative change in spending that results from an initial spending change. The marginal propensity to consume (MPC) is the fraction of additional income that is spent. A tax cut can also increase disposable income and consumption, or it can increase investment spending. Again, there is a multiplier process.

- If equilibrium is greater than full employment, there is inflationary pressure. The government can provide fiscal restraint by decreasing spending or increasing taxes. The multiplier will then work in reverse.

- If government spending and taxes are used as fiscal policy levers to change aggregate demand, it is likely that the government will experience a budget deficit or a budget surplus for any given year. A balanced budget is appropriate only if the level of aggregate demand is consistent with full-employment equilibrium.

Learning Objectives

After reading the chapter and doing the following exercises you should be able to:

1. Define what fiscal policy is.
2. Explain why fiscal policy might be needed.
3. Illustrate what the multiplier is and how it works.
4. Tell how fiscal stimulus or restraint is achieved.
5. Specify how fiscal policy affects the federal budget.

Using Terms to Remember

Fill in the puzzle on the opposite page with the appropriate terms from the list of Terms to Remember in the text.

Across

4. The fraction of each additional dollar of disposable income not spent on consumption.
5. Tax cuts or spending hikes intended to increase aggregate demand.
7. The total quantity of output demanded at alternative price levels.
12. Equal to exports minus imports.
13. The part of disposable income that is not spent.
14. The combination of price level and real output that is compatible with both aggregate demand and aggregate supply.
15. A tax hike or decrease in government spending intended to decrease aggregate demand.
16. Expenditure by consumers on final goods and services.

Down

1. The fraction of additional income spent by consumers.
2. The after-tax income of consumers.
3. Tends to increase when corporate taxes are cut.
6. The amount by which government expenditures exceed government revenues in a given time period.
8. The difference between full-employment output and the amount of output demanded at the current price level.
9. The excess of government revenues over government expenditures.
10. Indicates how much total spending will change in response to an initial spending change.
11. An example is a decrease in government spending to reduce inflation.

Puzzle 12.1

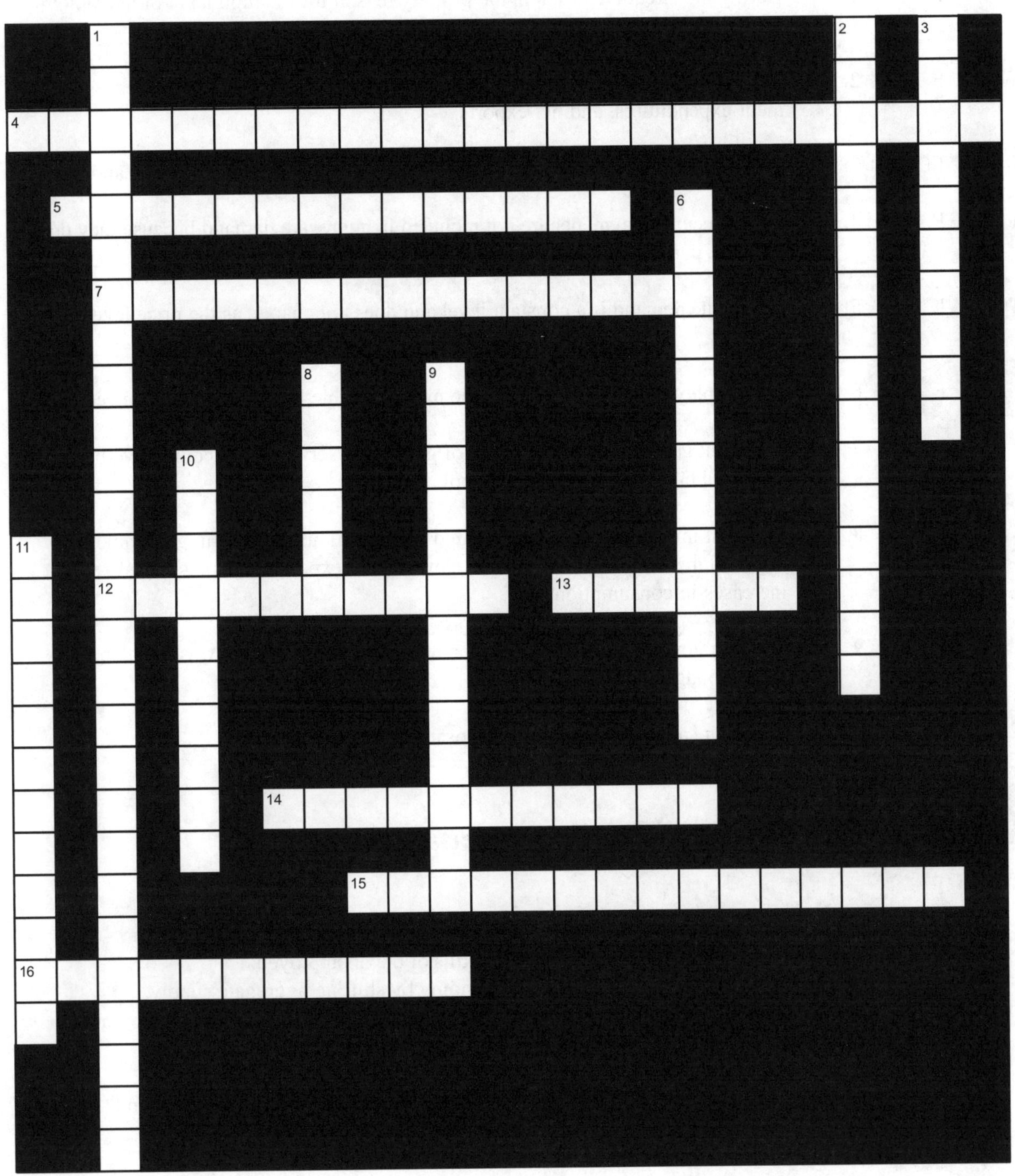

True or False: *Circle your choice and explain why any false statements are incorrect.*

T F 1. During the Great Depression, the primary reason for the high level of unemployment was because aggregate supply was insufficient.

T F 2. The four components of aggregate demand are consumption, investment, government expenditures, and net exports.

T F 3. To an economist, the term *investment* refers to the purchase of stocks and bonds.

T F 4. Social security payments are *not* included in aggregate demand because they do not reflect a purchase of goods and services.

T F 5. Aggregate demand is a constant level and does *not* change as the price level changes.

T F 6. Full-employment GDP is always the most desirable level of GDP for an economy.

T F 7. The GDP gap represents the value of goods and services that could have been produced but were *not* because people are lazy.

T F 8. The total impact on aggregate demand because of an increase in government expenditures includes both the new government expenditures plus all subsequent increases in consumption.

T F 9. The best government policy during a recession, *ceteris paribus*, is to balance the federal budget.

T F 10. A tax cut causes a decrease in disposable income.

Multiple Choice: *Select the correct answer.*

_______ 1. In developing his theory of unemployment during the Great Depression, Keynes:
(a) Focused primarily on improving the skills of the unemployed.
(b) Focused on the stimulation of the economy by shifting aggregate supply.
(c) Explained how aggregate demand could be inadequate to ensure full employment.
(d) Dealt with the causes of unemployment, but not the policies to correct it.

_______ 2. Which type of expenditure is typically the largest component of aggregate demand?
(a) Consumption.
(b) Government expenditures.
(c) Business investment.
(d) Net exports.

_____ 3. Which of the following is possible at the intersection of aggregate supply and aggregate demand?
(a) Full employment, but not unemployment or inflation.
(b) Unemployment, but not inflation or full employment.
(c) Inflation and full employment, but not unemployment.
(d) Inflation, full employment, or unemployment.

_____ 4. When aggregate demand exceeds the full-employment level of output, the result is:
(a) Significant unemployment.
(b) A higher average price level.
(c) Higher inventory levels.
(d) A recession.

_____ 5. Keynes argued that the level of economic activity is primarily related to:
(a) Aggregate demand.
(b) Aggregate supply.
(c) The money supply.
(d) Interest rates.

_____ 6. If an economy has a GDP gap, such that equilibrium output is less than full-employment output, which of the following fiscal policies will reduce the gap?
(a) A tax increase.
(b) An increase in the money supply.
(c) A reduction in Social Security payments.
(d) An increase in government expenditures on highways and bridges.

_____ 7. Which of the following explains why the multiplier effect exists?
(a) The circular nature of the economy.
(b) The fact that money is spent and respent multiple times.
(c) One person's spending becomes another person's income.
(d) All of the above.

_____ 8. Which of the following would be a Keynesian solution for inflation?
(a) Increase transfer payments to those people hurt by inflation.
(b) Decrease government expenditures and let the multiplier work.
(c) Restrict foreign imports into the country.
(d) Do nothing because the economy is inherently stable.

_____ 9. If consumers spend 80 cents out of every extra dollar of disposable income then:
(a) The MPS is 0.80.
(b) The MPC is 0.20.
(c) The multiplier is 8.0.
(d) The MPC is 0.80.

_____ 10. If government spending increases by $35 billion and the MPC is 0.90, what would the total change in spending be for the economy, *ceteris paribus*?
(a) $31.5 billion.
(b) $35 billion.
(c) $350 billion.
(d) $315 billion.

_______ 11. Refer to Table 12.1 in the text. The change in spending in the second cycle caused the aggregate demand curve to shift to the right by:
(a) $100 billion.
(b) $400 billion.
(c) $75 billion.
(d) $175 billion.

_______ 12. Which of the following economies has the largest multiplier?
(a) Economy A with an MPC of 0.80.
(b) Economy B with an MPS of 0.25.
(c) Economy C with an MPS of 0.50.
(d) Economy D with an MPC of 0.60.

_______ 13. Which of the following provides fiscal stimulus to the economy?
(a) Higher interest rates.
(b) Increased government purchases.
(c) Increased imports.
(d) More efficient employment of resources.

_______ 14. The amount of additional aggregate demand generated by increased government spending depends on:
(a) The marginal propensity to consume.
(b) The number of spending cycles that occur in a given period of time.
(c) The size of the initial increase in government spending.
(d) All of the above.

_______ 15. During an inflationary period it is appropriate for the government to pursue policies that:
(a) Stimulate aggregate demand.
(b) Reduce aggregate demand.
(c) Make budget deficits larger.
(d) Eliminate the public debt.

_______ 16. Which of the following will definitely reduce a budget deficit and provide fiscal restraint?
(a) Greater government spending and lower taxes.
(b) Greater government spending and higher taxes.
(c) Lower government spending and lower taxes.
(d) Lower government spending and higher taxes.

_______ 17. When we compare the total impact on aggregate demand of a $60 billion decrease in government expenditures and a $60 billion increase in taxes we find that the:
(a) Total impact on aggregate demand of the two policies will be the same.
(b) Total impact on aggregate demand will be the same but in opposite directions.
(c) Decrease in government expenditures will have a greater total impact on aggregate demand.
(d) Increase in taxes will have a greater total impact on aggregate demand.

_______ 18. Suppose government spending decreases by $12 billion, and the MPC is 0.75. What is the total impact on aggregate demand as a result of this action, *ceteris paribus*?
(a) A decrease of $12 billion.
(b) A decrease of $48 billion.
(c) An increase of $9 billion.
(d) An increase of $12 billion.

_______ 19. Fiscal policy is most effective in changing the level of real output without causing inflation when the aggregate supply curve is:
(a) Horizontal.
(b) Vertical.
(c) Upward sloping.
(d) Fiscal policy has no effect on inflation, regardless of the slope of the aggregate supply curve.

_______ 20. During a recession the appropriate fiscal policy would be for the federal government to:
(a) Balance the budget.
(b) Run a budget surplus.
(c) Run a budget deficit.
(d) Leave the budget alone.

Problems and Applications

Exercise 1

The following exercise shows how the multiplier works and how to calculate it.

1. Suppose the economy is initially at full employment. Then suddenly it experiences a $100 billion decrease in business expenditures because of a decrease in stock market prices. Follow the impact of this sudden change through the economy by completing Table 12.1. (Refer to Table 12.1 in the text if you need help.) Assume the marginal propensity to consume is 0.80. (*Hint*: Consumption will decrease in each round by the "change in spending" in the previous cycle times the MPC.)

Table 12.1

Spending cycle	*Drop in investment expenditure*	*Change in spending (billions of dollars per year)*	*Cumulative decrease in aggregate spending (billions of dollars per year)*
First cycle:	GDP gap emerges	$100	$100
Second cycle:	consumption drops by	________	________
Third cycle:	consumption drops by	________	________
Fourth cycle:	consumption drops by	________	________
Fifth cycle:	consumption drops by	________	________
Sixth cycle:	consumption drops by	________	________
Seventh cycle:	consumption drops by	________	________

2. Compute the multiplier. ________

3. Multiply $100 billion by the multiplier.________

4. What is the total change in aggregate spending after an infinite number of spending cycles? ________

5. T F A large portion of the total change in aggregate spending in Question 4 is due to the multiplier effect.

Exercise 2

Reread the News Wire article in the text titled "Here Comes the Recession." Then answer the following questions using Figure 12.1 for Question 1.

Figure 12.1

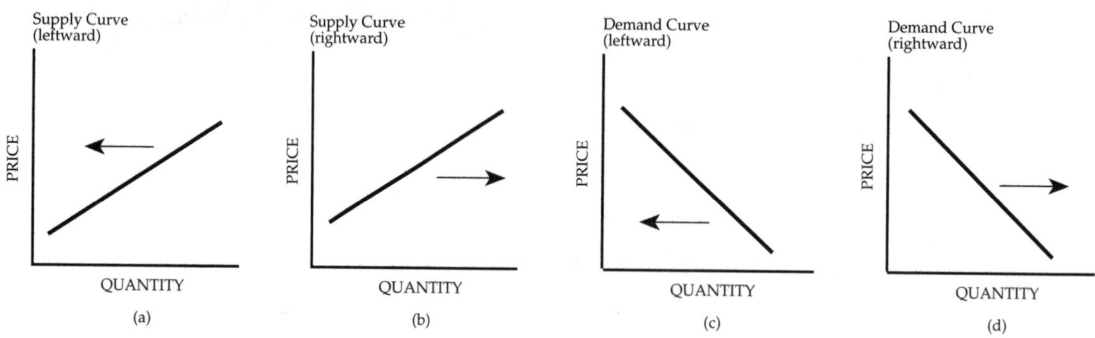

1. Which of the diagrams in Figure 12.1 best represents the shift that can be expected as a result of the change in consumer spending discussed in the article?
   a b c d (circle one)

2. What has happened to home prices that contributed to the change in consumer spending?

   ____

3. Why is consumer spending so important to the economy? ______________________

   ____

Exercise 3

This exercise shows how the multiplier works to eliminate a GDP gap.

Refer to Figure 12.2 to answer the following questions. Assume the MPC equals 0.75 and the current level of aggregate demand is equal to AD_1.

Figure 12.2

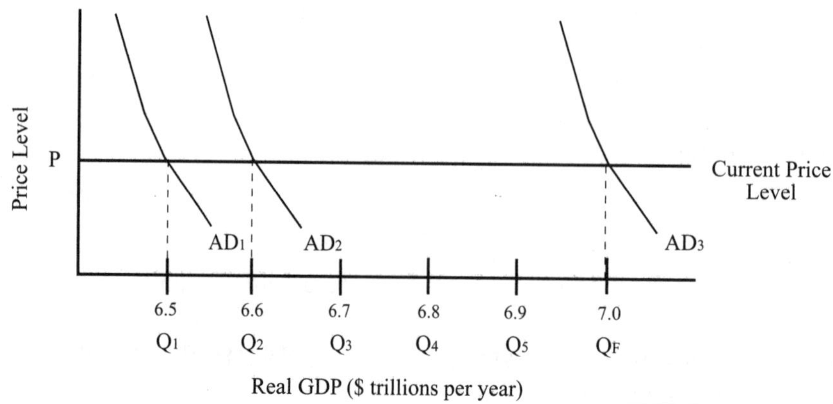

1. What is the equilibrium level of real GDP if aggregate demand is equal to AD_1? ____________

2. What is the full-employment level of real GDP? ____________

3. What is the size of the GDP gap? ____________

4. What is the value of the multiplier? ____________

5. An increase in government spending of $125 billion would cause consumption to increase by $_______ billion in the second spending cycle.

6. An increase in government spending of $125 billion would cause a cumulative increase in aggregate demand equal to $_______ billion and would result in an equilibrium real GDP equal to $_______ trillion.

Common Errors

The first statement in each "common error" below is incorrect. Each incorrect statement is followed by a corrected version and an explanation.

1. Government deficits always lead to inflation. *Incorrect!*
Government deficits may result from government spending to reach full employment with price stability. *Correct!*
The focus should be on what is happening to aggregate demand, not just deficits, when looking for the sources of inflation. By looking at the deficit, it is impossible to tell if the economy is at full employment or not. If there is a shortfall in AD, government spending and resulting deficits may restore full employment with price stability! If the economy is already at full employment, inflation can result from increased consumption, investment, or export expenditures, just as much as it can from increased government spending. It is easy to point the finger at the government and forget the contribution to inflation of all of the sectors of the economy.

2. When a person invests in the stock market, investment expenditure is increased. *Incorrect!*
The purchase of stocks has only an indirect relationship to investment expenditure in the economy. *Correct!*
Investment expenditure refers to purchases of new capital goods (plant, machinery, etc.) or inventories. A purchase of stock represents a transfer of ownership from one person to another. Sometimes such purchases are called "financial investments," but they do not represent economic investment.

3. Aggregate demand rises when people buy more imports. *Incorrect!*
Aggregate demand falls when people buy more imports, *ceteris paribus*. *Correct!*
Students often think of imports as expenditures and therefore believe that increased spending on imports will have the same effect on the economy as an increase in consumption. Expenditures on imports, however, do not generate domestic income. If imports increase, they do so at the expense of purchases of U.S. goods, meaning fewer jobs in the United States. Because employment declines, there is less income with which to consume goods; consumption falls and so does aggregate demand.

4. Macro equilibrium and full employment are always the same. *Incorrect!*
Macro equilibrium and full employment are determined in different ways. *Correct!*
Macro equilibrium occurs where aggregate demand and aggregate supply intersect. Full

employment refers to the use of all available resources in production. If macro equilibrium does not occur at full employment there is a GDP gap.

5. If the government increases spending and taxes by the same amount, there will be no effect on aggregate spending. *Incorrect!*
If the government increases spending and taxes by the same amount, aggregate spending will increase. *Correct!*
The increase in government spending works its way through the economy causing an increase in consumption and aggregate spending. The tax increase is paid for by a reduction in consumption and a reduction in saving, so consumption decreases by less than the increase in taxes. This means that the spending increase has a greater impact than the tax increase and aggregate spending increases.

~ ANSWERS ~

Using Terms to Remember

Across

4. marginal propensity to save
5. fiscal stimulus
7. aggregate demand
12. net exports
13. saving
14. equilibrium
15. fiscal restraint
16. consumption

Down

1. marginal propensity to consume
2. disposable income
3. investment
6. budget deficit
8. GDP gap
9. budget surplus
10. multiplier
11. fiscal policy

True or False

1. F During the Great Depression, the primary reason for the high level of unemployment was because aggregate *demand* was insufficient.
2. T
3. F Investment is business expenditure on buildings, equipment, and inventory.
4. T
5. F Aggregate demand is a schedule showing the quantity of output demanded at various price levels.
6. T
7. F The GDP gap represents the gap between the economy's ability to produce and the amount of output people are willing to buy.
8. T
9. F It is appropriate for the budget to be unbalanced in a period of inflation or recession.
10. F A tax cut causes an *increase* in disposable income.

Multiple Choice

1. c	5. a	9. d	13. b	17. c
2. a	6. d	10. c	14. d	18. b
3. d	7. d	11. c	15. b	19. a
4. b	8. b	12. a	16. d	20. c

Problems and Applications

Exercise 1

1. **Table 12.1 Answer**

Spending cycles	*Amount*	*Cumulative decrease in aggregate spending*
First cycle:	$100.00	$100.00
Second cycle:	80.00	180.00
Third cycle:	64.00	244.00
Fourth cycle:	51.20	295.20
Fifth cycle:	40.96	336.16
Sixth cycle:	32.77	368.93
Seventh cycle:	26.22	395.15

2. Multiplier = 1 ÷ (1 - MPC) = 1 ÷ (1 - 0.8) = 5
3. 5 x $100 billion per year = $500 billion per year
4. $500 billion
5. T

Exercise 2

1. c (*Ceteris paribus*, a decrease in consumer confidence causes a leftward shift of aggregate demand.)
2. "Housing prices are sliding, diminishing the value of the asset that's the biggest factor in Americans' personal wealth."
3. Consumer spending accounts for " . . . about three-quarters of U.S. economic activity."

Exercise 3

1. $6.5 trillion
2. $7.0 trillion
3. $7 trillion - $6.5 trillion = $500 billion
4. Multiplier = 1 ÷ (1 - MPC) = 1 ÷ (1 - 0.75) = 4
5. $125 billion x 0.75 = $93.75 billion (Refer to Table 12.1 in the text.)
6. 4 x $125 billion = $500 billion; $7.0 trillion

CHAPTER 13

Money and Banks

Quick Review

- Money facilitates market exchanges and allows for specialization. It makes an economy more efficient than one that relies on barter. Anything that serves simultaneously as a medium of exchange, a store of value, and a standard of value can be thought of as money.

- The money supply (M1) is composed of transactions accounts, currency in circulation, and traveler's checks.

- The banking system can create money by making loans. When a bank decides to make a loan, it simply credits the transactions account of the borrower. Because transactions accounts are included in M1, this deposit causes an increase in the money supply.

- In the United States, the Federal Reserve System requires banks to maintain some minimum ratio of bank reserves to total deposits. Any reserves above the required level are considered to be excess reserves. A bank may use its excess reserves to make new loans.

- As the new loans are spent, the dollars flow back into the banking system and additional loans are made. This process continues to happen over and over again and is known as *deposit creation.*

- The banking system as a whole can increase the volume of deposits by the amount of the excess reserves times the money multiplier. The money multiplier is equal to 1/required reserve ratio.

- Banks perform a strategic role in the economy by transferring money from savers to spenders and by creating additional money through lending. An increase in the money supply, because of deposit creation, leads to an increase in aggregate demand. A reduction in the money supply leads to a decrease in aggregate demand.

- Deposit creation is constrained by the willingness of market participants to use and accept checks. It is also constrained by the willingness of businesses and individuals to borrow and the willingness of banks to make loans. Regulations of the Federal Reserve System also limit deposit creation.

Learning Objectives

After reading the chapter and doing the following exercises you should be able to:

1. Detail what the features of "money" are.
2. Specify what is included in the "money supply."
3. Describe how a bank creates money.
4. Explain how the money multiplier works.
5. Discuss why the money supply is important.

Using Terms to Remember

Fill in the puzzle on the opposite page with the appropriate terms from the list of Terms to Remember in the text.

Across

2. Total reserves minus required reserves.
3. Assets held by a bank to fulfill its deposit obligations.
4. An account that allows direct payment to a third party.
5. Represent a leakage from the flow of money because they cannot be used to make loans.
6. Tends to increase with an increase in the money supply because new loans are used to purchase additional goods and services.
9. The reciprocal of the required reserve ratio.

Down

1. The process by which bank lending causes the money supply to increase.
3. The direct exchange of one good for another without the use of money.
7. The ratio of a bank's reserves to its total transactions deposits.
8. Currency held by the public plus balances in transactions accounts.
9. Throughout history gold coins, tobacco, and bullets have functioned in this role.

Puzzle 13.1

True or False: *Circle your choice and explain why any false statements are incorrect.*

T F 1. Money facilitates exchanges between market participants.

T F 2. Only currency and coins serve as money in the U. S. economy.

T F 3. To be money, an item must be accepted in exchange for goods and services, maintain its value over a period of time, and provide a standard for the measurement of the value of goods and services.

T F 4. Credit cards are a form of money because they facilitate exchanges.

T F 5. Changes in the supply of money affect the price level, employment, and output by shifting the aggregate supply curve.

T F 6. The Federal Reserve System has the primary responsibility of managing the money supply in the United States by changing transactions account balances.

T F 7. When a bank makes a loan, it is creating money.

T F 8. When you deposit $20 in coins into your checking account, M1 increases immediately.

T F 9. The lower the minimum reserve ratio, the smaller the deposit-creation possibilities are for the banking system.

T F 10. A primary function of banks is to transfer money from savers to borrowers.

Multiple Choice: *Select the correct answer.*

_______ 1. Alex watches her friend's children and the friend walks Alex's dog instead of paying her. This is an example of:
(a) Swap.
(b) An efficient exchange.
(c) Barter.
(d) A market transaction.

_______ 2. Which of the following is a necessary characteristic of money?
(a) It must serve as a medium of exchange.
(b) Its value must be backed by gold and silver.
(c) The government must declare it to have value.
(d) It must be printed by the government.

_______ 3. Almost all of the U.S. money supply (M1) is in the form of:
(a) Credit card and savings account balances.
(b) Cash and traveler's checks.
(c) Transactions and savings account balances.
(d) Currency in circulation and transactions-account balances.

_______ 4. If Tameika takes $400 out of her savings account and hides it in her cookie jar in the form of cash, M1 will:
(a) Decrease by $400.
(b) Increase by $400.
(c) Not change in size.
(d) Increase by more than $400.

_______ 5. Money creation occurs when:
(a) A person puts cash in a bank.
(b) A person deposits a payroll check into their checking account.
(c) Banks make loans to borrowers.
(d) The Federal Reserve System increases the reserve requirement.

_______ 6. The main goal of bank managers is to:
(a) Minimize the bank's reserve ratio.
(b) Create money.
(c) Lend all of the bank's deposits.
(d) Earn a profit.

_______ 7. The legal minimum-reserve ratio is set by:
(a) The commercial banks.
(b) The U.S. Treasury.
(c) The Federal Reserve.
(d) Congress.

_______ 8. Which of the following is the correct way to calculate excess reserves?
(a) The minimum-reserve requirement times transactions-account liabilities.
(b) Total reserves minus required reserves.
(c) Total reserves minus the legal minimum-reserve ratio.
(d) Total reserves plus required reserves.

_______ 9. A bank may lend an amount equal to its:
(a) Excess reserves.
(b) Total reserves.
(c) Total assets.
(d) Required reserves.

_______ 10. Suppose the total amount of transactions-account balances for all the banks in the banking system is $3 million and that the minimum reserve ratio is 0.07. The amount of required reserves for the banking system is equal to:
(a) $21,000,000.
(b) $2,100,000.
(c) $428,000.
(d) $210,000.

_______ 11. The term *fractional reserves* refers to:
(a) Reserves that are split among many banks.
(b) Reserves that are a fraction of total deposits.
(c) The ratio of required reserves to total loans.
(d) Reserves that are split among different types of accounts.

_______ 12. If the minimum reserve ratio is 12 percent, the money multiplier is:
(a) 8.33.
(b) 12.00.
(c) 0.83.
(d) 1.20.

_______ 13. Banks are required to keep a minimum amount of funds in reserve because:
(a) The bank may be robbed.
(b) Holding reserves encourages a bank to create money.
(c) Holding reserves allows a bank to have a large impact on aggregate demand.
(d) Depositors may decide to withdraw funds.

_______ 14. If there were no minimum reserve requirement in the banking system, the potential ability of banks to create money would be:
(a) Zero.
(b) Unlimited.
(c) Limited by the amount of deposits.
(d) Limited by the number of banks in the banking system.

_______ 15. Suppose a bank has $40 million in deposits, a required reserve ratio of 15 percent, and total reserves of $10 million. This bank has excess reserves of:
(a) $4 million.
(b) $6 million.
(c) $10 million.
(d) $15 million.

_______ 16. Suppose Jon finds $100 in the pocket of his jacket and deposits the money into his checking account. The bank must hold 6 percent of this deposit as required reserves. What is the approximate potential increase in the money supply because of this deposit?
(a) $94.
(b) $1,567.
(c) $1,667.
(d) $100.

_______ 17. Suppose the entire banking system has a required reserve ratio of 8 percent. How much can the money supply increase in response to a $2 billion increase in excess reserves for the whole banking system?
(a) $160 million.
(b) $2 billion.
(c) $25 billion.
(d) $16 billion.

_______ 18. Which of the following is a constraint on deposit creation?
(a) The willingness of consumers and firms to accept checks in payment for goods and services.
(b) The willingness of consumers, businesses, and governments to borrow.
(c) The willingness of banks to loan money to qualified borrowers.
(d) All of the above.

_______ 19. Banks perform the essential function of:
(a) Transferring funds from savers to spenders.
(b) Transferring funds from spenders to savers.
(c) Keeping the money supply constant.
(d) Lending funds to the Federal Reserve Banks.

_______ 20. An increase in the amount of bank loans should shift the aggregate:
(a) Supply curve to the left.
(b) Supply curve to the right.
(c) Demand curve to the left.
(d) Demand curve to the right.

Problems and Applications

Exercise 1

Use the information from the balance sheet in Table 13.1 to answer Questions 1–5.

Table 13.1 Bank of Arlington

Assets		*Liabilities*	
Required reserves	$200,000	Transactions accounts	$1,000,000
Other assets	$800,000		
Total	$1,000,000	Total	$1,000,000

1. Suppose that the Bank of Arlington is just meeting its reserve requirement. The reserve ratio must be _________, and the money multiplier must be _________.

2. To be in a position to make loans, the Bank of Arlington must acquire some (required reserves, excess reserves).

3. If we assume that the reserve ratio changes to 15 percent, the Bank of Arlington would now have required reserves of __________ and excess reserves of __________.

4. With a 15 percent reserve ratio the Bank of Arlington is in a position to make new loans totaling __________.

5. With a 15 percent reserve ratio, the entire banking system can increase the volume of loans by __________.

Exercise 2

This exercise shows how the multiplier process works.

Assume that all banks in the system lend all of their excess reserves, that the reserve ratio for all banks is 0.25, and that all loans are returned to the banking system in the form of transactions accounts. Use the information from the balance sheets in Table 13.2, Table 13.3, Table 13.4, and Table 13.5 to answer Questions 1–6.

Table 13.2 Initial balance sheet for Bank A, Bank B, & Bank C

Assets		*Liabilities*	
Required reserves	$25,000	Transactions accounts	$100,000
Excess reserves	0		
Other assets	$75,000		
Total	$100,000	Total	$100,000

1. Juan takes $10,000 out of his cookie jar and deposits it into a transactions account in Bank A. Fill in the blanks in Bank A's balance sheet in Table 13.3 after the deposit. (Remember that some of the deposit will show up in required reserves and the remainder will become part of excess reserves.)

Table 13.3 Bank A balance sheet after Juan's deposit

Assets		*Liabilities*	
Required reserves	$______	Transactions accounts	$______
Excess reserves	$______		
Other assets	$75,000		
Total	$______	Total	$______

Now assume Bank A lends all of its excess reserves to Kim, who spends the money on a car. The car dealership deposits the money into its transactions account in Bank B. Bank B's initial balance sheet is the same as Bank A's initial balance sheet.

2. Fill in the blanks in Bank B's balance sheet after the car dealership makes its deposit.

Table 13.4 Bank B balance sheet after car dealership's deposit

Assets		*Liabilities*	
Required reserves	$______	Transactions accounts	$______
Excess reserves	$______		
Other assets	$75,000		
Total	$______	Total	$______

Now assume Bank B lends all of its excess reserves to Latoya, who spends the money on college tuition. The university deposits the money into Bank C. Bank C's initial balance sheet is the same as Bank A's initial balance sheet.

3. Fill in the blanks in Bank C's balance sheet after the university makes its deposit.

Table 13.5 Bank C balance sheet after the university's deposit

Assets		*Liabilities*	
Required reserves	$______	Transactions accounts	$______
Excess reserves	$______		
Other assets	$75,000		
Total	$______	Total	$______

4. Add together the potential increase in loans for each bank because of the initial $10,000 deposit made by Juan.

   Bank A is able to lend $_________.
   Bank B is able to lend $_________.
   Bank C is able to lend $_________.

   Total loans made possible so far are equal to $_________.

5. The money multiplier for this exercise equals _________.

6. The potential deposit creation for the entire banking system in this exercise is ________________.

Exercise 3

This exercise focuses on the reserve requirement and its impact on the money supply.

1. Given the following reserve ratios, calculate the money multiplier for each.

   a. Reserve ratio = 12 percent   Money multiplier = _______
   b. Reserve ratio = 10 percent   Money multiplier = _______
   c. Reserve ratio = 5 percent   Money multiplier = _______

2. As the reserve ratio decreases, the money multiplier (increases, decreases).

3. As the money multiplier increases, potential deposit creation (increases, decreases).

4. T F A decrease in the reserve ratio allows the banking system to increase the money supply through deposit creation.

Common Errors

The first statement in each "common error" below is incorrect. Each incorrect statement is followed by a corrected version and an explanation.

1. Banks cannot create money. *Incorrect!*
   Banks can and do create money. *Correct!*

Banks and other depository institutions are very important participants in the money-supply process. They are able to lend excess reserves to borrowers. The borrowed money is added to customers' transactions accounts, and these accounts are part of the money supply, just like the printed money in your wallet. Thus, banks create money, but only in response to borrowers' demands for it. Without customers "demanding" loans, banks wouldn't be able to create money.

2. Banks hold your deposits in their vaults. *Incorrect!*
Banks (and other depository institutions) do not hold your deposits in their vaults. *Correct!*
Banks (and other depository institutions) are required by law to hold a fraction of the deposits they receive as reserves. The remaining portion of any deposit may be used by the bank to generate a profit, such as making a loan. Banks hold a portion of their required reserves in their vault, but most of the required reserves are kept in an account at the Federal Reserve bank.

3. Gold and silver are intrinsically valuable and necessary to secure the value of money. *Incorrect!*
Currency has value only because people accept its role as a medium of exchange, a store of value and a standard of value. *Correct!*
Precious metals such as gold and silver have been used to back many currencies in the past, but they do not back the dollar today. The dollar has value because people accept it as money. This acceptance actually implies a level of faith in the U.S. government. During periods of calamity and fear, precious metals are hoarded because people believe in their value. Precious metals then take on the role of a store of value.

4. Banks are responsible for storing all the money that is deposited with them so that it is available on demand. *Incorrect!*
Banks are responsible for storing a fraction of the money that is deposited with them and are allowed to lend out the remainder. *Correct!*
Banks actually make the economic system more efficient by transferring money from savers to spenders through lending. Banks earn interest on the money they lend and can then pay interest on deposits placed in the bank. If banks did not perform the lending function, individuals would lend money to one another, which would be much less efficient. By making loans, banks increase the money supply, which allows the economy to be much larger than it would be if this lending did not occur.

~ ANSWERS ~

Using Terms to Remember

Across

2. excess reserves
3. bank reserves
4. transactions account
5. required reserves
6. aggregate demand
9. money multiplier

Down

1. deposit creation
3. barter
7. reserve ratio
8. money supply
9. money

True or False

1. T
2. F Cash makes up a portion of our money supply, but transactions accounts are also a significant component of M1.

3. T
4. F Credit card balances are a loan that must be repaid using cash or check.
5. F Changes in the supply of money affect the price level, employment, and output by shifting the aggregate *demand* curve.
6. T
7. T
8. F Currency in circulation (the $20 in coins) is already part of M1 so M1 does *not* change immediately.
9. F The lower the minimum reserve requirement, the greater the deposit-creation possibilities are for the banking system.
10. T

Multiple Choice

1. c	5. c	9. a	13. d	17. c
2. a	6. d	10. d	14. b	18. d
3. d	7. c	11. b	15. a	19. a
4. b	8. b	12. a	16. b	20. d

Problems and Applications

Exercise 1

1. 0.20; 5
2. Excess reserves
3. $150,000; $50,000
4. $50,000
5. $333,333.33 (excess reserves x money multiplier)

Exercise 2

1. **Table 13.3 Answer**

Assets		*Liabilities*	
Required reserves	$27,500	Transactions accounts	$110,000
Excess reserves	$7,500		
Other assets	$75,000		
Total	$110,000	Total	$110,000

2. **Table 13.4 Answer**

Assets		*Liabilities*	
Required reserves	$26,875	Transactions accounts	$107,500
Excess reserves	$5,625		
Other assets	$75,000		
Total	$107,500	Total	$107,500

3. **Table 13.5 Answer**

Assets		*Liabilities*	
Required reserves	$26,406.25	Transactions accounts	$105,625.00
Excess reserves	$4,218.75		
Other assets	$75,000.00		
Total	$105,625.00	Total	$105,625.00

4. Bank A is able to lend $7,500.00.
   Bank B is able to lend $5,625.00.
   Bank C is able to lend $4,218.75.
   Total loans made so far are equal to $17,343.75.
5. 1 ÷ reserve ratio = 1 ÷ 0.25 = 4
6. Potential deposit creation = initial excess reserves x money multiplier = $7,500 x 4 = $30,000

Exercise 3

1. a. 8.33
   b. 10
   c. 20
2. Increases
3. Increases
4. T

CHAPTER 14

Monetary Policy

Quick Review

- The Federal Reserve System (Fed) controls the money supply by limiting the amount of loans that the banking system can provide from any given level of reserves, and it also controls the amount of reserves in the system.
- The Federal Reserve System is composed of twelve regional banks located across the country. The regional banks provide several services for the private banks in their region including check clearing, holding bank reserves, providing currency, and providing loans to the private banks.
- The Board of Governors of the Federal Reserve System is the key decision-maker in setting monetary policy. Board members are appointed by the president of the United States for fourteen-year terms.
- There are three primary levers of monetary policy: reserve requirement, discount rate, and open-market operations. Changing the reserve requirement changes both the money multiplier and the level of excess reserves in the banking system. It is the least frequently used tool.
- Private banks can borrow reserves from the Fed at the discount rate. The Fed can change the discount rate, which makes it more or less expensive for banks to borrow from it. Banks can also borrow reserves from other private banks at the federal funds rate.
- The principal monetary policy tool is open-market operations, which involves the buying or selling of U.S. government bonds in the open market by the Fed.
- The goal of monetary policy is to provide the appropriate level of aggregate demand (AD) in the economy to achieve the output, employment, and price level goals. Expansionary monetary policy shifts the AD curve to the right; restrictive policy shifts it to the left.
- The slope of the aggregate supply (AS) curve determines the impact of a given shift in AD. If AS is upward sloping then an increase in output is accompanied by an increase in the price level.
- Advocates of "discretionary" monetary policy argue that the Fed should be free to counter market instability by changing the growth rate of the money supply. Advocates of fixed "rules" believe the Fed should simply keep the money supply growing at a constant rate. They argue that the Fed itself is a source of instability.

Learning Objectives

After reading the chapter and doing the following exercises you should be able to:

1. Describe how the Federal Reserve is organized.
2. Identify the Fed's three primary policy tools.
3. Explain how open-market operations work.
4. Tell how monetary stimulus or restraint is achieved.
5. Discuss how monetary policy affects macro outcomes.

Using Terms to Remember

Fill in the puzzle on the opposite page with the appropriate terms from the list of Terms to Remember in the text.

Across

3. The most frequently used monetary policy tool.
5. Monetary policy may be used to shift the _________ curve.
6. The Federal Reserve System can use its powers to alter the _________.
8. The interest rate charged by the Fed for reserves it lends to private banks.
9. The use of money and credit controls to change the macroeconomy.
10. Held by banks either as vault cash or as deposits at the regional Federal Reserve bank.

Down

1. The effect of an aggregate demand shift on prices and output depends on the shape of the _________ curve.
2. The number of deposit dollars that the banking system can create from $1 of excess reserves.
4. The rate at which private banks lend reserves to other banks.
7. Bank reserves in excess of required reserves.

Puzzle 14.1

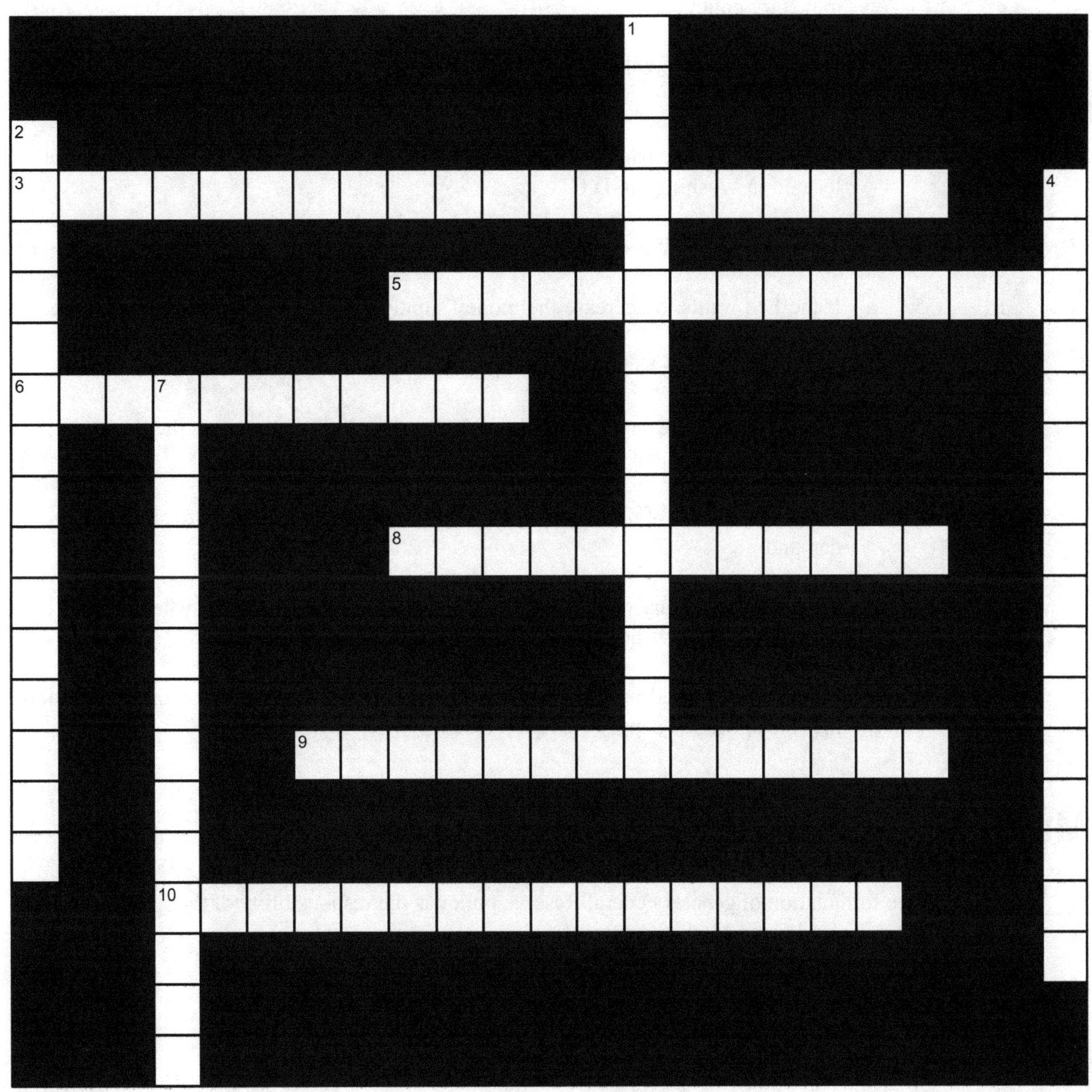

True or False: *Circle your choice and explain why any false statements are incorrect.*

T F 1. The Federal Reserve's control over the money supply is the key mechanism of monetary policy.

T F 2. Monetary policy involves the use of federal government spending to change the money supply.

T F 3. The Fed is not one bank but is actually twelve regional banks with central control located in Washington, D.C.

T F 4. The regional Fed banks hold deposits for private banks but not for individuals.

T F 5. If the Fed wants to decrease the money supply, it can decrease the discount rate.

T F 6. Profit-maximizing banks hold a large amount of excess reserves.

T F 7 When the Fed sells bonds, the quantity of transactions accounts in the banking system decreases and the quantity of loans decreases.

T F 8. The effectiveness of monetary policy depends solely on its ability to shift aggregate demand.

T F 9. Restrictive monetary policy is most effective in reducing inflation when the aggregate supply curve is horizontal.

T F 10. Proponents of fixed rules for monetary policy base their position on the assumption that the aggregate supply curve is vertical.

Multiple Choice: *Select the correct answer.*

_______ 1. The formulation of general Federal Reserve policy is the responsibility of the:
(a) Federal Open Market Committee.
(b) Board of Governors.
(c) Federal Advisory Council.
(d) Regional Federal Reserve banks.

_______ 2. Which of the following serves as the central banker for private banks in the United States?
(a) The twelve regional Federal Reserve banks.
(b) The Executive Branch of the government.
(c) The Board of Governors of the Federal Reserve System.
(d) The Federal Open Market Committee.

_______ 3. Suppose Amy receives a check for $500 from a bank in Dallas. She deposits the check into her account at a New York bank. The New York bank is likely to collect the $500 from the:
(a) U.S. Treasury.
(b) Central Federal Reserve bank in Washington, D.C.
(c) New York regional Federal Reserve bank.
(d) Federal Reserve Board of Governors.

_______ 4. Members of the Federal Reserve Board of Governors are:
(a) Selected by each new president when they appoint their cabinet.
(b) Selected by majority vote at the same time the U.S. president is elected.
(c) Appointed to seven-year terms by Congress.
(d) Appointed for one fourteen-year term by the U.S. president.

_______ 5. Which of the following is *not* a service performed by the Federal Reserve banks?
(a) Clearing checks between commercial banks.
(b) Holding reserves of commercial banks.
(c) Providing currency to commercial banks.
(d) Lend money to individuals.

_______ 6. Which of the following is *not* one of the tools of monetary policy used by the Fed?
(a) Expulsion from Fed membership.
(b) Changing the reserve requirement.
(c) Changing the discount rate.
(d) Performing open-market operations.

_______ 7. A change in the reserve requirement is the tool used least often by the Fed because it:
(a) Does not affect bank reserves.
(b) Can cause abrupt changes in the money supply.
(c) Does not affect the money multiplier.
(d) Has no impact on the lending capacity of the banking system.

_______ 8. Suppose that the banking system has total deposits of $50 billion, a reserve requirement of 0.20, and reserves of $10 billion. If the Fed lowers the reserve requirement to 0.10, the money supply could potentially increase by as much as:
(a) $50 billion.
(b) $5 billion.
(c) $100 billion.
(d) $60 billion.

_______ 9. Suppose that the Fed increases excess reserves in the banking system by $2 billion by buying $2 billion worth of bonds. Assuming the reserve requirement is 0.25, the money supply could potentially increase by as much as:
(a) $2 billion.
(b) $12.5 billion.
(c) $8 billion.
(d) $5 million.

_______ 10. Refer to the News Wire article in the text titled "Beijing Seeks to Cool Prices by Reining In Bank Lending." Which of the following could also be used to achieve contractionary monetary policy?
(a) A decrease in the discount rate.
(b) An increase in personal income taxes.
(c) An increase in the sale of bonds by the Fed.
(d) A decrease in immigration restrictions.

_______ 11. If the Fed wants to decrease the money supply, it can:
(a) Decrease the reserve requirement.
(b) Increase taxes.
(c) Buy bonds in the open market.
(d) Raise the discount rate.

_______ 12. When the Fed wants to increase the lending capacity of banks, it:
(a) Reduces the reserve requirement.
(b) Raises the discount rate.
(c) Reduces the tax rate.
(d) Sells securities.

_______ 13. When the Fed raises the discount rate, this policy:
(a) Reduces the cost of borrowing from the Fed for member banks.
(b) Increases the level of reserves in the banking system.
(c) Is an indication that the Fed wants to shift aggregate demand to the right.
(d) Is a signal that the Fed is moving toward a more restrictive monetary policy.

_______ 14. The monetarist aggregate supply curve is:
(a) Perfectly vertical at the natural rate of unemployment.
(b) Upward-sloping to the right.
(c) Flat until full employment is reached.
(d) Flat.

_______ 15. Refer to Figure 14.6 in the text. The shift in aggregate demand from AD_1 to AD_2 could have been caused by:
(a) Expansionary monetary policy or contractionary fiscal policy.
(b) Contractionary monetary policy or expansionary fiscal policy.
(c) Expansionary monetary or fiscal policy.
(d) Contractionary monetary or fiscal policy.

_______ 16. The policy lever most commonly used by the Fed is:
(a) Changes in the discount rate.
(b) Buying and selling securities.
(c) Changes in the reserve requirement.
(d) Foreign-exchange operations.

_______ 17. Expansionary monetary policy will:
(a) Decrease bank lending capacity.
(b) Raise interest rates.
(c) Shift aggregate demand to the left.
(d) Encourage people to borrow and spend more money.

_______ 18. An increase in the money supply will:
(a) Always cause inflation.
(b) Never cause inflation.
(c) Cause inflation only if aggregate supply is horizontal.
(d) Cause inflation if aggregate supply is upward sloping.

_______ 19. The vertical aggregate supply curve implies that in the long run:
(a) The rate of unemployment can be permanently reduced by more expansionary monetary and fiscal policies.
(b) The Federal Reserve can bring the economy to equilibrium by altering the money supply.
(c) Monetary policy only affects the rate of inflation.
(d) Discretionary monetary policy affects output.

_______ 20. Tight monetary policy:
(a) Reduces aggregate demand and increases inflationary pressures.
(b) Reduces both aggregate demand and inflationary pressures.
(c) Increases both aggregate demand and inflationary pressures.
(d) Increases aggregate demand and reduces inflationary pressures.

Problems and Applications

The three exercises below demonstrate how monetary policy might work in a hypothetical situation.

Exercise 1

The focus of this exercise is the reserve requirement and its impact on deposit creation.

Suppose the Fed wishes to expand M1. Carefully read the assumptions below and then work through the exercise step-by-step to achieve the policy objective. Assume:

- The banks in the system have initially $300 million of transactions-account liabilities.
- The banking system initially has no excess reserves.
- The initial reserve requirement is 0.20.
- The banks make loans in the full amount of any excess reserves that they acquire.
- All loans flow back into the banking system as transactions accounts.

The combined balance sheet of the banks in the system is shown in Table 14.1.

Table 14.1 Balance sheet of banking system when reserve requirement is 0.20 (millions of dollars)

Assets		*Liabilities*	
Total reserves	$60	Transactions accounts	$300
Required = $60			
Excess = $0			
Securities	$100		
Loans	$140		
Total	$300	Total	$300

1. Suppose the Fed lowers the reserve requirement to 0.10. How many dollars of excess reserves does this create? $ ____________.

2. How large are required reserves now? $ ____________.

3. How large are total reserves now? $ ____________.

4. What is the additional lending capacity of the banking system due to the change in the reserve requirement from 0.20 to 0.10? $ ____________.

5. Reconstruct the balance sheet in Table 14.2 to show the new totals for the accounts affected in the banking system because of the loans generated in Question 4 above.

Table 14.2 Balance sheet of banking system when reserve requirement is 0.10 (millions of dollars)

Assets		*Liabilities*	
Total reserves	$______	Transactions accounts	$______
Required $_____			
Excess $_____			
Securities	$______		
Loans	$______		
Total	$______	Total	$______

6. The money supply (M1) has expanded by $ ____________.

7. Total reserves have increased by $ ____________.

8. Loans have increased by $ ____________.

Exercise 2

The focus of this exercise is open-market operations and the impact on the money supply.

Suppose the banking system faces the balance sheet given in Table 14.3 and suppose further that:

- The banking system initially has no excess reserves.
- The reserve requirement is 0.25.
- The banks make loans in the full amount of any excess reserves that they acquire.
- All loans flow back into the banking system as transactions accounts.

Table 14.3 Balance sheet of banking system (millions of dollars)

Assets		*Liabilities*	
Total reserves	$75	Transactions accounts	$300
Required = $75			
Excess = $0			
Securities	$100		
Loans	$125		
Total	$300	Total	$300

1. Suppose the Fed Open Market Committee buys $10 million of securities from the commercial banking system. This action causes excess reserves to increase by $ ____________.

2. Complete the balance sheet in Table 14.4 after loans have been made. Assume the banking system expands its loans and transactions accounts by the maximum amount. (*Remember:* The reserve ratio is 0.25.)

Table 14.4 Balance sheet of banking system after expansion of loans and deposits (millions of dollars)

Assets		*Liabilities*	
Total reserves	$______	Transactions accounts	$______
Required $_____			
Excess $_____			
Securities	$______		
Loans	$______		
Total	$______	Total	$______

3. As a result of the open-market operations, the money supply has expanded by a total of $ ____________.

4. Total reserves have increased by $ ____________.

5. Loans have increased by $ ____________.

Exercise 3

This exercise examines what might happen if the Fed decided to decrease the discount rate.

1. A decrease in the discount rate would cause M1 to (increase, decrease, stay the same).

2. This change in the money supply would cause aggregate (demand, supply) to shift to the (left, right).

3. What other actions could the Fed take to achieve the same impact on aggregate demand?

____

4. Suppose aggregate demand shifts to the right. Determine the change to the equilibrium price level and output level (increase, decrease, or no change) for each of the aggregate supply curve shapes in Table 14.5.

Table 14.5

Aggregate supply curve	*Change in price level*	*Change in output level*
upward sloping	____________	____________
horizontal	____________	____________
vertical	____________	____________

Exercise 4

Reread the News Wire article in the text titled "Fed Cuts Key Interest Rate Half-Point to 1 Percent." Then answer the following questions.

1. Which rates did the Fed cut? ____

2. How will banks be affected by the cuts? ________________________________

   ____

3. According to the article, ". . . the central bank has dramatically ______________ direct loans to banks . . ." *Ceteris paribus*, bank borrowing from the Fed causes a(n) (increase; decrease) in aggregate demand.

Common Errors

The first statement in each "common error" below is incorrect. Each incorrect statement is followed by a corrected version and an explanation.

1. Bank reserves are required for the safety of depositors' money. *Incorrect!*
   Bank reserves are for control of the money supply. *Correct!*
   Many people have the idea that bank reserves provide for the safety of depositors' money. They don't. The amount of demand deposits is several times larger than the amount of reserves. The FDIC provides for safety of deposits by insuring them. Reserves are not principally for depositors' safety.

2. Deposits of cash are necessary to start the process of lending and deposit creation. *Incorrect!*
   To start the lending process, the banks must acquire reserves from outside of the banking system. *Correct!*
   Many find it difficult to understand that for deposit creation to occur, the banking system needs only to acquire reserves from outside the system or to stretch existing reserves further. It may acquire reserves by selling a security to the Fed or by borrowing from the Fed. When an individual bank acquires reserves from another bank its reserves increase, but the other bank's reserves shrink. Thus, the system has no more reserves after the transaction than it had before, and so the system's lending capacity is unchanged.

3. When the Fed sells government bonds in open market operations, it is increasing the money supply. *Incorrect!*
   When the Fed sells government bonds in open market operations, it is decreasing the money supply. *Correct!*
   When the Fed sells a bond, money is paid to the Fed by the purchaser. This money is then kept by the Fed and is no longer part of the money supply because it is out of circulation. The money supply decreases.

4. Monetary policy is easy to determine and administer. *Incorrect!*
   Monetary policy is difficult to determine and administer. *Correct!*
   There are many variables involved in monetary policy that make it difficult to prescribe and implement. These variables include the timing and duration of a particular policy, unanticipated events on the fiscal side, and problems abroad. The Fed's policy-makers analyze the available data and do the best they can to achieve a given objective, which often involves compromises. The process is much more complicated than it seems.

~ ANSWERS ~

Using Terms to Remember

Across

3. open-market operations
5. aggregate demand
6. money supply
8. discount rate
9. monetary policy
10. required reserves

Down

1. aggregate supply
2. money multiplier
4. federal funds rate
7. excess reserves

True or False

1. T
2. F Monetary policy involves the use of money and credit controls to change the money supply.
3. T
4. T
5. F If the Fed wants to decrease the money supply, it should increase the discount rate.
6. F Profit-maximizing banks try to keep their excess reserves as low as possible.
7. T
8. F The effectiveness of monetary policy depends on its ability to shift aggregate demand and the shape of the AS curve.
9. F Restrictive monetary policy is most effective in reducing inflation when the aggregate supply curve is *vertical*.
10. T

Multiple Choice

1. b	5. d	9. c	13. d	17. d
2. a	6. a	10. c	14. a	18. d
3. c	7. b	11. d	15. c	19. c
4. d	8. a	12. a	16. b	20. b

Problems and Applications

Exercise 1

1. $30 million
2. $30 million
3. $60 million
4. $300 million
5. See Table 14.2 Answer.
6. $300 million
7. Zero
8. $300 million

Table 14.2 Answer (millions of dollars)

Assets		*Liabilities*	
Total reserves	$60	Transactions accounts	$600
Required = $60			
Excess = $0			
Securities	$100		
Loans	$440		
Total	$600	Total	$600

Exercise 2

1. $10 million

2. **Table 14.4 Answer (millions of dollars)**

Assets		*Liabilities*	
Total reserves	$85	Transactions accounts	$340
Required = $85			
Excess = $0			
Securities	$90		
Loans	$165		
Total	$340	Total	$340

3. $40 million
4. $10 million
5. $40 million

Exercise 3

1. Increase
2. Demand, right
3. An open-market purchase of government securities or a decrease in the reserve requirement

4. **Table 14.5 Answer (millions of dollars)**

Aggregate supply curve	*Change in price level*	*Change in output level*
upward sloping	increase	increase
horizontal	no change	increase
vertical	increase	no change

Exercise 4

1. Its target for the federal funds rate and the discount rate
2. It will cost banks less to borrow reserves from other banks and from the Fed.
3. Increased; increase

CHAPTER 15

Economic Growth

Quick Review

- Economic growth refers to increases in real GDP. Growth is desired by virtually every society because it provides for possible improvements in the standard of living.
- In the short run, economic growth can be achieved by increased capacity utilization, represented by a movement toward the production possibilities curve.
- In the long run, growth requires an increase in capacity itself, represented by a rightward shift of the production possibilities curve. This results in a rightward shift in the long-run aggregate supply curve as well.
- GDP per capita is a basic measure of living standards. GDP per worker is a measure of productivity. Increases in productivity, rather than increases in the quantity of available resources, have been the primary source of U.S. economic growth in the past.
- The sources of productivity gains include improved labor skills, increased investment and the resulting increase in the nation's capital stock, technological advances, and improved management skills and techniques.
- Government policies play a role in fostering economic growth. Policies that encourage growth include education and training, immigration, and programs that promote investment and saving. All of these can lead to increases in both the quality and quantity of resources available.
- Macroeconomic policies should be evaluated in terms of their effect on long-run aggregate supply. Budget deficits may reduce the level of economic growth through "crowding out." This occurs when increased government spending, financed by borrowing, causes a reduction in the level of private investment. Budget surpluses can increase economic growth and cause "crowding in."
- Government regulation may also inhibit economic growth. Regulation of both factor and product markets tends to raise production costs and reduce supply.
- Continued economic growth is desirable as long as it brings a higher living standard for a country and an increased ability to produce and consume goods and services that society desires.

Learning Objectives

After reading the chapter and doing the following exercises you should be able to:

1. Specify how economic growth is measured.
2. Describe what GDP per capita and GDP per worker measure.
3. Illustrate how productivity increases.
4. Explain how government policy affects growth.
5. Discuss why economic growth is desirable.

Using Terms to Remember

Fill in the puzzle on the opposite page with the appropriate terms from the list of Terms to Remember in the text.

Across

1. The actual quantity of goods and services produced, valued in constant prices.
4. Average GDP.
7. All persons over the age of 16 who are working for pay or looking for work.
8. The alternative combinations of goods and services that could be produced in a given time period with all available resources and technology.
12. Percentage change in real GDP from one period to another.
13. The proportion of the adult population that is employed.

Down

2. An expansion of production possibilities.
3. Output per unit of input.
5. Income minus consumption.
6. A decrease in private-sector borrowing and investment because of increased government borrowing.
9. The current dollar value of output produced within a country's border.
10. Expenditures on new plant and equipment.
11. An increase in private-sector borrowing and spending because of a decrease in government borrowing.

Puzzle 15.1

True or False: *Circle your choice and explain why any false statements are incorrect.*

T F 1. Nominal GDP is used to measure economic growth.

T F 2. When an economy moves from a point inside its production possibilities curve to a point on the curve, potential GDP has increased.

T F 3. In order for an economy to produce a combination of goods and services beyond its current production possibilities curve, its productive capacity must increase.

T F 4. When population grows by a larger percentage than nominal GDP does, GDP per capita increases.

T F 5. A major goal of short-run economic policy is to achieve full employment.

T F 6. A shift of the production possibilities curve outward corresponds to an increase in aggregate demand.

T F 7. Long-run economic policy attempts to shift the production possibilities curve outward.

T F 8. If the literacy rate increases, the production possibilities curve will shift to the right.

T F 9. Overall, immigration has had a negative impact on the U.S. economy over time.

T F 10. Deregulation can lead to an increase in the aggregate supply curve by lowering production costs.

Multiple Choice: *Select the correct answer.*

_______ 1. When an economy is producing inside its production possibilities curve, this is an indication that:
(a) There are not enough resources available to reach the production possibilities curve.
(b) More output could be produced with existing resources.
(c) The level of technology is limiting the level of production.
(d) Workers are lazy or unskilled.

_______ 2. In order to produce a combination of goods and services outside of the current production possibilities curve, an economy would have to:
(a) Use more of its existing resources.
(b) Raise the prices of goods and services so that firms would produce more.
(c) Find more resources, for example, for such a combination to be possible.
(d) It will never be able to produce a combination of goods and services outside its current production possibilities curve.

_______ 3. A major goal of short-run macroeconomic policy is to:
   (a) Shift the production possibilities curve outward.
   (b) Shift the aggregate supply curve to the left.
   (c) Shift the aggregate demand curve to the left.
   (d) Move toward the production possibilities curve.

_______ 4. Economic growth in the long run:
   (a) Shifts the production possibilities curve outward.
   (b) Moves the economy along the production possibilities curve.
   (c) Moves the economy onto the production possibilities curve.
   (d) Shifts the aggregate supply curve to the left.

_______ 5. When the production possibilities curve shifts outward, we can conclude that:
   (a) GDP per capita has definitely increased.
   (b) Output has definitely increased.
   (c) Aggregate supply has definitely increased.
   (d) Population has definitely increased.

_______ 6. Real GDP is better than nominal GDP in making comparisons of GDP over time because:
   (a) Nominal GDP can increase simply because of price increases.
   (b) Real GDP is not affected by output changes.
   (c) Nominal GDP is the hypothetical output that would be produced at full employment.
   (d) Real GDP is not affected by changes in productivity or the size of the labor force.

_______ 7. Which of the following is definitely true if nominal GDP increases?
   (a) The living standard has improved.
   (b) The quantity of output has increased.
   (c) The production possibilities have increased.
   (d) The value of output has increased.

_______ 8. Suppose that real GDP in an economy is expected to increase at a consistent 4 percent annually in the future. Use the "rule of 72" as explained in the text to estimate how many years it will take for production to double.
   (a) 4 years.
   (b) 8 years.
   (c) 18 years.
   (d) 72 years.

_______ 9. Growth in GDP per capita is attained only when:
   (a) There is growth in population.
   (b) There is growth in output.
   (c) The growth in population exceeds output growth.
   (d) The growth in output exceeds population growth.

_______ 10. Which of the following is the best measure of the living standard for an economy?
   (a) GDP per worker.
   (b) GDP per capita.
   (c) Rule of 72.
   (d) Population growth rate.

_______ 11. In many less developed countries GDP per capita is declining because:
(a) Population growth is greater than the growth in GDP.
(b) Population growth is negative.
(c) Capital investment is zero.
(d) GDP is declining.

_______ 12. Which of the following is likely to contribute to an improvement in the productivity of labor?
(a) A reduction in the amount of capital per worker.
(b) An increase in the money supply.
(c) Greater government spending on welfare.
(d) Greater expenditures on training and education.

_______ 13. According to the text, over time which of the following is responsible for the greatest contribution to economic growth in the United States?
(a) Increases in the quantity of labor.
(b) Increases in the amount of capital per worker.
(c) Research and development that result in innovation and improvements.
(d) Improved labor skills due to increased education and training.

_______ 14. More technically-advanced capital makes its contribution to productivity by:
(a) Reducing population growth.
(b) Enhancing labor productivity.
(c) Reducing profits for businesses.
(d) Increasing nominal GDP.

_______ 15. Continual increases in GDP per capita are most likely to come from:
(a) Increases in output per worker.
(b) Increases in the employment rate.
(c) Decreases in population growth.
(d) Increases in inflation.

_______ 16. Productivity is likely to increase because of all of the following *except*:
(a) More research and development.
(b) Improvements in the management of labor.
(c) Savings incentives.
(d) Stricter immigration policies.

_______ 17. Which of the following does *not* affect the aggregate supply curve?
(a) Immigration policies.
(b) Minimum-wage laws.
(c) The reserve requirement.
(d) Marginal tax rates.

_______ 18. Which of the following policies is most likely to increase the aggregate supply curve?
(a) Stricter occupational safety regulations.
(b) A cut in the capital gains tax.
(c) An increase in the minimum wage.
(d) An increase in the discount rate.

_______ 19. Which of the following statements is true regarding the "crowding out" effect?
(a) It results in dollars being diverted from business investment to government spending.
(b) It always acts as a constraint on economic growth.
(c) It occurs at any point in the business cycle.
(d) All of the above.

_______ 20. The current problems in the United States of congested highways, poor air quality, and global warming are primarily the result of:
(a) Too many goods and services.
(b) The mix of output produced.
(c) Too much government regulation.
(d) Excessively high levels of GDP per capita.

Problems and Applications

Exercise 1

This exercise focuses on the difference in short-run versus long-run growth.

Refer to Figure 15.1 to answer Questions 1-4.

Figure 15.1

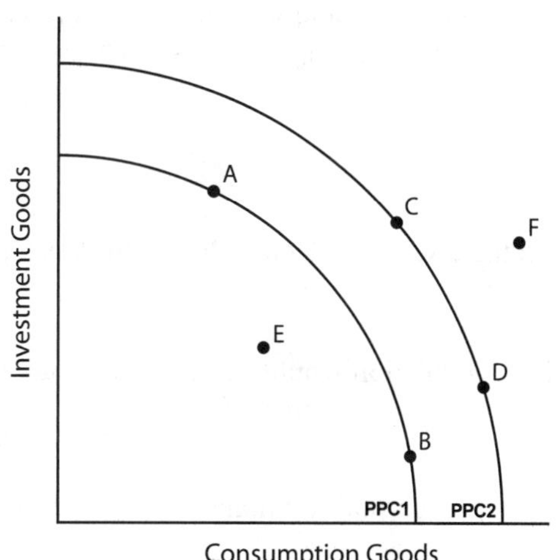

1. Assume the economy is producing at point *E*, and the productive capacity is represented by PPC1. A movement to point *B* represents an increase in (short-run, long-run) growth.

2. If the productive capacity is represented by PPC1, the movement from point *E* to point *B* results in increased output because of (increased use of existing capacity, increased capacity).

3. Assume the economy is now producing at point *B*, and is using all of its productive capacity. A movement to point *D* is possible if the economy experiences (short-run, long-run) growth.

4. Assume point *B* initially represents full employment. Movement to point *D* means that output has increased because of (increased use of existing capacity, increased capacity). This type of growth implies a (leftward, rightward) shift of the long-run _______________________ curve.

Exercise 2

The following exercise shows how GDP can be used to indicate the living standard and the rate of economic growth in an economy.

1. Using the data in Table 15.1, calculate the U.S. GDP per capita for 2007 and 2012. Record your answers in Table 15.1. (Answers may differ slightly due to rounding.)

Table 15.1

	2007	*2012*	*Percentage change*
(1) U.S. GDP (billions of dollars)	$14,029	$15,682	______
(2) U.S. population (thousands)	301,696	314,278	______
(3) U.S. GDP per capita (dollars per person)	$______	$______	______

2. According to Table 15.1, the U.S. living standard (increased, decreased, stayed the same) from 2007 to 2012.

3. Using the data in Table 15.1, calculate the percentage change in U.S. GDP, U.S. population, and U.S. GDP per capita from 2007 to 2012. Record your answers in Table 15.1.

4. From 2007 to 2012, what was the average annual growth rate for U.S. GDP? __________

5. If the growth rate calculated in Question 4 was the *actual* growth rate each year *not the average*, how long should it take for GDP to double according to Table 15.1 in the text? __________

Exercise 3

Reread the News Wire article in the text titled "House Poised to Pass STEM Immigration Bill" and answer the following questions.

1. Based on the article, which population would be allowed to stay in the United States?

   ____

2. Why do you think this immigration policy emphasizes degrees in the STEM disciplines?

   ____

Common Errors

The first statement in the "common error" below is incorrect. The incorrect statement is followed by a corrected version and an explanation.

1. Labor productivity increases when more output is produced per dollar of wages. *Incorrect!*
   Labor productivity increases when more units of output are produced per unit of labor. *Correct!*
   Productivity changes are not directly related to wage levels. Wage levels reflect a large number of influences embodied in the demand and supply curves for labor. Productivity, however, is a physical measure of the relationship between units of product and the amount of labor needed to produce the product.

2. Zero economic growth impacts all income groups equally. *Incorrect!*
Zero economic growth has a greater negative impact on low-income groups than on high-income groups, in general. *Correct!*
Zero economic growth means that GDP does not change from one year to another. If population grows by even the slightest amount, then GDP per capita must decrease. The only way that lower-income groups could have more would be if higher-income groups took less.

3. Zero economic growth would alleviate the world's pollution problem. *Incorrect!*
The only way to alleviate the world's pollution problem is through economic growth. *Correct!*
Zero economic growth might maintain pollution at its current level, but it would not decrease pollution. However, as the economy grows, new technology allows existing resources to be used more efficiently thus creating less pollution. The economy can actually reduce the level of pollution as it grows.

4. The world will run out of resources eventually. *Incorrect!*
The world will begin using its resources more efficiently before it runs out of resources. *Correct!*
The world will stop relying on theoretically exhaustible resources long before they run out. At some point it will become cheaper to recycle, substitute new resources, and develop new technology than to rely on the current resources that are in jeopardy of being depleted. For example, as energy costs continue to increase, there is more incentive to move to renewable energy resources such as solar and wind power.

5. A centrally planned economy can easily improve economic growth by shifting toward a market-based economy. *Incorrect!*
A centrally planned economy *cannot* easily improve economic growth by shifting toward a market-based economy. *Correct!*
The shift from a centrally planned economy to a market-based economy may result in an improvement in economic growth, but certain criteria are necessary. These criteria include a well defined property rights system and a legal system that is devoid of corruption. Without these fundamental principles, investors will lose faith in the economy and will not make the necessary investments. Without investment, economic growth will halt or even contract. This has been demonstrated by the Russian economy.

~ ANSWERS ~

Using Terms to Remember

Across

1. real GDP
4. GDP per capita
7. labor force
8. production possibilities
12. growth rate
13. employment rate

Down

2. economic growth
3. productivity
5. saving
6. crowding out
9. nominal GDP
10. investment
11. crowding in

True or False

1. F Real GDP, *not* nominal GDP, is used to measure economic growth.
2. F Potential GDP increases only when the production possibilities curve shifts outward.

3. T
4. F In order for GDP per capita to grow, nominal GDP must grow by a larger percentage than population.
5. T
6. F A shift of the production possibilities curve outward corresponds to an increase in aggregate supply.
7. T
8. T
9. F Immigration has significantly increased the labor force and contributed to the outward shift of the U.S. production possibilities curve over time.
10. T

Multiple Choice

1. b	5. c	9. d	13. c	17. c
2. c	6. a	10. b	14. b	18. b
3. d	7. d	11. a	15. a	19. a
4. a	8. c	12. d	16. d	20. b

Problems and Applications

Exercise 1

1. Short-run
2. Increased use of existing capacity
3. Long-run
4. Increased capacity, rightward, aggregate supply

Exercise 2

1. **Table 15.1 Answer**

	2007	*2012*	*Percentage change*
(1) U.S. GDP (billions of dollars)	$14,029	$15,682	11.8%
(2) U.S. population (thousands)	301,696	314,278	4.2%
(3) U.S. GDP per capita (dollars per person)	$46,500	$49,898	7.3%

2. Increased
3. See Table 15.1 Answer.
4. 2.4 percent (11.8 ÷ 5 = 2.36 or 2.4)
5. Appromimately 30 years (72 ÷ 2.4) using the rule of 72

Exercise 3

1. Foreign students who graduate from qualified U.S. schools with degrees in advanced technical areas or the STEM disciplines.
2. Because an increase in the number of workers with training in the STEM fields means an increase in human capital, which contributes to economic growth.

CHAPTER 16

Theory and Reality

Quick Review

- Government policy-makers have many tools with which to design and implement the ideal "package" of macro policies.
- The basic tools of fiscal policy are taxes and government spending. Automatic stabilizers, such as income taxes and unemployment benefits, help to stabilize any disruptions in the economy by responding automatically to changes in national income.
- Monetary policy, controlled by the Federal Reserve, uses open-market operations, changes in the discount rate, and occasional changes in the reserve requirement to impact the macroeconomy. Both monetary and fiscal policy shift the aggregate demand curve.
- Supply-side policy focuses on shifting the aggregate supply curve, which allows for economic growth. Tax cuts, government deregulation, education, training, and research are supply-side tools.
- To end a recession, we can cut taxes, increase government spending, or expand the money supply. To curb inflation, we can reverse each of these policy levers. To overcome stagflation, fiscal and monetary policies can be combined with supply-side incentives.
- Recurring economic slowdowns with accompanying increases in unemployment and nagging inflation suggest that obstacles may stand in the way of successful policy-making. In addition, there are opportunity costs for all policy decisions, and economic goals may even conflict with one another.
- Policymaking is an inexact science for many reasons. Measurement problems exist because data are incomplete and take months or years to report. Furthermore, we must rely on inherently uncertain forecasts about the economy, and we are unsure just how the economy will respond to specific policy choices. Implementation problems occur because of the time it takes Congress and the president to agree on an appropriate plan of action. Finally, there is always the chance that any policy may be more politically motivated than economically desirable.
- Those who favor discretionary policies believe that active intervention is necessary. Others believe fine-tuning is not possible and favor fixed policy rules.

Learning Objectives

After reading the chapter and doing the following exercises you should be able to:

1. Identify the major tools of macro policy.
2. Explain how macro tools can fix macro problems.
3. Depict the track record of macro outcomes.
4. Describe major impediments to policy success.
5. Discuss the pros and cons of discretionary policy.

Using Terms to Remember

Fill in the puzzle on the opposite page with the appropriate terms from the list of Terms to Remember in the text.

Across

1. Alternating periods of expansion and contraction in the economy.
3. Government spending and receipts that occur because of a change in the business cycle.
5. Begins on October 1 for the U.S. federal government.
6. The attempt to correct even small changes in the macroeconomy.
7. Equal to 1 ÷ (1 - MPC).
10. The goal of __________ is to increase aggregate supply.
11. The Federal Reserve uses monetary policy tools to change the __________.
12. The simultaneous occurrence of substantial unemployment and inflation.

Down

2. Occurs because of the mismatch between worker's skills and the available jobs.
4. The use of open-market operations, discount-rate changes, and reserve requirements to change the macroeconomy.
8. The difference between full-employment GDP and equilibrium GDP.
9. The use of government spending and taxes to change the macroeconomy.

Puzzle 16.1

True or False: *Circle your choice and explain why any false statements are incorrect.*

T F 1. The failure of macroeconomic policy is reflected in the fact that since World War II, the ups and downs of the business cycle have become more severe.

T F 2. The federal budget contains the details of fiscal policy.

T F 3. Automatic stabilizers tend to exaggerate the business cycle.

T F 4. During a period of inflation, monetarists advocate a policy of patience.

T F 5. Good economic policy and political objectives often conflict.

T F 6. The shape of the aggregate demand curve is the most important determinant of the effectiveness of fiscal and monetary policy.

T F 7. Stagflation is caused by a leftward shift of the aggregate supply curve.

T F 8. "Fine-tuning" the economy is a generally accepted approach to macro policy because time lags in implementation are not a problem.

T F 9. The Fed uses monetary policy in an effort to change interest rates and ultimately shift the aggregate demand curve.

T F 10. Macroeconomic forecasts from different computer models often differ because they are based on different macroeconomic theories (e.g., Keynesian, supply-side).

Multiple Choice: *Select the correct answer.*

_____ 1. Which of the following is an accurate statement concerning the performance of macroeconomic policy in the United States?
(a) We consistently reach our goals of full employment, price stability, and economic growth.
(b) The business cycle is no longer an issue.
(c) Fiscal and monetary policy are no longer used.
(d) The ups and downs of the business cycle have been less severe since World War II.

_____ 2. Which of the following is most likely to advocate the use of fine tuning?
(a) Supply-siders.
(b) Classical economists.
(c) Keynesians.
(d) Monetarists.

_____ 3. As the economy grows out of a recession, automatic stabilizers cause:
(a) Larger budget deficits.
(b) Government spending to decrease.
(c) The money supply to increase.
(d) Tax revenues to be reduced.

_______ 4. When the Fed cuts interest rates, it is attempting to:
(a) Increase aggregate demand.
(b) Increase aggregate supply.
(c) Decrease aggregate demand.
(d) Decrease aggregate supply.

_______ 5. Fiscal and monetary policy are most effective in reducing inflation when the aggregate:
(a) Supply curve is horizontal.
(b) Supply curve is vertical.
(c) Supply is upward sloping but not vertical.
(d) Demand curve is vertical.

_______ 6. Which of the following is considered an appropriate policy by a modern Keynesian during an inflationary period?
(a) Expand the money supply and increase government spending.
(b) Expand the money supply and decrease government spending.
(c) Contract the money supply and increase government spending.
(d) Contract the money supply and decrease government spending.

_______ 7. Expansionary fiscal and monetary policy are *not* effective in increasing the level of output when the aggregate:
(a) Supply curve is horizontal.
(b) Supply curve is vertical.
(c) Supply is upward sloping but not vertical.
(d) Demand curve is vertical.

_______ 8. The News Wire article in the text titled "Tough Calls in Economic Forecasting" basically says that:
(a) Recessions are frequent and easy to predict.
(b) All past recessions have been predicted in advance.
(c) Economic assumptions are accurate in predicting recessions.
(d) Recessions cannot be accurately predicted.

_______ 9. Refer to Table 16.3 in the text. Fed policy during this period can be described as:
(a) Consistently expansionary.
(b) Consistently restrictive.
(c) At times expansionary; at other times restrictive.
(d) Following fixed rules.

_______ 10. Based on supply-side policy, the aggregate supply curve should be shifted to the ________ during periods of inflation and to the ________ during a recession.
(a) Right; left.
(b) Left; right.
(c) Right; right.
(d) Left; left.

_______ 11. Supply-side policy is designed to:
(a) Move the economy from a point inside the production possibilities curve to a point on it, and shift the aggregate supply curve to the left.
(b) Move the economy from a point inside the production possibilities curve to a point on it, and shift the aggregate supply curve to the right.
(c) Shift the production possibilities curve outward and shift the aggregate supply curve to the left.
(d) Shift the production possibilities curve outward and shift the aggregate supply curve to the right.

_______ 12. Which of the following is the monetarist policy for fighting a recession?
(a) Decrease government spending.
(b) Patience (i.e., laissez-faire approach).
(c) Provide tax incentives to increase investment.
(d) Contract the money supply at a more rapid rate.

_______ 13. Which of the following could be both a supply-side and a fiscal policy tool during a recession?
(a) Tax cuts.
(b) Deregulation.
(c) Worker training programs.
(d) Liberalized immigration laws.

_______ 14. Which of the following would be recommended by supply-siders to fight stagflation?
(a) Raise tax rates.
(b) Increase the money supply.
(c) Deregulation.
(d) Increase government expenditure.

_______ 15. Refer to Table 16.2 in the text. Fiscal policy during this period can be described as:
(a) Consistently expansionary.
(b) Consistently contractionary.
(c) Following fixed policy rules.
(d) Expansionary in some cases and contractionary at other times.

_______ 16. Many economists argue that the CPI overstates inflation by two to three percentage points. From the point of view of those designing economic policy, this is an example of:
(a) A goal conflict.
(b) A measurement problem.
(c) A design problem.
(d) An implementation problem.

_______ 17. The problem of deciding whether to provide aid to foreign countries when there are unresolved problems at home is an example of:
(a) A goal conflict.
(b) A measurement problem.
(c) A design problem.
(d) An implementation problem.

_______ 18. The time it takes for Congress to deliberate over fiscal policy is an example of:
(a) A goal conflict.
(b) An implementation problem.
(c) A design problem.
(d) A measurement problem.

_______ 19. The political business cycle refers to:
(a) The ups and downs in overall business activity.
(b) The political independence of the Fed's Board of Governors.
(c) The concept of politicians stimulating the economy before an election, then tightening fiscal policy afterward.
(d) Illegal behavior on the part of politicians.

_______ 20. Advocates of fixed policy rules believe:
(a) That discretionary policies can improve macro outcomes.
(b) Appropriate macro policy includes a constant increase in the money supply.
(c) Appropriate macro policy includes a constant balance in the federal budget.
(d) The economy is better off if discretionary policy is abandoned.

Problems and Applications

Exercise 1

This exercise will help you recognize the inherent tradeoffs in the economy.

Table 16.1 presents hypothetical data on interest rates, government expenditures, taxes, exports, imports, investment, consumption, a price index, and unemployment for four levels of equilibrium income (GDP). These items appear frequently in newspaper articles about the economy.

Table 16.1 Level of key economic indicators, by GDP level (billions of dollars per year)

Interest rate	15%	11%	7%	3%
Government expenditures	$500	$500	$500	$500
Taxes	300	400	600	700
Budget balance	_____	_____	_____	_____
Exports	300	300	300	300
Imports	260	280	300	320
Investment	100	200	300	500
Consumption	4,000	4,500	5,000	6,000
Nominal GDP	_____	_____	_____	_____
Price index	1.00	1.00	1.02	1.10
Real GDP (constant dollars)	_____	_____	_____	_____
Unemployment rate	10%	8%	5%	3%

1. Compute the federal budget balance, nominal GDP, and real GDP in Table 16.1, for each interest rate level.
(*Hint:* Remember the formula $C + I + G + [X - M] = \text{GDP}$)

2. Which policy is most likely being used to achieve each of the situations in Table 16.1?
   (a) Supply-side policy.
   (b) Monetary policy.
   (c) Wage and price controls.
   (d) Labor policy.

3. Which of the following statements best explains why the amount paid in taxes might change as the level of GDP changes in Table 16.1?
   (a) As taxpayers' incomes rise, their marginal tax rates rise.
   (b) Taxpayers experience stagflation as income increases.
   (c) The income tax is regressive.
   (d) The work effort of taxpayers increases as the marginal tax rate rises.

4. The most likely explanation for why the price index changes as the level of GDP changes, as shown in Table 16.1, is that:
   (a) People receive greater income so they can be more discriminating buyers and find the lowest prices.
   (b) Firms receive more orders so productivity rises allowing inflation to ease.
   (c) Businesses receive greater income so they have an incentive to expand capacity and must pass the cost of the increased capacity on to consumers in the form of higher prices.
   (d) People receive greater income so they spend it, and if the economy is near full employment, prices begin to rise.

5. The most logical reason for why unemployment changes as the level of GDP changes, as shown in Table 16.1, is that as GDP rises:
   (a) People do not need jobs and leave the labor force.
   (b) Automatic stabilizers provide increased benefits to the unemployed, keeping them out of the labor force.
   (c) Aggregate demand rises, stimulating the derived demand for labor.
   (d) Inflation causes real income to fall and employment to decrease.

Exercise 2

This exercise shows the difficulties faced by policy-makers because of the inevitable tradeoffs that exist in the economy.

Table 16.2 presents data on government expenditure, taxes, a price index, unemployment, and pollution for four levels of equilibrium income (GDP). These items appear frequently in newspaper articles about the economy.

Table 16.2 Level of key economic indicators, by GDP level (billions of dollars per year)

Indicator	*Nominal GDP*			
	$120	*$160*	*$200*	*$240*
Government expenditure	$0	$20	$35	$50
Taxes	18	24	30	36
Budget balance	____	____	____	____
Price index	1.00	1.00	1.02	1.20
Real GDP (constant dollars)	____	____	____	____
Unemployment rate	15%	7%	4%	3.5%
Pollution index	1.00	1.10	1.80	1.90

1. Compute the federal budget balance and real GDP in Table 16.2 for each level of nominal GDP.

2. Choose the government expenditure level that is best at accomplishing all of the following goals, according to Table 16.2. $ ___________
   - Lowest level of taxes.
   - Lowest pollution index.
   - Lowest inflation rate.

3. Which of the following might induce a policy-maker to choose a higher government expenditure level than the one that answers Question 2?
   (a) High unemployment.
   (b) An inability by government to provide public goods and services.
   (c) Low real income.
   (d) All of the above.

4. Choose the government expenditure level that is best at accomplishing all of the following goals, according to Table 16.2. $ ___________
   - Lowest unemployment rate.
   - Largest amount of government spending.
   - Highest level of real income.

5. The policy that best satisfies the goals in Question 4 is most likely to result in:
   (a) Rapid economic growth accompanied by inflation.
   (b) A recession.
   (c) Stagflation.
   (d) Deflation.

6. Choose the government expenditure level that is best at accomplishing all of the following goals, according to Table 16.2. $ ___________
   - The best attempt at a balanced federal budget.
   - Reasonably low levels of pollution.
   - Price stability.

7. At which government expenditure level does full employment occur? (Use 4 percent unemployment as full employment.) $ ___________

8. If you are a policy-maker faced with the alternatives in Table 16.2, can you say that one of the government expenditure levels is clearly better than all the others? ________

Exercise 3

This exercise tests your ability to choose the appropriate policy initiative to overcome various undesirable economic conditions.

Choose a policy from the list below that would be appropriate to correct the economic conditions at the top of Table 16.3. Place the letter of each item only once in Table 16.3.

a. Deregulation.
b. Discount rate reduced.
c. Discount rate raised.
d. Government spending reduced.
e. Government spending raised.
f. Open-market operations (Fed buys government securities).
g. Open-market operations (Fed sells government securities).
h. Reserve requirement raised.
i. Reserve requirement reduced.
j. Job and skill training.
k. Tax cuts.
l. Tax incentives to alter the structure of supply and demand.
m. Tax incentives to encourage saving.
n. Tax increases.

Table 16.3 Economic policies

	Recession	*Inflation*	*Stagflation*
Fiscal policy	1.________	6.________	
	2.________	7.________	
Monetary policy	3.________	8.________	
	4.________	9.________	
	5.________	10.________	
Supply-side policy		11.________	12.________
			13.________
			14.________

Exercise 4

Reread the News Wire article titled "Budget Deficit Sets Record in February" in the text.

1. Based on the article, how large does the Obama administration expect the budget deficit to be for the 2010 budget year? ____________________

2. According to the Obama administration, why are the budget deficits necessary? ____________

____

3. T F The 2009-2012 budget deficits were caused by the 2008-2009 recession and the federal government's fiscal stimulus.

Common Errors

The first statement in each "common error" below is incorrect. Each incorrect statement is followed by a corrected version and an explanation.

1. Fiscal and monetary policies should be consistently applied to stimulate the economy. *Incorrect!*
   Fiscal and monetary policies must be tailored to the specific economic problems faced by the economy. *Correct!*
   The government sometimes needs to apply apparently contradictory monetary and fiscal policies in order to attain quite different goals. For example, an expansionary fiscal policy may be needed to stimulate the economy, but a contractionary monetary policy may be needed to raise interest rates so that foreign capital will be attracted to U.S. financial markets. A policy-maker must weigh the various goals and trade-offs and then decide on the appropriate mix of policies.

2. Fiscal, monetary, and stagflation policies are effective regardless of the current income level of the economy. *Incorrect!*
   The state of the economy in relation to full employment is important in determining the effectiveness of the various policies. *Correct!*
   If the economy is experiencing excess aggregate demand, wage-price controls will be ineffective in reducing inflation. At relatively low levels of GDP, however, wage-price controls can be effective in fighting inflation. Workforce policies are often more effective in matching people with jobs when many people are looking for work than when unemployment is low. It is easier for the government to increase expenditures to stimulate the economy when there is a recession than to cut expenditures to fight inflation.

3. Discretionary fiscal policies are better than automatic stabilizers for daily management of the economy. *Incorrect!*
   Automatic stabilizers are better than discretionary fiscal policies for daily management of the economy. *Correct!*
   There is a significant lag between the time when a problem is recognized in the economy and the development of a policy prescription to address the problem. During this time lag, the economy can change. By the time discretionary fiscal policies are in place and affecting the economy, the economic problem may no longer exist so the policies are inappropriate. As a result, automatic stabilizers are typically a much better way of addressing economic problems.

4. The government has the power to prevent unemployment and inflation but it chooses not to. *Incorrect!*
   The government has very little power to totally prevent unemployment and inflation. *Correct!*
   The government can use policies to address unemployment and inflation, but it cannot prevent these situations from occurring. The government has been relatively successful in reducing the magnitude and duration of unemployment and inflation through the use of monetary and fiscal policies.

~ ANSWERS ~

Using Terms to Remember

Across

1. business cycle
3. automatic stabilizer

Down

2. structural unemployment
4. monetary policy

5. fiscal year
6. fine tuning
7. multiplier
8. GDP gap
9. fiscal policy
10. supply side policy
11. money supply
12. stagflation

True or False

1. F The ups and downs of the business cycle have become less severe since World War II, possibly indicating partial success.
2. T
3. F Automatic stabilizers tend to *smooth out* the business cycle.
4. F During a period of inflation, monetarists advocate reducing the growth rate of the money supply.
5. T
6. F The shape of the aggregate *supply* curve is the most important determinant of the effectiveness of fiscal and monetary policy.
7. T
8. F "Fine-tuning" is not generally accepted because time lags in implementation are a problem (along with goal conflicts and measurement and design problems).
9. T
10. T

Multiple Choice

1. d
2. c
3. b
4. a
5. b
6. d
7. b
8. d
9. c
10. c
11. d
12. b
13. a
14. c
15. d
16. b
17. a
18. b
19. c
20. d

Problems and Applications

Exercise 1

1. **Table 16.1 Answer (billions of dollars per year)**

Interest rate	15%	11%	7%	3%
Budget balance	-$200	-$100	$100	$200
Nominal GDP	$4,640	$5,220	$5,800	$6,980
Real GDP (constant dollars)	$4,640	$5,220	$5,686	$6,345

At the 15% interest rate, the following calculations should have been made, in billions of dollars per year: Budget balance = $300 - $500 = -$200

Nominal GDP = $500 + $300 - $260 + $100 + $4,000 = $4,640

Real GDP = $4,640 ÷ 1.0 = $4,640

2. b
3. a
4. d
5. c

Exercise 2

1. **Table 16.2 Answer (billions of dollars per year)**

Indicator	*Nominal GDP*			
	$120	*$160*	*$200*	*$240*
Budget balance	$18	$4	-$5	-$14
Real GDP (constant dollars)	$120	$160	$196	$200

2. $0
3. d
4. $50 billion
5. a
6. $20 billion
7. $35 billion
8. No

Exercise 3

Table 16.3 Answer

	Recession		*Inflation*		*Stagflation*	
Fiscal policy	1. k 2. e	Tax cuts Government spending raised	6. n 7. d	Tax increases Government spending reduced		
Monetary policy	3. b 4. f 5. i	Discount rate reduced Open-market operations (Fed buys government securities) Reserve requirement reduced	8. c 9. g 10. h	Discount rate raised Open-market operations (Fed sells government securities) Reserve requirement raised		
Supply-side policy			11. m	Tax incentives to encourage saving	12. a 13. l 14. j	Deregulation Tax incentives to alter the structure of supply and demand Job and skill training

Exercise 4

1. $1.56 trillion
2. ". . . to get the country out of the deepest recession since the 1930s."
3. T

SECTION IV International

CHAPTER 17

International Trade

Quick Review

- The trade balance for any country is the difference between its exports and imports. Since the mid-1970s, the United States has experienced a trade deficit.

- Without trade, each country's consumption possibilities are limited to its production possibilities. With trade, a country may concentrate its resources on the goods it produces relatively efficiently. Trade allows for specialization and increases total world output. For each country, consumption possibilities will exceed production possibilities.

- For trade to be mutually beneficial each country must exploit its comparative advantage. Comparative advantage is based on relative efficiency in production. If Country A produces a specific good and in doing so gives up less in terms of other goods than Country B gives up to produce the same good, then Country A has a comparative advantage. Comparative advantage relies on a comparison of relative opportunity costs.

- For trade to be mutually beneficial, the terms of trade—the rate at which one good is exchanged for another—must lie between the opportunity costs for each of the individual countries. The closer the terms of trade are to the slope of a country's production-possibilities curve, the fewer benefits it receives, and vice versa.

- Not everyone benefits from trade. Those involved in import competing industries will object to trade because they may lose jobs to foreign producers. Those engaged in export industries will favor trade because jobs and profits are likely to increase.

- Tariffs discourage imports by making the goods more expensive. Quotas set a limit on the quantity of a particular good that may be imported. Nontariff barriers also restrict trade.

- When goods are traded between countries, there is an exchange of currency. The exchange rate is the price of one currency in terms of another currency. A currency will appreciate or depreciate in value based on the supply and demand for the currency. If a nation's currency appreciates, its goods become more expensive for foreigners and it exports less, *ceteris paribus*. The opposite is true if the currency depreciates.

- The World Trade Organization (WTO) polices world trade and can cite countries for trade agreement violations.

Learning Objectives

After reading the chapter and doing the following exercises you should be able to:

1. Summarize U.S. trade patterns.
2. Explain how trade increases total output.
3. Tell how the terms of trade are established.
4. Discuss how trade barriers affect market outcomes.
5. Describe how currency exchange rates affect trade flows.

Using Terms to Remember

Fill in the puzzle on the opposite page with the appropriate terms from the list of Terms to Remember in the text.

Across

1. The alternative combinations of goods and services that could be produced in a given time period with all available resources and technology.
3. Cannot be greater than a country's production possibilities without trade.
5. A decrease in the value of a currency relative to another.
7. An imbalance experienced by the United States since the mid-1970s.
13. An increase in the value of one currency relative to another.
14. The quantity of good A that must be given up in exchange for good B when countries engage in trade.
15. When a country's exports exceed its imports.
16. When a country can produce more of a good than another country with the same amount of resources.

Down

2. When the opportunity cost of producing a good is lower in one country than in another.
4. The quantity of one good that must be given up in order to produce one more unit of another good.
6. The price of one country's currency in terms of another country's currency.
8. Can be determined by the intersection of demand and supply curves.
9. A tax on imported goods.
10. Goods and services purchased from foreign sources.
11. A limit on the quantity of a good that may be imported in a given time period.
12. Goods and services sold to foreign buyers.

Puzzle 17.1

True or False: *Circle your choice and explain why any false statements are incorrect.*

T F 1. The United States imports goods and services from other countries, but it exports almost no U.S. goods and services to foreign countries.

T F 2. Because one country's imports are another country's exports, overall world trade must balance.

T F 3. Because world resources are limited, when two nations trade, consumption for one nation will increase, but consumption for the other nation must decrease.

T F 4. The main reason why countries specialize and trade with each other is so they can get goods and services they cannot produce themselves.

T F 5. Without trade, it is impossible for a country to consume a mix of goods and services beyond its production possibilities curve.

T F 6. If a country has a comparative advantage in the production of a good, then it can produce the good with fewer absolute resources than its trading partners.

T F 7. In establishing the "terms of trade," a country will not give up more for a good in trade than it would give up if it produced the good itself.

T F 8. When a country specializes and trades, everyone in the country is better off.

T F 9. Compared to a free-trade situation, tariffs and quotas reduce world output and lower living standards.

T F 10. *Ceteris paribus*, if the value of a nation's currency increases, its exports will decrease, and its imports will increase.

Multiple Choice: *Select the correct answer.*

_______ 1. Which of the following statements about U.S. trade is true?
(a) The United States typically has a trade surplus in goods.
(b) The United States typically has a trade deficit in services.
(c) The United States has a trade deficit with each of the countries it trades with.
(d) The United States typically has a trade deficit in goods and a trade surplus in services.

_______ 2. Suppose the country of Montgomery uses all of its available resources and technology. It has specialized in the production of a good but has not yet entered into trade. At this point, Montgomery has:
(a) Moved to a level of production outside its production possibilities curve.
(b) Shifted its production possibilities curve outward.
(c) Moved along its existing production possibilities curve.
(d) Moved to a level of consumption outside its production possibilities curve.

_______ 3. Referring to the previous question, suppose that Montgomery now trades with another country. We can say that Montgomery has:
(a) Moved to a level of production outside its production possibilities curve.
(b) Shifted its production possibilities curve outward.
(c) Moved along its existing production possibilities curve.
(d) Moved to a level of consumption outside its production possibilities curve.

_______ 4. World output of goods and services increases with specialization because:
(a) The world's resources are being used more efficiently.
(b) Each country's production possibilities curve is shifted outward.
(c) Each country's workers are able to produce more than they could before specialization.
(d) The world's workers are being exploited by rich countries.

_______ 5. In the absence of trade, a country's consumption possibilities are:
(a) More than its domestic production possibilities.
(b) Equal to its domestic production possibilities.
(c) Less than its production possibilities.
(d) Unlimited, since the terms of trade are not a constraint.

_______ 6. "Absolute advantage" refers to:
(a) The ability of a country to produce a specific good with fewer resources than other countries can.
(b) The ability of a country to produce a specific good at a lower opportunity cost than its trading partners can.
(c) Total market domination by one country in the production a certain good or service.
(d) The ability of a country to guarantee itself very favorable terms of trade at the expense of its trading partners.

_______ 7. To say that a country has a comparative advantage in the production of wine is to say that:
(a) It can produce wine with fewer resources than any other country can.
(b) Its opportunity cost of producing wine is greater than any other country's.
(c) Its opportunity cost of producing wine is lower than any other country's.
(d) The relative price of wine is higher in that country than in any other.

Suppose the production possibilities for producers in China and Mexico are as indicated in Table 17.1. The table reveals that China can produce 2 toasters or 10 pounds of cotton, and Mexico can produce 1 toaster or 8 pounds of cotton. Refer to Table 17.1 to answer Questions 8-11.

Table 17.1 Output per worker-day in China and Mexico

Country	*Toasters (perday)*	*Pounds of cotton (per day)*
China	3	12
Mexico	1	6

_______ 8. Which of the following statements is true?
(a) Mexico has an absolute advantage in the production of both cotton and toasters.
(b) Mexico has an absolute advantage in the production of cotton only.
(c) China has an absolute advantage in the production of toasters only.
(d) China has an absolute advantage in the production of both cotton and toasters.

_______ 9. Which of the following is a true statement?
(a) The opportunity cost of toasters is higher in China than in Mexico.
(b) The opportunity cost of toasters is lower in China than in Mexico.
(c) It is impossible to tell anything about opportunity cost from the information given.
(d) China has a comparative advantage in the production of cotton.

_______ 10. Which of the following statements is true?
(a) Mexico should specialize in the production of cotton and import toasters from China.
(b) Mexico should specialize in the production of toasters and import cotton from China.
(c) Mexico should import both toasters and cotton from China.
(d) Mexico cannot compete with China; protectionist trade barriers should be implemented.

_______ 11. Which of the following statements is true concerning the terms of trade between Mexico and China?
(a) Mexico should *not* give up more than 1/8 of a pound of cotton to get 1 toaster.
(b) Mexico should *not* give up more than 10 pounds of cotton to get 1 toaster.
(c) Mexico should *not* give up more than 8 pounds of cotton to get 1 toaster.
(d) Mexico should *not* give up more than 1/5 of a pound of cotton to get 1 toaster.

_______ 12. The World Trade Organization (WTO) was created:
(a) Because nations thought a stronger mechanism was needed to enforce free trade agreements.
(b) To replace GATT.
(c) To assist a country if it believes its exports are being unfairly excluded from another country's market.
(d) All of the above.

_______ 13. Suppose that Brazil has a comparative advantage in coffee and Mexico has a comparative advantage in tomatoes. Which two of the following groups will be worse off if these two countries specialize and trade?
(a) Brazilian tomato producers.
(b) Brazilian coffee producers.
(c) Mexican tomato producers.
(d) Mexican coffee producers.

_______ 14. If we could add all the gains of international trade then subtract all the losses, the net result would be:
(a) Zero; the gains and losses would cancel out.
(b) Positive; a net gain for the world and each country.
(c) Negative; a net loss for the world and each country.
(d) Positive some years and negative other years.

_______ 15. Protectionism achieves which of the following goals?
   (a) Greater consumption possibilities through greater specialization.
   (b) Protection of comparative advantage.
   (c) Protection from microeconomic losses.
   (d) Protection of absolute advantage.

_______ 16. Tariffs result in:
   (a) Higher employment and output in protected industries than would otherwise be the case.
   (b) Lower domestic prices than those that would prevail in their absence.
   (c) A stimulus to efficient American firms that are not protected.
   (d) A more efficient allocation of resources than would occur in their absence.

_______ 17. As trade restrictions are eliminated, increased imports:
   (a) Lower competition in product markets.
   (b) Leave the composition of the GDP unchanged.
   (c) Redistribute income out of import-using industries.
   (d) Alter resource allocation away from import-competing industries.

_______ 18. Which of the following policies is least desirable, from a consumer's point of view?
   (a) Tariffs on imported goods.
   (b) Quotas on imported goods.
   (c) No trade.
   (d) Free trade.

_______ 19. When the U.S. dollar loses value compared, for example, to the euro:
   (a) U.S. producers and workers in export industries will lose.
   (b) U.S. producers and workers in export industries will gain.
   (c) U.S. consumers of European products will gain.
   (d) European tourists coming to the United States will lose.

_______ 20. Exchange rates are affected by:
   (a) The supply of a currency, but not the demand.
   (b) The demand for the currency, but not the supply.
   (c) Either the supply or demand for a currency.
   (d) Neither the supply nor demand for a currency.

Problems and Applications

Exercise 1

This exercise shows how trade leads to gains by all trading partners through specialization and comparative advantage.

1. Suppose that Japan has 20 laborers in total and that the United States has 40 laborers. Table 17.2 represents the different levels of productivity for the two countries. (*Be careful:* The table tells you that one worker in Japan can produce 2 motorcycles per day *or* 10 bicycles per day, *not* 2 motorcycles *and* 10 bicycles!)

Table 17.2 Output per worker-day in the United States and Japan

Country	Motorcycles (per day)	Bicycles (per day)
Japan	2	10
United States	1	8

Draw the production possibilities curves for each country in Figure 17.1. Assume constant costs of production.

Figure 17.1

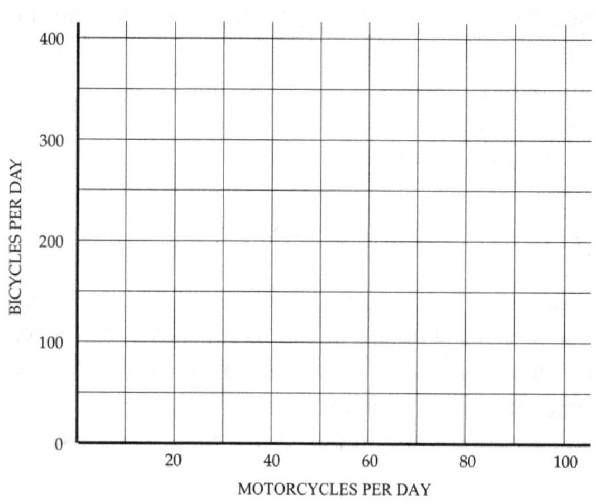

2. Suppose that before trade Japan uses 12 laborers to produce bicycles and 8 laborers to produce motorcycles. Suppose also that in the United States 20 workers produce bicycles and 20 produce motorcycles. Complete Table 17.3.

Table 17.3 Output produced and consumed without trade

Country	Motorcycles (per day)	Bicycles (per day)
Japan	____	____
United States	____	____
Total	____	____

3. Before trade, the total output of motorcycles is __________ ; of bicycles __________.

4. What is the opportunity cost of one motorcycle in Japan? __________ In the United States? __________

5. What is the opportunity cost of one bicycle in Japan?__________ In the United States?__________

6. If Japan and the United States specialize according to their respective comparative advantages, Japan will produce __________ and the United States will produce __________. They will do so because the opportunity cost of bicycles in terms of motorcycles is (lower, higher) in the United States than in Japan, and the opportunity cost of motorcycles in terms of bicycles is (lower, higher) in Japan than in the United States.

7. After specialization, the total output of motorcycles is __________ and the total output of bicycles is__________ . (*Hint:* Twenty Japanese produce only motorcycles, and forty Americans produce only bicycles.)

8. After specialization, there is an increase of __________ bicycles and __________ motorcycles compared to the previous level of output. (*Hint:* Compare answers to Questions 3 and 7.)

Exercise 2

This exercise focuses on how the terms of trade are determined. Use the data from Exercise 1 above.

If Japan and the United States are to benefit from the increased production, trade must take place. The Japanese will be willing to trade motorcycles for bicycles as long as they get back more bicycles than they could get in their own country.

1. The terms of trade will be between 1 motorcycle equals ____ bicycles and 1 motorcycle equals ____ bicycles.

2. If the terms of trade were 4 bicycles equals 1 motorcycle:
   (a) Neither country would buy bicycles but both would buy motorcycles.
   (b) Neither country would motorcycles but both would buy bicycles.
   (c) Both countries would buy bicycles and motorcycles.
   (d) Neither country would buy motorcycles or bicycles.

3. Suppose that both countries agree that the terms of trade will be 6 bicycles equal 1 motorcycle. Let Japan export 20 motorcycles per day to the United States. Complete Table 17.4. Assume that Japan produces 40 motorcycles per day and the United States produces 320 bicycles.

Table 17.4 Consumption combination after trade

Country	*Motorcycles (perday)*	*Bicycles (perday)*
Japan	_____	_____
United States	_____	_____
Total	40	320

4. As a result of specialization and trade, the United States has the same quantity of motorcycles and _____ more bicycles per day. (Compare Tables 17.3 and 17.4.)

5. As a result of specialization and trade, Japan has the same number of bicycles and _____ more motorcycles per day.

   Now suppose that at the exchange rate of 6 bicycles to 1 motorcycle, Japan would like to export 10 motorcycles and import 60 bicycles per day. Suppose also that the United States desires to export 90 bicycles and import 15 motorcycles per day.

6. At these terms of trade there is a (shortage, surplus) of motorcycles.

7. At these terms of trade there is a (shortage, surplus) of bicycles.

8. Which of the following terms of trade would be more likely to result from this situation?
   (a) 5 bicycles equal 1 motorcycle.
   (b) 6 bicycles equal 1 motorcycle.
   (c) 7 bicycles equal 1 motorcycle.

Exercise 3

Reread the News Wire article in the text titled "Obama Cuts Sour Deal on Sugar." Then answer the following questions.

1. According to the article, what do price supports and import quotas essentially guarantee sugar beet and cane producers? ____________________

2. How does this policy affect American families? ____________________

3. How does this policy negatively impact some American workers? ____________________

   ____

Common Errors

The first statement in each "common error" below is incorrect. Each incorrect statement is followed by a corrected version and an explanation.

1. A country must have an *absolute advantage* in order to gain from trade with another country. *Incorrect!*
   A country must have a *comparative advantage* in order to gain from trade with another country. *Correct!*
   Mutually advantageous trade requires only that the opportunity costs of producing goods differ between the two countries, *ceteris paribus*. Another way of stating this is that the production-possibilities curves of the two countries must have different slopes. These two circumstances are indicated in Figure 17.2. In diagram (a), Country B has an absolute advantage over Country A, but the production-possibilities curves have the same slope. Mutually advantageous trade is *not* possible. In diagram (b), each country has a comparative advantage because the production-possibilities curves of the two countries have different slopes. Mutually advantageous trade is possible.

Figure 17.2

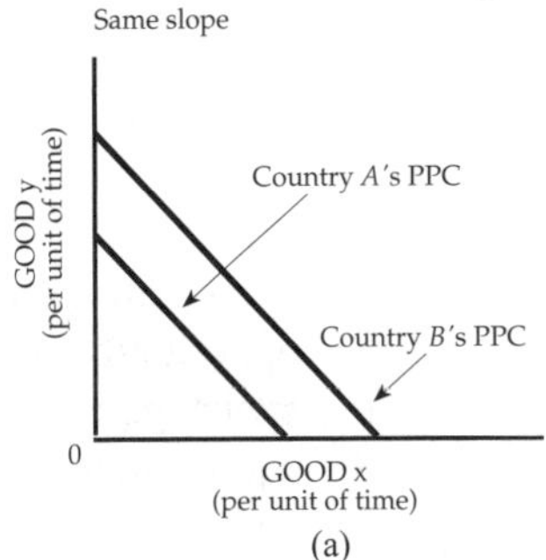

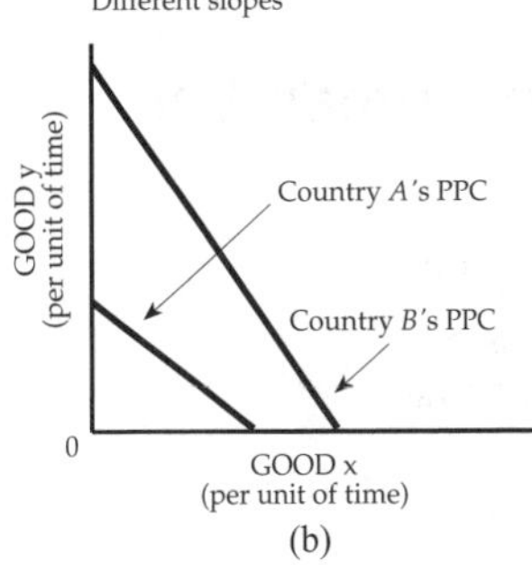

2. Foreign trade costs a country jobs. *Incorrect!*
Although jobs may be lost, new ones will be created by the opportunities opened up with trade. *Correct!*

When countries specialize and trade according to the law of comparative advantage, some particular workers and firms may be hurt by imports, but the economy as a whole gains by trade. More output per resource input will be attainable. Because the economy is able to reach full employment with trade as well as without trade, there is no reason to assume there will be fewer jobs.

3. A country is well-off only as long as it exports more than it imports. *Incorrect!*
Countries may, at times, be well-off when they experience a trade surplus; they may also be well-off when they have a trade deficit. *Correct!*

Both trade deficits and trade surpluses can be problems if either situation persists for a long period of time. Trade surpluses mean that a country is giving more of its limited, precious resources in trade than it is acquiring from other countries. The currencies of deficit countries tend to depreciate, which means they will be unable to buy as many foreign goods with a unit of currency.

4. Countries tend to enter into trade to get things they cannot produce themselves. *Incorrect!*
Countries very often trade for things they could produce themselves. *Correct!*

Be careful! Countries often trade for things they could produce themselves, because the relative costs of domestic production would be prohibitive. Take baskets as an example. U.S. producers could certainly produce baskets if they really wanted to. The technique is not difficult to learn and the materials are abundant. But baskets do not lend themselves to machine production, and hand labor is expensive in the United States. The cost in terms of goods forgone would be tremendous. (So would the price of baskets.) The United States is better off specializing in goods such as computers, where it has a comparative advantage, and trading for baskets, where it does not have a comparative advantage.

5. Protectionism only affects the workers in the protected industry and the domestic consumers of the protected commodity. *Incorrect!*
Protectionism affects the protected market plus other related markets. *Correct!*

Protectionism and the resulting price and output changes will set off additional changes in related markets. Higher prices for a protected product lead consumers to look for lower priced substitutes. An increase in demand for substitute products causes changes in that market and other related markets. In the case of sugar, corn-based high-fructose corn syrup is a sugar substitute. Corn farmers now lobby in favor of the sugar quota because it causes demand for corn to increase, which increases the price of corn. Similar impacts can be expected in foreign markets because of the sugar quota.

~ ANSWERS ~

Using Terms to Remember

Across

1. production possibilities
3. consumption possibilities
5. currency depreciation
7. trade deficit
13. currency appreciation
14. terms of trade
15. trade surplus
16. absolute advantage

Down

2. comparative advantage
4. opportunity cost
6. exchange rate
8. equilibrium price
9. tariff
10. imports
11. quota
12. exports

True or False

1. F It is true that U.S. imports exceed U.S. exports, but U.S. *exports* are equal to about 10 to 11 percent of U.S. GDP.
2. T
3. F Because of specialization, total world output will increase and consumption for both trading partners can increase.
4. F The main reason countries specialize and trade is because total output, income, and living standards are increased.
5. T
6. F If a country has a comparative advantage in the production of a good, then it can produce the good at a *lower opportunity cost* than its trading partners.
7. T
8. F When a country specializes and trades, the *country as a whole* is better off, but some individuals or industries may be worse off.
9. T
10. T

Multiple Choice

1. d	5. b	9. b	13. a, d	17. d
2. c	6. a	10. a	14. b	18. c
3. d	7. c	11. c	15. c	19. b
4. a	8. d	12. d	16. a	20. c

Problems and Applications

Exercise 1

1. **Figure 17.1 Answer**

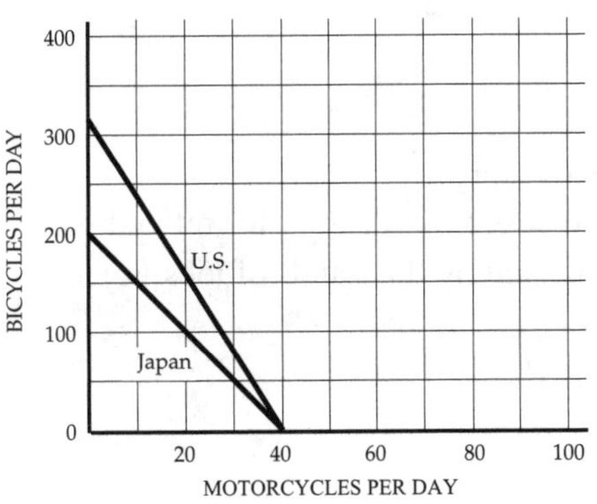

2. **Table 17.3 Answer**

Country	*Motorcycles (per day)*	*Bicycles (per day)*
Japan	16	120
United States	20	160
Total	36	280

3. 36; 280
4. 5 bicycles; 8 bicycles
5. One-fifth of a motorcycle; one-eighth of a motorcycle
6. Motorcycles; bicycles; lower; lower
7. 40; 320
8. 40; 4

Exercise 2

1. 5; 8
2. a
3. **Table 17.4 Answer**

Country	*Motorcycles (per day)*	*Bicycles (perday)*
Japan	20	120
United States	20	200
Total	40	320

4. 40
5. 4
6. Shortage. The Japanese wish to export fewer (10) motorcycles than Americans want (15).
7. Surplus. The Americans wish to export more (90) bicycles than the Japanese want (60).
8. c

Exercise 3

1. 80 percent market share
2. American families pay higher prices at the grocery store.
3. "Artificially high domestic sugar prices raise the cost of production for refined sugar, candy . . . Higher costs cut into profits and competitiveness, putting thousands of jobs in jeopardy."